OH GOD! WHAT HAVE WE DONE?
Misadventures, Bras and Mostly Bad Ideas

True tales of how mommyhood hijacked our careers, our relationships...and our lingerie!

Yvonne Parks and Stephanie Duprie Routh

Published by
Rene' Marcelle Publishing
Austin, Texas

Copyright © 2017 by Yvonne Parks and Stephanie Duprie Routh

All rights reserved.

Published in the United States of America. ISBN-13:978-0-9975043-1-6

Disclaimer: This is not a work of fiction. Everything described herein actually happened as described (more or less), to the best of the authors' recollections. The authors kept their names throughout but changed the names of all other guilty parties and innocent bystanders. Mostly because the authors recall some lawyer telling them it might be a good idea to do that.

DEDICATION

To our husbands and high-maintenance children, we dedicate this book to you. And as you read it, keep two things in mind: yes, it's all true—you really did do these things—and no, you can't sue us (we checked). Thanks for all your patience in letting us take so many weekends away from you to work on the book...it was hard for two BFF's to give up laundry, cooking, cleaning, and chauffeuring to spend time together laughing, writing, and drinking margaritas. But we did it all for you (no, really)!

In all seriousness, we love you very much. Thanks for charming us, inspiring us, loving us, and for just being wonderful you.

To our mothers, we offer our sincere thanks for having the good sense to become English teachers and offering so many wonderful, constructive criticisms of our nascent writing efforts in high school...we think it might have paid off. If we become wildly successful, we'll buy you each a condominium on a lake somewhere. (No, really.)

Yvonne would also like to thank her sister and her cousin "Liz" for providing subject matter for the book (without intending to, of course) and for reading through early versions of the manuscript (but neither of you is getting a condominium).

We would also like to send virtual high-fives to Dave in Serbia for the cover design!

"One thing they never tell you about child raising is that for the rest of your life at the drop of a hat you are expected to know your child's name and how old he or she is."

-Erma Bombeck

"Oh God! What have I done?"

-Moms everywhere (and, in particular, Stephanie and Yvonne, on numerous occasions)

Table of Contents

PROLOGUE	10
PART ONE	13
CHAPTER ONE: OUT OF THE CLOSET	15
CHAPTER TWO: LEARNING TO JUGGLE	25
CHAPTER THREE: A DECADE PAST	43
PART TWO	51
CHAPTER FOUR: THE TRUTH ABOUT CHILDBIRTH	53
CHAPTER FIVE: TOP TEN LISTS FOR LADIES ONLY	61
CHAPTER SIX: ARE THOSE GUYS STALKING ME?	69
CHAPTER SEVEN: MATING RITUALS	79
PART THREE	83
CHAPTER EIGHT: A WHOLE NEW WORLD	85
CHAPTER NINE: BABY BOOM	100
CHAPTER TEN: WEDDINGS AND MOTHER'S DAY	114
CHAPTER ELEVEN: THEY DIDN'T LEARN THAT FROM ME	127
CHAPTER TWELVE: CAN I BLAME THIS ON THE KIDS?	140
CHAPTER THIRTEEN: LIFE CYCLES	147
PART FOUR	157
CHAPTER FOURTEEN: AGING GRACEFULLY	159
PART FIVE	195
CHAPTER FIFTEEN: LEARNING FROM OUR CHILDREN	197
CHAPTER SIXTEEN: IT'S A TRIP	207

CHAPTER SEVENTEEN: AM I LOSING MY MIND?	221
PART SIX	**233**
CHAPTER EIGHTEEN: ON THE ROAD AGAIN	235
CHAPTER NINETEEN: I'LL TAKE ALL THE HELP I CAN GET	248
CHAPTER TWENTY: ROAD TRIP	257
CHAPTER TWENTY-ONE: THEY GROW UP SO FAST	269
CHAPTER TWENTY-TWO: SHOP 'TILL I DROP	291
CHAPTER TWENTY-THREE: BACK WHERE WE STARTED	303
ABOUT THE AUTHORS	**305**

PROLOGUE

Subject : BUTTONS

Steph,

Hey-haven't heard from you in a while. Let me guess. You've been out of the country with your husband and rug rats on yet another rip-roaring adventure. I'm right, aren't I? I won't tell you that you suck. You know you do.

Want to know what I've been doing? Of course you do. I've been picking buttons up off the floor for the last half hour, wondering what on earth possessed me to provide a bucket of them to my girls. I mean, really. Exactly what did I think was going to happen when I handed over at least five hundred tiny objects to two smiling preschoolers bent on destruction and mayhem? Was I so naïve as to think that the dastardly duo might actually work quietly on their fine motor and sorting skills at the kitchen table while I tried to find my bed under a whole mountain range of their laundry? Why, yes! Yes, I was.

I should know better by now, shouldn't I?

So far, I've found a trail of buttons all over the floor from the kitchen to the dining room, down the hall past the family room, and right into the bathroom to end, rather inexplicably, behind the toilet. Of the girls, I have seen no sign. Perhaps I am meant to be misled by this trail, thrown off their scent.

But if I hide out here in my office to try to catch up on e-mail, they'll come looking for me. It's the surest method of any I've tried to guarantee that they'll come running. Not that I really want to see them anytime soon, but still, I'm their mother and all. I should probably be apprised of their whereabouts on a somewhat regular basis.

The button trail reminded me of something that I haven't thought about in years. Do you remember when we met? You and I were the first two kids dropped off to Mrs. Nelson's kindergarten class on our inaugural day of school.(Probably the first and last time you and I were both early for something.) So there you were, sitting at a table, sorting buttons, when my mom walked me in and Mrs. Nelson introduced us. Remember? We were so shy together, sorting buttons…it was the beginning of a beautiful—and highly entertaining—friendship!

Great. As predicted, the girls have found me. And with pockets filled with buttons. And dirt and rocks and sand from the backyard. How cute.

Now they're whining about something.

And here I was prepared to tell you all about the exciting events of the past few weeks: the latest notices we received from the architectural review committee regarding our little weed problem (and no, not the kind that might draw the attention of the DEA); how my monthly vet bill for prescription dog food for three canines rivals my monthly grocery bill for four people; and how last week I went home almost naked—again—from the doctor's office when Emma puked all over me during the interminable wait for the M.D. (those paper gowns at the pediatrician's office are really not made for plus-sized moms—they gave me two and I still made an almost R-rated exit from the office). Cool stuff.

So, do drop me a line and tell me all about your new passport stamps. Please? I'm begging here.

Oh, crap. Now they're crying. Something about being hungry or some such nonsense. Remind me again why I ended up the stay-at-home mom of two, with no real career to speak of? I forget.
yp

PART ONE

(A long time ago in a lifetime far, far away…)

CHAPTER ONE: OUT OF THE CLOSET

SUBJECT: FIRST DATE

Yvonne,

I'm happy to report I have quashed the attorney and have officially been on my first "un-official date" with Pierce. You were right—those attorney types are probably best left to their own devices. It seems the one I chose to date, among other things, had a habit of sharing his briefs. Luckily Pierce, a non-legal type, asked me out on an "un-official" date.

This is what happened: Pierce calls me on a Tuesday night when I was working late and asks, "Are you a Republican or a Democrat?" Truthfully, I say I vote for the person, not the party. This is met with silence. Okay, I'm thinking… this is off to a good start. He then asks if I'd like to accompany him to a private fundraising dinner with the Governor on Wednesday night. I respond that I will have to check my calendar and get back to him. What I was thinking, I'll never know! What on earth would do I have to do on a Wednesday night? It's not like my social calendar is overrun with appointments or dates. Anyway, I call back the next day and we are set to meet on Wednesday.

Now, let me remind you that I live in Po-dunk-Ville, where the only store with clothing is a Walmart. Not that I'm dissin' Wallyworld clothes, but I just didn't think that would be upscale enough for dinner with the Governor. Let me remind you that it is Tuesday and the date is tomorrow— on Wednesday. That being said, I do what any self-respecting girl would do: feign an illness, play hooky from work that afternoon, and high-tail it to the nearest mall in search of "the little black dress."

After visiting several stores, I decide the little black dress is a figment of someone's imagination. Everything I find was too business-like, too trampy, too much cleavage, not enough cleavage, too short, too morbid, too frumpy, too everything but right. I finally decide on a navy number, erring on the conservative side.

Wednesday evening arrives and I dash home to get dressed for the un-official date. I only have half an hour to get dressed and then head to Pierce's house. It is a challenge for me indeed, as I'm always late. I'm pulling on my pantyhose, which I hate, only to pull too hard and have them rip in half. Fine. I'm going hose-less, which actually suits me better. I'm painting on my makeup as fast as I can only to realize Lady Gaga makes an appearance in the mirror where my face should be. Wash off. Restart. This time I try for "simple yet elegant." Better. I jump into my Ford truck, a stick-shift without air and zoom to Austin. About halfway there I realize whatever hairstyle I thought I had is now blown into oblivion. Sweat pours down my face and into what little cleavage shows in my conservative, navy cocktail attire. It's only 105 degrees and I'm stuck in rush hour traffic trying to get to a date.

After half an hour of stop and go with a stick shift and a clutch, I get off the freeway and find my way into Pierce's neighborhood. I take the wrong turn—of course and backtrack and try again. I arrive —only twenty minutes late— looking like a calico cat with black mascara and orangey base streaks down my face. My hair gives Albert Einstein a run for his money, and I have acquired a lovely aroma thanks to the commingling of sweat and perfume.

Pierce graciously waits as I use the powder room to try and freshen up a bit. I splash water on my face and my hair. I transform myself into a no-makeup, no-hairstyle, and - hopefully- no-odor escort. We proceed to dinner, at which I have two glasses of wine instead of food. My nerves are shot, buried, dug up and shot again. Conversation with the Governor centers, of all things, on the illustrious high school mascot of Po-dunkville—the Ducks.

So I guess I proved what a great date I am. Brilliant conversationalist (please refer back to the Ducks), gorgeous arm candy (particularly after sweating off all the makeup), and a model of decorum (especially after two glasses of wine on an empty stomach). I hope the evening wasn't a total disaster as I would really like to go out with Pierce again. Maybe next time I'll suggest it be just the two of us on a boat on Lake Travis—just in case he's a little bit shy about taking me out in public again.

Must run. I have makeup work to do after recovering from my "afternoon illness"! Talk to you soon. S.

SUBJECT: RE: FIRST DATE

Steph,

Way to go for dumping the lawyer! They make terrible mates. Just ask my husband.

As for the "non-date" date with Pierce, at least your brush with the Governor wasn't as embarrassing as mine. Back in college, I ran into him—almost literally—on a plane to a presidential inauguration. I looked like a clown on the run from Barnum and Bailey's in a bright purple pant outfit, a hot pink ski jacket, and—because my mother insisted that it would be snowing in D.C.—ridiculous snow boots. Who does that? Like we were going to be wading through snow banks in the airport terminal or something. Not one of my finer sartorial moments.

Kudos for pulling yourself together so quickly—and may you be blessed with air conditioning on your second date!
yp

SUBJECT: SECOND DATE

Yvonne,

I am a bit befuddled about this entire dating process. As it were, I was dating the lawyer almost exclusively (well, exclusive on my part anyway) before I dumped the two-timer. During my stormy relationship with him, I had multiple offers from Neanderthals, married men, seventy-year old men clothed in overalls or leisure suits, and persons (I dare not call them men) who were fresh from the movie Deliverance. I cannot recall a single, respectable, age-appropriate guy in waiting during all this time.

Now that I've had one official "unofficial" date with Pierce, who seems like a trustworthy guy, I wonder if we're really in line for a second. I know I was a bit scary at first glance, the night I arrived to attend the Governor's fundraiser, but I thought I recovered quickly. Since then I have suggested lunch meetings, to discuss business of course, but no dice. Rejection. Rejection. Rejection. So last week I decided to up the ante.

I am sitting in a local restaurant having a beer with a friend when I see Pierce outside at the ATM machine. I decide to ask him to join us. I leave the restaurant and rush over, hoping he doesn't drive away before I get there. He is standing outside his car getting cash when I approach. Careful. I remind myself not to sound desperate. I casually remark on how hot the weather is and how work has slowed. I ask if he has seen the Governor recently. Beginning to drown in a pool of sweat, I flippantly ask him if he might join us.

He says no, he has work to do. Ugh! Who, in the late afternoon has work to do? I am skipping out early on a Thursday — why can't he? Anyway, as I look down dejected, I notice he is wearing sandals and that his big toe is painted with silver, glittery polish. Oh, I can't pass this one up!
"So, is that it?" I ask. "Are you taking your first steps on coming out of the closet? Is that why you are not interested in going out with me again? I was simply your cover at the political event, was I not?" He roars with laughter, turning the deepest shade of red you can imagine. He explains that his nieces had been in town the weekend before and they were "practicing" on him. Hmmm...

True or false, at this point, I wasn't sure. I guess I will just have to keep searching the field for anyone respectable until Mr. Pierce comes around. Well, at least I hope he does...Talk to you soon. S.

SUBJECT: RE: SECOND DATE

Steph,

Assuming he's not, in fact, preparing to come out of the closet (and I might be concerned about that—hello—glitter nail polish??), the problem with Pierce must be your politics. If you can't agree with his, just lie about it. You can always vote in secret.

I'm kidding, of course! Never base a relationship on a lie; truth should be the bedrock of your bond…yada, yada, yada.

Good luck! Keep me posted. yp

SUBJECT: PIERCE UPDATE

Yvonne,

Hey there! I thought I might send a quick hello to see how things are going in Frisco. My life here has been a series of mishaps or interesting events, as the case may be. You be the judge. After all, you are the attorney! In the space of one weekend, I have managed to climb around an attic in stilettos, drop a bra (twice), and learn a little more than I should about Mr. Pierce.

Since I am getting absolutely nowhere with Mr. Pierce and the dating scene, I decide to make a go on my own with other potential dates. Mistake. I should know by now that my sense of direction sucks. I have not performed the dating ritual in some time. Nevertheless, I am determined not to just sit at home this weekend. So…

Thursday afternoon, a male colleague of mine invites me to his office for a drink after work. Sure, I think. What could come of it? After all, he is married and I am not interested. But, he is an expert at banter, which I truly enjoy. A drink, some lively conversation and debates over the political state of things should be fun before I head home. So I go.

Everything goes along as I expect until he sees his wife's car pull into the parking lot. "Quick! Into this hallway and up the stairs!" This is all I hear as I am shoved through the door. In and up I go to discover he has hidden me in the attic of his office building. I am so shocked I can not even protest. After all, I thought this was an innocent meeting. Below, I can hear his wife making all kinds of accusations and think better of going out to defend myself. Instead, I poke around the loft as quietly as I can and find a little wooden bench among the insulation and old files. I make myself comfortable while I wait for a signal that the coast is clear.

It must have been the drink or the extremely long day at work because I fall asleep. In the attic. The next thing I hear is the whistle of the eleven o'clock train! What now? I have not been rescued! What a fine mess! Again I ask, what now? And, WHERE THE HECK DID HE GO?

I stomp down the attic stairs hoping no vigilante wife waits below. Thankfully, all is quiet. I know the building has an alarm system. Great. Is it armed or not? I call one of my girlfriends in an act of desperation. What do I do? If I open the door to leave and the alarm sounds, the police will arrest me for breaking and exiting. What a great situation for a city employee. If I stay all night, his entire office staff will wonder how I entered the building in the first place and above all, what am I doing there in yesterday's clothes.

My friend advises me to leave the building and run like the wind. I take her advice and manage a clean getaway, the alarm wailing in my dust. I will not be mentioning this encounter at work the next day. And, I would not be having any more drinks with that wife-bound lunatic!

On Friday, I persuade the only other single girl in town that I know to go with me to Austin to a dance club. We are to meet at a restaurant, have a respectable dinner and then head to the club for a night of trolling. I figure a public place will be a much better venue for actually getting to talk to a guy than in the attic from the night before.

Typically, I am running late from a work meeting that ran long. Instead of dressing at home, I plan on changing at the restaurant before heading out to the dance club. All is going relatively smoothly. I meet my friend; we eat; I head to the ladies room to change. One minor, critical mistake—I drop my bra in the toilet. You know, those bathroom stalls are not made for a full dress change! I debate what to do next. Do I leave the bra for the next unsuspecting visitor? Do I fish it out (eeewww)? If I do fish it out, then what? Being one of my better pieces of lingerie, I decide I cannot live without it. Time to go fishing.

After pulling the sopping wet undergarment from the toilet, I wring it out and wonder how to get it out of the restaurant. After all, I do not want to put it in my bag with my 'dry clean only' suit! There is scarcely enough room in my purse for a tube of lipstick, much less a full-sized bra, and the dress I am wearing does not have much material to speak of, much less pockets! So, as discreetly as I can I put the bra between the suit bag and my purse. Halfway through the middle of the restaurant, in full view, the bra falls to the floor with a loud "splat." Crap.

"Oh dear. I ate too much. Had to make a little room." This is the best I can do as the surrounding diners look on in amusement. I wish all my food went to my boobs instead of my hips. It would make an hourglass achievement something to really strive for in my every day life.

My friend and I go to the bar. It is quite crowded. We dance. Men buy us drinks. All seems to be going along just fine. After a few hours, I happen to see someone familiar. It is Mr. Pierce. He is out with the guys doing the same thing we are. We actually have a conversation, which goes well. (Maybe the drinks are helping.) Anyhow, during the course of our conversation, Pierce tells me the most amusing story. Translation: too much information.

He is on his way to a meeting with the Mayor of Brenham when he has to use the bathroom. He can't wait for the nearest town or gas station. So, as with any man whose motto is "the world is my urinal," he pulls onto the side of the road and begins to relieve himself. Along comes a highway patrol car. In a hurry, Pierce zips up and jumps into his car. He has not, however, bothered to finish his business. So now, he is on his way to a meeting with the powers that be with a very noticeable wet spot in front. He does what any 'y'- chromosome person would do in the blistering heat of a Texas September. He turns the heater in his car on full blast and aims the vents at his trousers. Now he has added a lovely aroma to his already disheveled attire. Despite the crispy pants and the eau-de-urine cologne, the meeting with the city officials went off as expected. Is this the guy I secretly desire? Convince me otherwise before it is too late!

Saturday, I swear off men and spend time at home with the rose bushes and the barbecue grill. It turned out to be an even trade. Instead of yet another dating faux pas, I had scratched arms and hands and burnt steak to show for my efforts. Oh well. I better go. The day is growing short. Let me know how you are doing soon. S.

SUBJECT:RE: PIERCE UPDATE

Steph,

Wow. My life is really dull compared to yours. I cannot believe the guy left you in his office attic. That's called FALSE IMPRISONMENT!! Get a lawyer and sue (but not me…I don't do that kind of law…conflict gives me hives). You did at least give the guy a call and chew him out, didn't you? But more importantly, you're not seriously going to wear that bra again, are you? It's gotta be at least a Level 3 biohazard. (BTW, really cool comeback in the restaurant. A better one would have been to wave the bra in the air while yelling at your friend, "Hey wait up! I found your bra on the bathroom floor—don't you want it back?")

So I just have to ask, what exactly is it about Pierce that has drawn your interest? Between the glittery toenail polish and the wet pants, it can't be his hygiene and neat personal appearance. Sense of humor, maybe? Just curious!

Keep me posted. And don't go fishing out any more bras from public toilets. Your mom would be appalled, you know. yp

CHAPTER TWO: LEARNING TO JUGGLE

SUBJECT: WHY I MAY JOIN CONVENT

Steph,

I'm writing to procrastinate. It has come to my attention that I am not very proficient at juggling 40 different tasks at once, particularly since one of those tasks includes running a struggling law practice. I offer evidence below in support of my conclusion:

1) Jack made the following announcement at breakfast this morning: "I don't mean to criticize, but I'm down to my last t- shirt and underwear."

My response: "I have a day open three weeks from tomorrow in which I plan to do laundry. Turn your dirty clothes inside out in the interim and get double use out of them (but institute Level 3 biohazard protocols)." Unfortunately, this suggestion was not received as well as I had hoped. He's threatening to send his t-shirts and tighty-whities to the dry cleaners now. On the upside, if he does, I can use that day three weeks from now to engage in other equally mindless tasks.

2) It's my turn to host our neighborhood ladies group for Bunco tomorrow. As hostess, my duties include buying and wrapping the party gifts, cleaning my house, setting up tables, and providing a spread that will fortify 16 ladies for a raucous night of dice-throwing. Thus far, I have done

approximately NONE of these things.

3) Jack has made the following announcement/inquiry at least three times since last week: "I'm almost out of deodorant. When are you going to the store?"

My response: "Use mine-you'll get used to the floral scent. I'll get there when I get there."

Jack didn't seem to appreciate my brilliant idea, but I'm sure he'll see the wisdom of it when people start avoiding his cubicle at work and holding their noses as he walks by.

4) I'm meeting clients tonight for an estate planning document execution ceremony. Each client will sign five documents, witnessed by several people, all under my expert supervision. Guess how many documents are fully edited, printed, and ready to go? Correct. That would be zero.

Given the above, I am quite sure that a jury could find by a preponderance of the evidence that I am unfit as a housewife and attorney, and that I should probably be committed to the care of a convent to spend my days in sackcloth picking potatoes and carrots.

Actually, it does have some appeal . . . so long as I don't get laundry duty.

Here's hoping that your week is not so crazy that you would find a celibate existence gardening in sackcloth an appealing alternative to life in the fast lane.
yp

SUBJECT: RE: WHY I MAY JOIN CONVENT

Hi there! It sounds as if there are not enough hours in the day for you either. I thought it was just me! Luckily, I do not have the Level Three Biohazard men's underwear to contend with on my laundry watch! And as for the stress-induced preparation for the Bunco game, here's a bit of advice from the single scene: Go out! There is no cleaning before or after and you have someone else serve you food and drinks! It's well worth the $$. I can't comment on the deodorant issues because (ashamedly) I have to admit that I have on occasion had to borrow the hygienic necessity from the opposite sex! On that note, I better get busy or my hours will quickly be gone as well. Talk to you soon. S.

SUBJECT: IT'S OFFICIAL-I'M A REAL WOMAN

Steph,

Hey! Exciting news. We bought a new car yesterday. Or as Jack insists, a "truck." We're the sort of people who keep a car until it's been run into the ground, so a new auto purchase is big news around here.

My official mode of transportation is now a dark green SUV. Jack's dubbed it the "baby-mobile." After a year and a half of trying, I don't know whether that's healthy optimism or merely wishful thinking. Of course, if and when it happens, we'll at least have the transportation thing down. Plenty of room for those baby torture contraptions known as "infant car seats." (Having been in more than one friend's car recently with a screaming infant strapped in tightly, I know exactly what I'm talking about.)

But the best part is, driving around in my truck that I've owned for all of 18 hours now, I finally feel like I'm on my way to becoming a full-fledged member of the distaff half of suburban society. The nice house in the nice neighborhood just isn't enough, you know. You have to have an SUV. And kids. Up until now, I think the ladies on the block have dubbed me, "The one who stays home…without kids," which, I've deduced, is a suburban euphemism for "not a real woman." Well, not anymore, girls. I've got the SUV. And I'm working on the kid thing. I'm at least half a real woman now.

But how stupid is that? According to the scuttlebutt around here, being a stay-at-home mom is the hardest thing ever, a job for Superwoman. Shouldn't being an attorney count for something? Even if I just work for myself, and even if it's only part time, I'm still working on a career here. It's not like I'm just lying around eating bonbons all day, you know (not all day, anyway). As if staying at home and taking care of minors could be that difficult. Try three years of torture known as "law school." Try working for a judge or two. Try explaining to an elderly woman hard of hearing and inclined to narcolepsy why she needs a power of attorney and what on earth that even means. Please. I'm doing important stuff here. So I already am a real woman. Kids — if and when they come — will just be icing on the cake.

The above diatribe notwithstanding, I think I need a nap. I'm so tired this morning. In point of fact, I'm still in my p.j.'s; the upside of having a home office and working part time, I suppose. Actually, I haven't found a down side — at least not yet. Unless you count the FedEx guy seeing me in said p.j.'s. That was a little embarrassing. And maybe the lack of steady income…a minor detail…

Well, back to work. Later.

yp

SUBJECT: RE: IT'S OFFICIAL-I'M A REAL WOMAN

Hi there! Congrats on the SUV-truck! Getting a new ride is always exciting and nerve-racking. Well, at least for me it is nerve-racking. The four occasions when I've picked up a new car, it has rained. No more nice and shiny.

One of these days I'll probably wind up smacking some innocent tree along the way because I am unaccustomed to the braking system. Oh well. I'd say keep up the efforts on becoming a 'real' woman, but that would be weird! Talk to you soon. S.

SUBJECT: WHY I SHOULD NEVER GET BETWEEN THE BEST MAN AND THE BRIDE'S UNDERWEAR

Steph,

Hey…I'm back from Austin. Got a little story for you, Aggies! (Don't you sometimes miss Friday night yell practice at A&M?) Kick back your heels—this one's a long one. BTW, sorry I couldn't meet up with you while I was in Austin. There just wasn't any time during the weekend from hell— think you'll see why…My "plan" was for both of us to get up at 4:45 a.m. Friday morning, get dressed, loaded, to the dog sitter's, to Jack's office, and to downtown Dallas for a court appearance on behalf of my one and only (and, I've decided, my first and last) criminal case—

all by 9 am. After that, Jack and I would part ways at the airport, him driving to Austin for the wedding rehearsal and me flying to Austin to grab my grandmother, who would fly with me to Mississippi to see my sister dance. On Saturday, I would fly to Austin in plenty of time to attend the wedding of Jack's brother.

This whole arrangement was to benefit me in any number of ways. A) I wouldn't have to attend the wedding rehearsal or dinner. After all, my sole wedding duty was to pass out corsages before the ceremony, and who really needs to practice that? B) I would be two states away for the inevitable argument between Jack and his brothers over whether Jack would attend the bachelor flesh festival following the rehearsal dinner Friday night, so I couldn't possibly be blamed if Jack chose, of his own accord, not to go. C) I wouldn't have to attend the bridal brunch the next morning that I myself was technically co-hosting, thus upping my reserves of patience and forbearance, which I would need for the wedding itself, to deal with the family disputes that were sure to visit the happy nuptials (just going on past experience here — never been part of ANYONE'S wedding where there wasn't a family squabble of some variety).

Well, that was the "plan," anyway. In hindsight, I don't think even Napoleon could have executed this plan had he been saddled with me as tactician, my husband as logistics expert, and our dogs as cargo. It was our very own Waterloo.

FRIDAY MORNING

I awaken forty-five minutes late and can't get Jack out of bed until 6:30. Perfect. We're supposed to be at the dog sitter's by now.

Because we're running so late, the task of packing the truck falls, unfortunately for all concerned, to Jack, who apparently finds it necessary to fold all the back seats down to enlarge the cargo hold—so the dogs get an upgrade from coach to first class. I would like to make it clear that I had no part in the loading. At all.

Finally packed, we pull out at 7:15 a.m. As we head down the very slight slope of the driveway, I hear the frantic scraping of three sets of paws all over the back of my brand- spanking new, three-day-old SUV. The boys can't find a foothold anywhere, of course, because Jack has neglected to place anything remotely resembling a towel or sheet on the slick mat covering the storage compartment. This inevitably results in dogs slamming helter-skelter into piles of bags, boxes, luggage, and clothing we need for the weekend. Tuffy lands on the beautiful black boucle knit dress and jacket I have selected for the wedding, digging his claws in to maintain his balance. Why my super- intelligent, brilliant, logical husband didn't place the dress under a plastic dry-cleaning bag is beyond me. No amount of coaxing or yelling can get Tuffy to stop prancing on my dress. And we haven't even left the alley yet.We're only an hour and fifteen minutes behind schedule, so we're not stressed or anything. (And we're certainly not sniping at each other over who bears the fault for our completely screwed up itinerary. Not rolling eyes at each other or huffing in silence, either. Not us.) On the drive to the dog sitter's, Kaiser takes great joy in perching his front paws (and claws) on the back window ledge and barking at each car that goes by. It's rush hour. You do the math. Every time I order him to stop, he gazes at me with mild disinterest and then resumes barking. He clearly has calculated that I, sitting WAY up front, could not possibly inflict much damage to him, located WAY back in the truck's rear end. His little claws do wonders for my brand-new interior and upholstery, and the scraping sound they make—kind of like nails on a chalkboard—really helps my blossoming headache.

We make it halfway through town when I realize that I left the directions and phone number to the doggie caregiver at home on the kitchen bar. My mistake, I admit. I'm not quite perfect, you know. Unfortunately, I compound my error by telling Jack of my memory lapse just as we approach the very last turn-around before hitting really heavy traffic. Seizing a dubious opportunity, Jack brakes hard, bringing the truck to a screeching halt, and then he burns rubber—that would be brand-new tire rubber, of course—to complete the U-turn. This well-executed maneuver throws Tuffy—his paws still embedded in my dress—into the very narrow space between the back of the driver's seat and the edge of the folded down back seat, where his fat belly gets him quite stuck. The truck's spin also knocks Kaiser from his perch on the window ledge (which is not such a bad result), but this causes him to slam into my extremely twitter-pated Scotty, who groans loudly and begins hyperventilating. But the dogs are not the only things thrown around.

Since I had not had time to supervise Jack's loading of the truck, and as we were running too late to feed the dogs breakfast before leaving, Jack did what I can only surmise must have seemed perfectly reasonable to the male mind: he filled the dogs' bowls with food, stacked them three high without covers, and then just set them down in the back of the truck.

As Jack performs his hairpin turn, the bowls go flying and dog food goes airborne. Landing EVERYWHERE. Expensive prescription dog food from the vet (a different kind for each dog—each with its own unique aroma, no less) now blankets the cargo hold. And not just the dry kind. Nope. Nothing but the best for our boys: aromatic canned food, topped off with yummy, gritty dry beef pebbles.

Chaos ensues as the three hungry dogs realize that a feast has literally landed at their collective feet, er, paws. Tuffy struggles mightily to free himself from his imprisonment between the seats, his claws still attached to my dress despite my constant shouting to get off. But food is a great motivator, so he succeeds in squirming his way out of the pit to gobble up more than his share, my dress in tow. Kaiser knocks Scotty off his feet (again) as he attempts to scarf up the most grub. And they all use our luggage and hanging clothes as serving dishes.

You should have seen it. And inhaled it. So much for that new truck smell.

As we head back to the house, Jack and I alternate between yelling at each other over who is to blame for this debacle (duh...him!) and laughing hysterically at our dogs, who are quite full and smug by the time we return home.

We have to unload EVERYTHING, clean out the back of the truck, and repack. Because we're rocket scientists, we throw two of the dogs into the muddy back yard during this frantic scrub job, but Scotty (being the only intelligent one of us) refuses to leave the truck. He jumps into my seat in front and won't budge, licking his chops and looking on nervously. He's huge, so I just give up trying to drag him out.

When we finish scraping dog food off the new upholstery

(nauseating job, I have to tell you), we re-pack the luggage— but under my expert supervision this time. We then coax Scotty (a.k.a., "the Furball") out of my seat and into the back with the other two, who, I might add, are now wet and muddy from the drizzle that began just as we were about to load them up, of course.

Plenty wet and disheveled ourselves, we hastily climb in and take off. Again. It's only after I buckle my seatbelt that I remember Scotty's horrible shedding problem. Too late. Dog hairs on car seat plus damp wool suit on rear-end? You do the math.

We finally get back on the road and manage to arrive at the dog sitter's home only two hours late. Of course, we both have monumental headaches thanks to Kaiser's incessant barking during the ride, but I have to say that the extreme nausea that hits shortly thereafter really helps distract me from my pain (attributable to wet dog smell and malodorous dog food, no doubt). Joy.

But God must have had his fill of humor for the morning and momentarily takes pity on us as there is—miracle of all miracles—no traffic at all on the tollway, and we manage to get downtown in record time. I drop Jack off at work and arrive right outside the courtroom at exactly 9:00 a.m., covered in the aforementioned dog hair and smelling slightly of wet dog. And seriously nauseated. Good times, good times.

My court proceeding turns out to last all of three minutes, thankfully. But that leaves me wondering why on earth I had bothered to come down here in the first place. Like we can't do this over the phone? And why am I not charging the client more for this? Am I stupid? Oh, wait, we've established that already, haven't we?

Anyway, the rest of the morning proceeds roughly as planned. I land in Austin, deplane, grab my grandmother, and hop another plane to Mississippi. My grandmother is the ultimate traveling partner for persons who enjoy being constantly embarrassed: never have so many insults and complaints to so many people in such a confined place and in such a small amount of time issued from so few persons (that would be one person, to be precise). She's a tornado of incivility, and woe to those unsuspecting souls who wander into her path.

FRIDAY NIGHT

I survive my grandmother's multiple diatribes during the flight (there's nothing like being a captive audience), we land in Mississippi, and we make it to my sister's college ballet performance-she is spectacular, as usual—a bright spot in an otherwise trying weekend.

Meanwhile, back on the ranch . . . er, Austin, Jack attends the wedding rehearsal folderol and, as predicted, quarrels with his brothers about the boob party. (For the record, I actually told him to go just to save himself the grief from his siblings, but I'm proud to say that he respected me enough to refuse to visit a strip bar. Do you think this means I have no hope of ever seeing the Chippendales?) But there's nothing like a good family fight before a wedding, don't you think? Especially if it's followed by another argument at the reception. Details to follow.

SATURDAY MORNING

An unseasonably cold Arctic front hits Mississippi in the wee hours. It's a little early for ice, but there it is, hanging out on the wings of the plane. Once the techs fix that problem, some other malfunction appears. In the crowded, smelly gate lobby, we sit, and we sit, and we sit. F...O...R...E...V...E...R. Then they finally let us on the plane, where we sit freezing our tails off for a further measure of F...O...R...E...V...E...R. In danger of missing the wedding altogether at this point, I ignore the prohibition against cell phone use on the runway to hastily arrange alternate transportation from the airport to the hotel, since by the time we land in Austin, my ride will be lined up in his place as groomsman at the alter. Thankfully, I don't get kicked off the plane for this.

This "alternate" transportation I procure takes the form of my very gracious aunt, who lives in Austin. This constitutes a dubious arrangement given that my grandmother and aunt are not on speaking terms at the moment. I was so looking forward to that chilly car ride after being stuck first in the smelly airport lobby and then in the freezing claustrophobic confines of the plane for an eon. And I am so freaking nauseated. What is up with this?We finally get airborne. We finally land in Austin. We finally find my aunt. I'm still nauseated. Conversation is, for the most part, civil on the interminable ride to the hotel. After waving goodbye to my aunt and my grandmother, with false mutual admonitions to get together like this more often, I make a beeline to my hotel room for a shower, because of course I didn't bother to do my hair before leaving Jackson, thinking I'd have plenty of time on the other end to attend to my coif.

I only have half an hour to spare to get beautiful. Under the best of circumstances, this is just not possible. You know I'm not the wash and wear type. Unless I'm trying to look like Roseanne Roseannadanna, that is. And I still have to sew glittery black buttons on my beautiful black dress to further accessorize the paw prints and essence of dog food. I cut some serious corners. Dry, frizzy, unconditioned hair? So be it. Quill-covered porcupine legs? The dress has an ankle-length skirt, after all. No harm, no foul.

And how am I going to get to the wedding now that almost everyone else is already there? With Jack's aunt, of course, who is also running late. She's a fun one. I've always found it high entertainment to watch a "discussion" between her and Jack's mom. The two sisters can be sitting at the same table, talking to each other for half an hour, and neither one will wander into the other's conversation. It's a little like listening to two different radio channels simultaneously.

Jack's aunt drives his sister and me (furiously sewing buttons on my dress jacket as we swerve up and down hills through Austin traffic) to the wedding locale, a graceful Victorian set on a lush hilltop. Quite beautiful. Sadly, I did not arrive soon enough to carry out my very important duties as chief flower presenter. But we do, miracle of all miracles, make it there before the wedding starts.The outdoor ceremony goes without a hitch—I have no idea how. Jupiter must have aligned with the Big Dipper. But there it is. The dinner reception . . . slightly different story.

Due to some managerial oversight, there's an open bar for all the alcohol you can possibly consume (indeed, the employees take great joy in foisting it upon unsuspecting teetotalers, like the preacher and his wife), but guests have to pay for a soda or juice. So all those who could pass for over 21 have no trouble whatsoever getting something to drink for free, but the younger kids are just out of luck. As Jack and I are drinking wine tonight (and are clearly not going to be carded), this does not present a problem for us.

I can tell that Jack's mom is so not happy that he and I are imbibing while dining at the same table as the Southern Baptist minister who officiated the ceremony, who, by the way, just happens to be your own dear brother's father-in-law. So during dinner we all talk about you, of course. Did you really hit a nude beach in Cancun?

The evening culminates in Jack and his big brother getting into a huge fight when I tip off the bride that big brother (the best man) and the groomsmen are about to abscond with all of her lingerie that she has packed for the honeymoon. Who wants to go to Jamaica with no underwear? It's not like lacy thongs are included in those "all-inclusive" resorts. But the best man doesn't appreciate my interference and calls me the "B" word. Jack, in turn, doesn't much appreciate that characterization of me in public, although, in private, he might be inclined to agree on occasion. Words are exchanged. Ultimatums are thrown down. Feelings get hurt. I laugh. Jack doesn't. (But I very much appreciate his sticking up for me!). We manage to avoid an all-out fist fight as the party breaks up.

So all's well that ends well, I suppose, or in the case of this wedding, just ends, anyway. After the weekend I have had, the prospect of returning home from Austin—even in a truck that reeks of dog food—seems glorious. But this thought lingers only until I get in the truck and the nausea returns. I blame it on the mingling of the dog food odor with some fragrant wedding greenery that Jack's mom insisted we swipe from the ceremony. But as luck would have it, purloined wedding cake is quite the antidote to nausea. I eat it all the way home to Dallas.

So. That was my weekend from hell. You know, right now, I don't think I ever want to go anywhere again. Or attend another family wedding. Which reminds me, have I mentioned that Jack's sister is getting married next month the day after Christmas and that I'm singing in the wedding?

Well, I've taken up enough of your day. And I'm supposed to be drafting my business forms. Or something useful like that. But what I really need is a nap. I'm so exhausted from the trip. Conveniently, I'm still in my P.J.'s, which has been officially approved as business casual attire at my office. It's so great to be the boss.

Catch you later. Have a great day!
yp

SUBJECT: RE: WHY I SHOULD NEVER GET BETWEEN THE BEST MAN AND THE BRIDE'S UNDERWEAR

Tears are rolling down my face I am laughing so hard!! Instead of 'why you should never...' I think you should just step aside and let the chips fall where they may. There is enough fodder in that family to have an entire bonfire!

As for the packing incident—too funny! I'm sure at the moment it was not the most hilarious thing you have ever heard, but it definitely is the most hilarious thing I have ever heard! Better run—will catch up later. S.

SUBJECT: WELL WHAT DO YOU KNOW

Dear Steph,

Big news! I'm expecting!!!!! A baby, in case that wasn't clear. We just found out a few days ago. Explains all that nausea, which has now hit full force. And as so many women through the ages have opined, "morning sickness" is a complete misnomer. This crap lasts all day. Ice cream seems to help. Lots of ice cream. With chocolate syrup. Someone suggested cheese, but that can't be right. It doesn't have sugar. Must have sugar . . .As it turns out, I was pregnant when we bought the "baby- mobile," which was perfect timing! On the downside, I was also pregnant when drinking two glasses of wine at Jack's brother's wedding. So now I get to worry for nine months that my drinking binge has caused fetal alcohol poisoning or some awful defect. A woman's body really ought to give some sort of signal that can't possibly be misinterpreted to let a newbie mom-to-be know in those first few weeks that she's got a stowaway on board. A bull's eye "birth" mark suddenly appearing across the abdomen would work well. Or maybe cup size should go up four sizes in two days. Something really obvious and unambiguous. None of this nausea crap or sore breasts or weepiness, which could be anything. Then again, maybe women who are trying to get pregnant just shouldn't be drinking two whole glasses of wine in the first place.

Nah, that can't be right.

I've been reading that pregnant women need lots of rest, so I've decided to give myself permission to sleep late and take a nap every day. And I think ice cream breaks every four hours are perfectly acceptable—after all, the baby needs lots of calcium. Signing off to grab some calcium and a nap!
yp

SUBJECT: RE: WELL WHAT DO YOU KNOW

WAY COOL! CONGRATULATIONS! You are going to be such a great mom. And how great is it that you get to eat ice cream and take naps whenever you feel like it?! Keep me posted on your progress. S.

SUBJECT: YOU KNOW YOU'RE A DOG LOVER WHEN

Steph,

Hey! Hope you're having a happy holiday season. We're great here. Still extremely nauseated. But otherwise great. Well, except for all the barking, which inspired my new list.

You know you're a dog lover when:

1. You agree to pet sit two super-high-maintenance dogs on top of keeping your own three high-maintenance dogs over the Christmas holiday, even though you're pregnant and very tired and very nauseated. And eight guests are coming to stay over for Christmas. And you're feeding twenty on Christmas Day. You hope everyone will welcome the dogs, but if they don't, you feel confident in telling them to take a hike.
2. You further agree to shred carrots twice a day to feed to the aforementioned guest dogs, even though you've never heard of dogs eating carrots and you nearly barf every time you get the peeler out (yes, they have to be peeled, then shredded) because the whole experience is so nauseating. And you're pretty sure you'll never eat carrots again.
3. In an attempt to surprise your mother-in-law (a seasoned grandmother already) with your good news of an impending

birth, you ask her if she'd like to be a grandmother again, and her immediate response is a horrified, "You're getting another dog?"

4. You don't mind (for the most part) hearing five dogs bark at you every single time you pass through the kitchen, or someone knocks on the door, or the phone rings, or a door closes, or you sneeze, or you flush the toilet. You decide that some dogs simply do not have discriminating hearing, and you resign yourself to wearing ear plugs for the duration of the holidays.

5. You limit your holiday activities outside the home so that you can closely monitor dog fights, water bowl levels, how much stuffing has been pulled out of the dogs' sleeping beds and shredded all over your kitchen, and, most importantly, so you can scoop poop and vacuum dog hair on an hourly basis.

Are we nuts or what? But they're just so sweet . . .
Merry Christmas! Happy New Year! yp

SUBJECT: RE: YOU KNOW YOU'RE A DOG LOVER WHEN

Nuts? Yes. Or maybe not. Maybe it is beyond "nuts." Yes, definitely I think that it is beyond "nuts." Maybe your dog fascination is a precursor to mommy-hood, and it is merely the first stage of the morphing process from successful attorney to crazed mommy.

I mean really—dogs are not that "sweet." Oh. And I have an entirely different vision of carrots now. Ewwww! You realize this will have to put your dog-obsession on a leash when baby arrives! Take care and milk the pregnancy for all it's worth! S.

CHAPTER THREE: A DECADE PAST

SUBJECT: CLASS REUNION

Steph,

Hey! I'm excited about our eleventh year high school "mini-reunion." How lame are we that our class couldn't even get a ten-year party together? Oh, wait. That was supposed to be the job of the senior class president, right? And I didn't win that election, right? So, hey — not my problem!!

It's unfortunate that I'm going to be as big as a blue whale when I see everyone, but there's not much I can do about that until after the birth, so I guess I won't worry about that problem either.

yp

SUBJECT: RE: CLASS REUNION

Hi there!

We are a lame class. Or, should that be we were a lame class? Regardless, I think we have held to our motto of "Don't do today what you can put off until tomorrow!" Funny, how the important lessons in high school seem to stick in your craw forever.

I am really looking forward to seeing you and everyone else. If it is okay with you, I'll head to Dallas on Saturday morning.

Pierce's sister is turning forty, which is a monumental occasion considering last year she was literally on her deathbed for a few months. Anyhow, I would like to see everyone coming in for her "surprise" party so I'll be in Austin Friday night. I'll see you Saturday!S.

SUBJECT: ON MY WAY

Hi there!

Just a quick note to let you know I am finally leaving for Dallas. Is it raining? My head is pounding and there is a dense fog outside—oh...my mistake. It is called a hangover. I went out last night for the surprise party. I know I did not get out of control. Pierce's mother was there for crying out loud! I know what has caused this tremendous headache and foggy vision. It was all the heavy bass-loaded music pounding in the smoke-filled bar, which caused me to have to scream to be cordial. The screaming, of course, required that I open my mouth widely, creating a vacuum that sucked as much smoke into my lungs as possible. The presence of the smoke, the screaming, and the incessant pounding of the bass drum has taken up residence in my psyche and will not leave. That is why I have a headache and blurry vision. Okay, is any of this making sense to you? I best just get on the road. I will be there eventually. The ETA is unknown at this point as I am sucking down forty-four ounces of pure caffeine disguised as coffee, which will inevitably cause bathroom breaks. So, see you soon! S.

SUBJECT: RE: ON MY WAY

Steph,

As you're no doubt on the road by now and should NOT be checking your e-mail, it's probably pointless to even bring this up, but . . . most normal families [and by "normal" I mean dysfunctionally normal—the stuff you find in most any family: serious father-son disagreements at holiday gatherings over things that happened a decade ago; cat fights among jealous, superficial females; an alcoholic or two drawing unwanted attention to the clan; and no more than three confirmed tax evaders] have get-togethers at really boring restaurants and/or have house parties. Any family that has a "reunion" at an ear-shattering, lung-damaging bar might warrant further investigation before plunging in too deep. Just something to ponder.

Can't wait to see you today!
yp

SUBJECT: RE: RE: CLASS REUNION

Steph,

I had a great time with everyone. I hope no one was too bummed out by my having to leave the partying at the West End early. Being nine months pregnant makes clubbing a bit of a challenge. Especially when all you can order is water, milk, or more water. And when the baby started "dancing" to the beat of the music, things became extraordinarily uncomfortable (and by "things," I mean my bladder, which has been squashed down to the size of a thimble). Based on her activity level at the bars, I'm a little worried that Claire might turn out to be a party girl!

Despite having done the good-mom-to-be thing by foregoing the hip partying with you guys in favor of resting my whale belly and tired dogs, I have still managed to wind up on bed rest for the remainder of this pregnancy. The day after y'all left, in fact. Preeclampsia, they tell me. Otherwise known as pregnancy-induced high blood pressure. I'm two weeks out from my due date. And I'm stuck in a horizontal position for almost 24/7 until then.

This is completely unacceptable, of course. I was right smack in the middle of some serious nesting when this hit, and now nobody will let me walk to the kitchen, much less reorganize the silverware drawer and clean out the fridge, both of which must absolutely be done before this baby comes. Why, you may ask? I confess I don't know. It's not like the baby will be sleeping in either the drawer of the refrigerator. But like the salmon instinctively knows to swim upstream, I just know in my gut that these things—and about fifty-two other super important tasks—have to be done!

So since no one will let me out of bed, I've begged my mom and my mom-in-law to come help satisfy my nesting urge. They're thrilled to help, of course. Being teachers, they neither one have anything better to do during their last few days of summer freedom before the school bell tolls than clean parts of my home that haven't seen a dust cloth since we moved in two years ago.

To be perfectly honest, I think they're a little worried that if they don't carry out my every domestic cleaning whim, I'll freak out.

They're absolutely right, but I'm not letting them know that I know that they know I'm a mental case. We're all just pretending that it's normal for me to want to alphabetize the soup cans in the pantry and to sort the new baby clothes and blankets not just by size but also by color, style, and function.

Well, enough about poor me, stuck in bed, my only companions a stack of unread novels and paperwork that I've been putting off for three years. I hope we can get everyone together again for a fifteenth or twentieth reunion. But knowing us, it'll be the nineteenth or the twenty-first. We were always such an offbeat, apathetic class. But who care, you know?
Yp

SUBJECT: RE: RE: RE: CLASS REUNION

Hi there!

I just wanted to say I had a great time at the mini-reunion. I had no idea that even though I was the tallest person from eighth grade until we graduated that I would now be a full foot shorter than anyone at the reunion. Wow!

As for apologizing for having to leave, do not worry. I will fill you in on what you missed.

Do you remember the guys singing and playing the guitar on your front lawn? One of them wants to be a country singer. So at the club he went on stage and did the karaoke thing. Not bad, I'll have to admit. And guts too. (Literally, both brevity and stomach, —out there for all to see.) If he wants to be a singer, he is going to have to learn to make the 'guts' look a lot more sexy than the "Hi, I am your plumber here to fix your sink. Do you want me to turn around?" look he had going that night.

Second, after the karaoke stint we moved to a different bar, a hip-hop place. It was all fun but immediately got funnier (well, for the rest of the group) when the bouncer approached Rachel. She was dancing, getting her groove on and this bouncer comes up to her with an underage teen in tow and says, "Is this your kid?" We were rolling! The laughs were coming so hard, tears were streaming and the guys were doubled over! Well, you remember Rachel—she is not going to take any flack! She went off on the bouncer in this twang that even I could barely understand. After a few rounds of "I yam barrelly old 'nough to be ennis baw, much less be 'is momma'" we decided it would be best if we moved on to another venue. So we went outside for some fresh air.

Once there, Abe had to bale due to girlfriend pressures which left Paul, Rachel and me. After approximately two more beers, we decided, no I decided, it was time to call it a night. My main reason was due to alcohol consumption the night before plus the alcohol consumption that night, AND I was starting to think I was blind for not hooking up with Paul! Okay. Didn't want to ruin a friendship over that! So, Rachel and I caught a cab and high-tailed it to your house at the respectable hour of 3:00 a.m. (Hope we didn't wake you.)

It was all great fun. Let's do it again in another eleven years!

S.

SUBJECT: RE: RE: RE: RE: CLASS REUNION

It's high school all over again. You guys were always going off partying without me! Whether I'm seventeen or twenty-nine, I guess I'm just not cut out to be a party girl. But why didn't y'all tell me all about this Sunday morning at breakfast? Always out of the loop . . .

Glad you had a great time, though!
Yp

PART TWO

CHAPTER FOUR: THE TRUTH ABOUT CHILDBIRTH

SUBJECT: CLAIRE'S HERE!

Steph,

Well, I survived childbirth. As did the baby, thankfully. I wasn't sure there for a while if either of us was going to make it to the end, but it's not as though those hospital people give you much of a choice, is it? You do as you're told or they threaten the scalpel, regardless of how worn out you are. But we'll get to that later.

Claire is so amazing. She's so tiny! She weighed less than six pounds at birth, so I can literally hold her up on my chest with only one hand. Her hair looks like spun gold. Everyone tells me it will all fall out soon. It hardly seems fair for a nearly bald baby to lose even more hair, but I don't make the rules, so I guess we'll take what we can get. Or lose what we have. Whatever.

She's so sweet and looks so gorgeous to me, although if I were being perfectly objective, I would have to say that she needs to be thrown in a dryer and fluffed up a bit. She's a little wrinkled! When she's awake, which isn't often unless it's nighttime, of course, she's so alert. She's quite fun to cuddle with, and her favorite spot seems to be on her daddy's chest.

Claire's not so much fun to feed, however. The "lactation consultants" (a really nice title someone came up with for "leaking boob experts") say that I can expect to be a little sore for a short while when feeding Claire. Well, if by "a little sore" they mean that I'm supposed to feel as though a vacuum suction cup lined with heavy-duty sandpaper is ripping out my nipples when she eats, then yeah. I'm a little sore. They said my soreness should only last for about a week. Well, it's been a week. And I'm still "a little sore." Way sore, to be perfectly honest. I had no idea that there could be so many ways to get it wrong when it comes to something as simple- sounding as nursing an infant. Of course, it could be that we're experiencing technical difficulties because Claire's tiny head and mouth are smaller than the feeding apparatus, as it were. In any event, I'm going to continue to play my role as the sacred cow and hope for the best. And take copious amounts of Tylenol.

Not willing to be the one woman in history to risk unraveling the very fabric of our feminine society by maintaining silence on this subject, I shall of course be obliged to disclose my own birthing tale to you. Not wanting to bore you, however, I'll just narrate the highlights. Those I recall, anyway.

Where to begin? The evening of July 26, at 7:00 p.m. seems as good a place as any to start. We were asked to arrive at the hospital a full 24 hours before Claire's birth. I can only assume that this was to ensure that we would not actually miss the birth ourselves. I was not in labor at all when I arrived but was forced into it by my doctor, who wielded a small pill in his gloved hands and knew exactly what to do with it to minimize my modesty and maximize my discomfort. While waiting for said pill to take effect, I endured being strapped to an uncomfortable hospital bed (is there any other kind?) and a miserable contraption known as a fetal monitor. For her part, Claire did not appear to enjoy the fetal monitor as much as I did, and she did her best to avoid it, thus causing me great abdominal stress and endless grief from the nurses who kept coming in to reposition it on my truly enormous whale of a white belly. I could have sworn I heard one nurse muttering on her way out, "Call me Ishmael."

A parade of relatives marched through the room that night — to encourage me, I suppose. The room offered a rather boring scene, at best, but was enlivened briefly by the appearance of Jack's aunt and uncle. The two were traveling by motorcycle on their way from Houston to somewhere up north for some sort of Harley-Davidson convention. Bedecked in black leather and fishnet hose (I kid you not), they entertained us for a while before getting back on the road.

At various points, my spectators left to get themselves something to eat for dinner. And despite being the one person in this ordeal who would be performing the most work (hence the term "labor"), I was the only one denied food of any kind, although the nurses graciously offered me ice chips. To top it all off, someone ordered my blood drawn, a hideous experience for me under the best of circumstances, which this clearly was not, and my arm was cuffed for the remainder of the ordeal due to the preeclampsia.

Jack, ever the great comfort and helpmate, played computer games while I stared at the ceiling most of the early nighttime hours. My nurses had instructed me to get some sleep, and even gave me something to help in that endeavor, but sleep I did not. It's rather difficult to doze when: A) you're starving;

B) your arm is being squeezed to pieces every ten minutes; C) the nurses keep coming in to readjust the fetal monitor on your huge belly every twenty minutes with rather cold hands (or sooner if Claire was being particularly difficult); and D) you're freaking scared about when that first contraction is going to hit and can't think about anything else.

And so it was that in the wee hours of the morning of the 27th, that first contraction hit. Almost immediately, we recalled Cindy, my doula (a personal child-birthing aide) to the hospital to help me handle the contractions. My goal was to have a "natural" childbirth, although clearly I was off to a bad start in that regard. But aside from being artificially induced into labor, being forced to stay in bed hooked to monitors and cuffs with no reprieve, and being given a cocktail of drugs for my various conditions that made me feel like a junior chemistry set experiment, I was bound and determined to get through this like a "real woman" (that term being defined here as one who labors and delivers without pain relief). You can stop laughing now.

I relied on Cindy to help me through the pain, which she did admirably, despite the constrictions under which we, and more specifically I, labored. Jack helped by reading an internal monitor (there was a fun experience-don't ask) and telling me when my next contraction was coming and how big it would get. Without him, of course, I would not have been able to figure these things out.

Several hours and several hundred excruciating contractions later, loaded up on one medicine to lower my blood pressure, which made me irritable, and another to increase my contractions, which also made me irritable, and strapped to oxygen for the baby's sake, which annoyed me to no end, I finally begged for mercy. I never really had anyone accurately explain the pain of a contraction to me prior to my own labor, which is why, I suppose, I thought I could do it without pain relief. But I can tell you even now, a week later, exactly what it felt like (and this in spite of the fact that I was promised that the memory of the pain would fade away almost immediately- you know, in retrospect, I really don't think these medical people always know what they're talking about). In any event, the pain of every contraction wrapped tightly around my entire torso like an iron corset that squeezed my body like a vise. But not just any vise. This one felt like it had been smoldering in flames. It burned. In short, it hurt like hell.

I really wanted to die. The hospital staff, however, felt this was not in my best interest at the time, so they gave me an IV pain reliever. This helped ever so much. Instead of being awake and in pain the entire time (because I had constant back labor pain between the contractions), the medicine caused me to fall asleep between the contractions, so that when I next awakened, it was at the height of a contraction, with no time to mentally or physically prepare for it at all. Because I fell into the pattern of sleeping, awakening to excruciating, unmanageable pain, then sleeping again, it felt as though there were no breaks between my misery. Everyone assured me that the pains were two minutes apart, but I didn't believe them, of course. I again wanted to die. And, again, no one thought that to be a tenable solution to the situation.

I never thought I would get to the point that I would let someone stick a needle in my back, but Jack, without consulting me, decided to put me out of my misery and called for the holy grail of labor relief, the epidural. In truth, I believe no small measure of self-interest motivated his decision. Though I have little memory of it, I am told that I bit and scratched him repeatedly during contractions when he ranged too close, and that I nearly bit my doula as well, which would have been terribly rude.

I was not pleased about being forced into an epidural with its foot-long needle and all, nor was I happy that I had to sit up, wrap my arms around my nurse's waist, lean over, and take a needle in the back—all during the middle of a very strong contraction. Apparently, this is the only way these anesthetists will perform the procedure (medical necessity or sadistic torture-you decide). As I hung onto my nurse for dear life, I involuntarily took that old commercial's quip to heart about "if you can pinch an inch" and very nearly performed a rudimentary tummy tuck on her as the needle went in. I did feel badly about that. No doubt she was bruised for days. She was very kind and did a wonderful job of coaching me through the pushing phase, from what I recall of it anyway, which came several hours after the peaceful rest brought on by the epidural.

With the pain gone after the application of the epidural, I no longer hated Jack and the anesthesiologist, and I was actually quite thankful to them both for putting an end to my grief. Or I would have been, anyway, had I been conscious, which I wasn't.

At around 5:30 p.m., (or so I deduced later), someone flipped on the lights, told me to wake up, and start pushing. This was most disorienting. Why they wouldn't let me just sleep through the pushing was beyond me. I tried to, but they wouldn't allow it. Everyone kept yelling at me to wake up. They reduced my epidural medication, however, and that got my attention.

It was determined that the baby was "sunny-side up" and had to be turned before delivery. This sounded to me like a job requiring more epidural medication, not less. But I lost that argument. The nurse put me up on some medieval torture device called a squat bar, and while I don't recall exactly what I did while hanging from it, I do remember it causing me to empty what few contents I had left in my stomach all over the floor (that would be ice chips, for the record), and then I had to endure a case of dry heaves.

It wasn't enough that I was naked, cold, and disoriented, neither was it sufficient that I was nauseated beyond belief, and yet starving and thirsty all at the same time. But to top it off, everyone kept yelling at me to push. Push what? I had no idea. Eventually, though, my nurse managed to calm me and I guess I performed as required, because after an hour and a half of this manic activity (so I'm told), and approximately 24 hours after our arrival to the hospital for this adventure of a lifetime, the doctor placed this warm, wiggly, wet baby on my somewhat flatter belly. And she was perfect. A bit disgusting until they cleaned her up, of course, but perfect, nonetheless.

I won't bore you with the cleanup detail (I don't even want to think about that placenta) or the recovery period, neither of which was nearly as comfortable as one might hope. I wish I could say that Claire's birth was a wonderful, fulfilling experience, but it was mostly a hellish nightmare. She, on the other hand, is a wonderful little person, and if I had to go through the whole thing all over again to get her here, I most certainly would. But I would get the epidural way earlier. Like when the first contraction hit.

Well, I promised only the highlights and so I have fulfilled my promise. But I have done my duty in adding my story to the annals of birthing history. And from it I hope you have deduced an important point or two: 1) birth control is always a good thing; and 2) an epidural, in spite of the terrifyingly long needle involved, is your best friend in the delivery room. Oh, and babies and birth are miracles of God, and the gift of life is a precious thing, and blah, blah, blah.

Well, my munchkin is apparently wailing in hunger and waits to torture me again. I shall bid you adieu.
Yp

SUBJECT: RE: CLAIRE'S HERE

Yvonne,

Ewwww!!! Okay—too much information. Birth control- GOOD; baby birth—not so good. Didn't you go to some kind of pre-delivery seminar to get the lowdown on the labor process before you were actually in the midst of it all? There are seminars about virtually everything and nothing. Surely there is something offered along the lines of, "Childbirth: Torture Like You've Never Known?" Nevertheless, I'm glad you survived, and I cannot wait to see Claire. I'm sure she is beautiful. And, I would venture to say you won't be doing that again anytime soon! (At least not on purpose!) Get some rest and write when you can. S.

CHAPTER FIVE: TOP TEN LISTS FOR LADIES ONLY

SUBJECT: TOP 10 THINGS I'VE LEARNED ABOUT BEING A NEW MOM

Dear Steph,

This whole new mom thing is great-extraordinarily tiring, but fun. I have learned so much already. Had a few missteps here and there, but I'm practically an expert now. And I'm so happy to share my knowledge with you, for future reference of course. Thus far, the wisdom I've gained from motherhood can be summed up as follows:

10. It's probably not a good idea to let the new dad videotape anything as incriminating as the new mom giving the baby her first full bath, particularly when the new dad is talking on the phone with an old pal while videotaping and is NOT helping clueless new mom AT ALL. When in doubt as to the next step, however, just keep washing the baby's hair. All fifty-three strands of it. Maybe not seventeen times though (Jack actually counted on the video replay—if Claire turns out bald and wants to know why, I'm blaming Jack and burning the incriminating tape).

9. Read infant care books with great caution and skepticism. They are full of insidious untruths designed to lure a new mom into thinking the physical toll of motherhood will be slight and that something must be terribly wrong with you if you don't fit the

model. For instance, the books say that nipples will be sore for a mere five to seven days from the start of nursing. I don't know what man started that ridiculous notion, but I'd like to string him up by his nipples and see how long his stay sore. Only five to seven days, I should think. Trust me when I say that strategic nursing anatomy remains sore for a full freaking month. And don't believe any book, however expertly written and informative it may seem, that tells you otherwise.

8. You are not crazy to fear that your peacefully sleeping infant three rooms away will somehow land in the hot kitchen oven if you turn it on to bake something for dinner. To keep from having panic attacks over this particular waking nightmare, simply do not cook during the postpartum period. Lock yourself and the baby in the room farthest away from the kitchen, especially if the new dad decides that he really must have a hot meal that requires the use of the oven. Have the new dad bring you the hot meal to enjoy in your room so that the oven will have a chance to cool down before you and the baby venture anywhere near the kitchen.

7. Riding in the car with a new baby is an unsettling experience, but one you can work through. Although you may fear that the new baby will choke to death in her car seat each and every time you apply the brakes, the constant, excruciating craning of your neck and arms to check on the infant's breathing will be reassuring to you, though possibly annoying to your infant.

It is not strictly necessary to stop every few blocks to climb in the back seat and check to see if the baby is still alive, but it is perfectly acceptable to do so — and to drive super slowly Ignore all the horn-honking behind you.

6. While out shopping with the new baby, make certain that you carry at least four EXTRA outfits with you in the diaper bag at all times. Within four minutes of arriving at a store, the first and cutest outfit you dressed the baby in that morning will get pooped on, thus necessitating a trip to the changing room, a room you'll become very familiar with. The second outfit (that's really darling, mind you) will be peed on while changing the infant out of the first and cutest poopy one, so you'll need that third outfit, a marginally interesting two- piece from some great aunt with little fashion sense that you didn't really expect to ever have to use. After already changing the infant twice, said infant will be starving from so much physical exertion, and you will have to feed said infant in the changing room, using the very sore feeding apparatus. Much spit up will ensue, of course, necessitating the fourth outfit, which is really only a glorified onesie. But feeding leads to more pooping and more leaking, so although you haven't made it out of the changing room yet, the fifth and final outfit at your disposal, inevitably a plain white, ill-fitting onesie, will be the one your baby dons for everyone to. see while shopping, which you can finally begin. That is, unless you also must change the onesie at some point, leaving your poor infant wrapped in nothing but swaddling clothes- conveniently, however, you will no doubt be in a store that carries at least rudimentary infant supplies and/or clothes (where else could you possibly go?) and can probably purchase something for the ride home.

5. When overzealous grandparents want time alone to cuddle your newborn baby, and they kick you out of the house, forcing you to go on a "date" with your spouse for the first time after the birth, do not make the mistake of going to see a horror movie. Especially one involving dead children. See a comedy instead.

Also, don't make the mistake of going out to dinner on your date. You won't hear a thing your husband says to you because you'll be concentrating on all the other people's babies, causing you to pine for your own defenseless infant left in the clutches of clueless grandparents. What do grandparents know about babies? You can't enjoy a meal when you're worried your baby will not survive until your return. And while constantly thinking about your baby, you'll leak all over the place from the very sore feeding apparatus, which is rather embarrassing.

4. It is perfectly normal to check your sleeping infant's breathing pattern every five minutes, day and night. You cannot be too careful in this area. Grabbing the peacefully sleeping baby up out of the bassinet as quickly as you can when you think she's not breathing is always the right thing to do, even when she's only been asleep for fifteen minutes and it took you two hours to get her to go to sleep in the first place. She'll stop screaming eventually, and you'll be so much more at peace knowing that she's breathing just fine.

3. If you have a newborn girl, and you dress her in pink and wrap her in a pink blanket and put a pink bow in her hair, and you carry a pink diaper bag, you will inevitably attract a large number of people for whom gender identification is somewhat challenging. This is especially true of the elderly, all men, and most children. Don't be surprised if you hear questions like, "What's his name?" and "Oh, he's so cute. His father must be so proud to have a son." Rather than embarrassing the person who asks about your "boy" by correcting the poor soul's misapprehension, simply tell them his name is "Max." Explain that you hope he'll be a football star some day and make his father proud. It's just easier. Trust me.

2. Germs are a major concern with any newborn. To minimize the risk that you'll be visiting the pediatrician every two weeks, set up rules for touching your infant. When visitors come to see your new baby, immediately direct them to the powder room, which should have industrial strength anti- microbial soap and disposable towels. Leaving a nailbrush out for guests is not a bad idea either. And surgical masks. Insist that all children under the age of eighteen simply stay away. Should any guest rub his or her nose while at your home, offer a wet wipe immediately. Under no circumstances allow anyone who touches his or her nose, hair, eyes, or feet to hold or touch the baby thereafter, wet wipes notwithstanding. Discourage visitors from touching the baby's hands, face, or head. Feet are safe to touch only if the baby is wearing socks, which will have to be immediately washed upon the exit of your guest. But it's best to wrap the baby in a blanket to discourage any kind of direct contact at all. In extreme cases, use the "nursing modesty" ploy to spirit your child away to safety in another room, then put her down for "a nap" until the offending guest leaves.

Explain that babies often scream in their sleep if the guest seems dubious about the reason you provide ("a nap") for the baby's failure to return to the room with you. An added bonus is that a screaming infant usually induces a quicker departure from said guest.

1. And finally, the number one thing I've learned about being a new mom is to relax and enjoy my baby. As long as I'm not suffering a panic or anxiety attack about the safety, health, or comfort of my little darling, and assuming I am not more than three feet away from my sweet baby, and provided there are no threatening guests with germs, and if I don't have to bathe the

baby, and if I know she's breathing okay, I am as happy as can be as a new mom-it's so relaxing! I highly recommend motherhood. Jack would like to add that he recommends a good therapist for new moms, which is ridiculous, of course. Who could possibly need a therapist when so she's deliriously happy?
yp

SUBJECT: TOP 10 THINGS I'VE LEARNED ABOUT BEING A NEW MOM

Wow! Considering I have no prospective babies in the near future, I'd like to just take this moment to breathe. Now, that I have done that I'd like to briefly note the top ten things I've learned being single...which isn't too far off from being a mom. Well, not yet anyway...

10. It's probably not a good idea to photograph or video ANYTHING! It's all incriminating, no matter how innocent you think it might be. Whoever invented the video recorder and made it available to the masses should have his life on constant "record." Oh, that's reality TV, isn't it?

9. Read all romance novels and historical fiction books with full confidence that everything in them has happened, will happen, or is happening in reality as you read. I can assure you that the life of the single female is almost always replicated in print under the guise of "fiction."

8. Most single people I know don't own an oven, so there is no fear there. Microwaves and take-out are the methods of choice when not dining in the actual restaurant. And, for clarification,

fast food drive thru's do count as edible when one is in a hurry. Plus, the happy meal toys score big points with your nephew when you visit!

7. Driving while blasting the radio is a perfect substitute for going to the gym so long as your head is bobbing and your fingers and toes are tapping. If you open your window, you also get the benefit of outdoor exercise.

6. It is critical that a single female be ready at all times for a change in venue. Hence, one must always have the gym clothes, a pair of stilettos, emergency make-up bag, hair brush, and sexy jeans in the backseat of one's vehicle. Don't worry if you think you need a shower first; it is perfectly acceptable to ditch the undergarments, splash some water on your face, and change clothes in a fast food restaurant or parking lot for that matter. If you get the opportunity to go out, don't miss it by having to prep for an hour!

5. Dates? What dates? Most of the time, single females are seeing horror movies alone, which is quite horrific in and of itself.

4. When one is single, sleep is inevitably taken for granted. Of course, it never occurs during the normal course of things. Usually, single people catch naps on buses in transit or while waiting on their boss, who is invariably late. Nighttime sleeping is usually done between the hours of 1:00 a.m. and 6:00 a.m. if it is a "work day." Otherwise, sleeping will happen sometime around 5:00 a.m. until 11:00 a.m.

3. If you have the chance, walk down Sixth Street in Austin or Bourbon Street in New Orleans. There, all gender identification

issues will be further complicated. Trust me on this. And, as a precaution, unless you want to dance with a man who thinks you are a man, a woman who thinks you are a man, a man who thinks you are a woman, or a woman who thinks you are a woman, DON'T — I repeat — DON'T go to a gay bar called the Forum on Halloween. I did. Fun, but quite confusing.

2. Germs. Again, don't go to the Forum on Halloween. There are no antibacterial soap dispensers, no hand towels, and no doors on the unisex stalls. There is, however, an attendant that can show you more than a few uses for duct tape.

1. Being single is not relaxing. Enjoyable at times, yes, but relaxing, no. After all, there are dates to acquire, a body to maintain, germs to eek out, and sleep to work into the schedule. In lieu of therapy, I suggest making the most of your time as a single person: translation — be a tramp — while you can! Eat all the crap you want, race to the gym, splash some water about, and head to the nearest bar for all-night dancing in hopes of finding the perfect partner with whom you will spend the rest of your life. It is a lot more fun than the traditional therapy and I would venture to say, cheaper.

See ya! S.

CHAPTER SIX: ARE THOSE GUYS STALKING ME?

SUBJECT: THE END OF YOUTH

Steph,

Hey! Thanks for the birthday card! It was sweet of you to remember. I can't believe I've hit thirty. I feel like my youth is over. Technically, I guess it was over some time ago, but "twenty-anything" sounds so much younger than thirty. I'll get over it in a couple of days. Or years.

I will be heading down to our old stomping grounds to visit family next week. Do you suppose even one thing will have changed at the high school? I'm guessing not. At least you and I can say that we've broken free—our children's grandparents and parents may have gone to the same high school, but our kids sure as heck won't.

I hope my little gold spider monkey (that's kind of what she looks like right now) will travel well. My mom ordered me to start packing today even though we are not leaving for several days. She seems to be under the impression that it will take that long for me to pack up all the baby's stuff. I have no idea why. The fact that there isn't a flat surface in my house that isn't covered in baby paraphernalia (all of which I consider absolutely essential) can't have anything to do with it. But since I'm now thirty, I surely don't have to take orders from her anymore, do I? Nah. I didn't think so.I'm off in search of a Dr. Pepper and some serious chocolate to counter my depression over aging. (I'm not really depressed, but I have to come up with an excuse to overindulge, and that one sounds as good as any.) And, if I'm up to it, I might ponder a packing list. Do you remember when we used to sit for hours working on our summer camp packing lists? Weren't we silly? How much could we possibly have needed? Catch you later.

Yp

SUBJECT: RE: THE END OF YOUTH

Hi there,

Don't sweat turning thirty. I had a hard twenty-nine so thirty will be a breeze for me! Have a safe trip. S.

SUBJECT: THE BEST LITTLE…NURSING STATION…IN TEXAS

Hi Steph,

Claire and I just got back from our marathon trip down to Taft to visit my grandmother. I'm exhausted. And mortified. And somewhat concerned Child Protective Services is going to come knocking on my door.

The best laid plans of mice and moms…
You probably aren't aware of this, but the preparation required to take a two-month old infant on a successful one- hour trip to the grocery store a mere mile away is a bit like mounting a K2 summit expedition. Aside from the complex provisioning involved (I think I've mentioned

a time or two the survival gear no diaper bag should be without), the timing of the outing must be planned with the utmost precision, as the narrow window of opportunity for a happy outing between feedings and poopings starts closing the second after the first feeding time is over. And woe unto the new mom who finds herself in a long checkout line with an overloaded cart when the baby decides she's absolutely starving to death and she's going to let the whole world know how unhappy she is about this sorry state of affairs—sort of like being stuck on a mountain between base camp and the next camp up when the storm hits. You either abandon all progress and retreat to base camp (leaving your cart full of unpaid groceries with a very putout bag boy while baby cries "Wee, wee, wee" all the way home), or you slog on up the mountain, punishing everyone in earshot (not to mention your starving, wailing infant) for your ineptitude. Speaking from experience…nightmare.

So knowing this, I approached taking said infant on a 425-mile car trip knowing it would require planning on the scale of mounting an Arctic expedition. I didn't really have high expectations. But who knew I'd fall so low?

So picture this. Claire and I are on the Austin-to-Dallas leg of our trip, and Claire is sleeping peacefully in the back seat. Perfect. I expertly calculate that she will wake up and need to nurse around the time we get to Hillsboro, which will be just the perfect place to stop and refuel. I pat myself on the back for having thought of such a great plan and for being such a wise and wonderful new mom. "I'm . . . Supermom."

So we're rolling along just fine on this beautiful autumn day (yes, I know…we don't really have autumn in Texas, but indulge me), and we get all the way to Hillsboro. It's time to stop. But Claire's still sleeping. Hmm. What to do, what to do? Stop and wake her up? That's a crapshoot—never know which baby will wake up when I do that. Baby Jekyll might wake up and coo and smile, or baby Hyde might appear and scream at me all the way back to Dallas for interrupting her beauty sleep. Decisions, decisions. What would Supermom do?

Having missed the last exit due to my utter inability to make a quick decision, I "decide" to keep on trucking. Well, lo and behold, approximately thirty seconds after making my so-called "decision"—and after passing any and all exits even remotely leading into the safe haven of Hillsboro—Claire wakes up. She's hungry, of course. Since I am Supermom, I naturally assume that I can handle this hiccup in my travel plans without much difficulty. There's bound to be a rest area or something ahead. Famous last words of car-bound parents.

So where to stop? No suitable exits in sight. The screaming intensifies, and Supermom's heart rate goes up significantly. But am I, in fact, Supermom? Do I really have a clue what I'm doing? What am I doing? What on earth have I done? Why didn't I stop and wake her up when I had the chance? What is wrong with me? How stupid can I be?

"It's okay, sweetie. Mommy will stop and feed you. I promise." Supermom's soothing verbal assurances have absolutely zero positive effect. If anything, the screaming ramps up. Supermom, the Super-Idiot, is positively frantic at this point.

What have I done to my poor baby? Where to stop? I search in vain for an exit. Hello, what idiot designed an interstate without exits? What if the next exit is twenty miles away? WHERE THE HECK AM I GOING TO STOP? WHY ARE THERE NO EXITS?

And then, through her tear-induced blurred vision, Supermom sees it. Could it be? Is it a sign? "Exit ahead." Well it's about freaking time! By now both baby and Supermom are in complete hysterics. How am I going to make it three more minutes with all this screaming????? We are going to die.

Shockingly, we make it to the exit without either of us expiring from all the screaming. We pull off the interstate, but the only place I see to park is a shady-looking truckers' stop. All the windows are boarded up; it looks like something from a Stephen King movie, except trucks are everywhere, so I know there must be people around. Obviously, it's not the ideal location to stop and nurse a baby. But I'm quite sure that one of us, if not both, will perish if I don't stop right this second and feed her.

So Supermom pulls into the parking lot, as far away from the building and as close to an exit as I can safely find. I rush out and unbuckle her from her infant seat in the back and try to maneuver the both of us into the front seat to nurse, no easy task with the steering wheel and all, but I have to be able to race out of there when the evil truckers start coming for us.

Just as I'm whipping it out to feed her and she's beginning to calm down, men start walking out of the building, staring at me as if I'm an alien... or an unlikely sex slave candidate. Supermom bravely tries not to panic. Again. I double, triple, quadruple check to see that the truck is locked, the motor's on, and we're ready to zip out in a heartbeat, infant seat be darned. I check the locks three more times. And as I feed Claire, I devise a sophisticated, mirror-viewing rotation system to keep track of anyone who might try a stealth approach to the truck. While I carry out this self-induced form of whiplash, I also nervously plot out six different emergency exits and try to determine the one nearest my position. (Where's a flight attendant when you need one?)

Claire takes absolutely forever to eat. I must have starved her. Oh God, what have I done? Are we going to make it out of here alive? Men continue to stare at us as they slowly saunter to their rigs. Where are the women? In an "equal- opportunity" world, shouldn't there be women truckers here? What is wrong with this place? I can't quite figure it out.

At this point, I recall with perfect clarity every horrific news story I've ever heard about a mom and her baby being abducted, molested, killed, etc. Oh my God, these men are plotting to kidnap my baby and me. I am now on the verge of an all-out panic attack because I, Supermom, have thoroughly convinced myself that Claire and I will be making the evening news headlines as missing and presumed dead. We're going to die.

Three years later, or so it seems, Claire finally finishes eating. I nervously examine the trucks and truckers and plot my next move. Can I safely get out of the car to put Claire back in her car seat? Are they close enough to get to me before I have time to dash back to the driver's side and jump in the truck? What if they kill me? What will happen to my precious Claire? Bravely, I take a deep breath and bound out of the truck with her poor little head bouncing on my chest (so now we both have whiplash) and, in world-record time, buckle her up and jump back in the truck. We zoom out of there like the proverbial bat out of hell, although as this place seems to be some sort of dump, maybe it's not so figurative. I don't even bother to buckle myself up until we're safely on the highway. Thank God. We're safe.

But now, I have a new worry: Child Protective Services is going to find out about this and take my baby away from me because I let her cry for what had to be half an hour before feeding her, and then I pulled in to feed her at a freaking horror movie truck stop. I'm a horrible mother. What if they take my baby?

Relaying all of this to my dad later that day, he informs me that the truck stop is a well-known strip joint and most likely doubles as a house of ill repute. This is news to me. But it explains a lot: the scary boarded up windows, the lack of female truckers, the creepy men. It all makes sense now. And the stares I got? Obviously, those cretins are not accustomed to seeing breasts utilized as a nutrient delivery system for infants in the parking lot of their local "gentlemen's" club, where no doubt a woman's bosom has other uses. Or… maybe they just wondered what this plus-size stripper was going to do with her baby during the lap dance portion of the show. In any event, I feel so much better now.But then again, this episode gives the CPS even more nails for my coffin. I mean, at the tender age of two months, I allowed my precious daughter to eat lunch at an alleged whorehouse. Who does that? Supermom? I don't think so. CPS will bring a SWAT team and take my baby. What have I done?

Well, I really need to go and take my medication now. And, BTW, I'm trusting that you won't report me to CPS about the whole whorehouse thing. Okay?

yp

SUBJECT: RE: THE BEST LITTLE...NURSING STATION...IN TEXAS

Hi there!

It's no wonder you weren't picked up by sex-starved truck drivers at the horror movie theater! I'm sure your constant head turning to check mirrors for attackers made you look like someone with an uncontrollable tick. Hilarious! I would have loved to be a fly in that car! On a different note, I think you may have a future in screenwriting. Take care and no more houses of ill repute for baby Claire until she's at least three. S.

SUBJECT: PUSHING FIFTY

Hi Yvonne,

How are you? I've been working a lot lately but really like doing so. My current job is...well, the job itself is fun. However, there is an underlying current that seems to continually resurface with me and it is quite evident at my current place of employment. To put this into perspective, I have to tell you that I am the only middle/upper manager in the company who is female. All other females are support staff. All the "worker bees" are male as are all other managers. You see, as in almost all of my "real" jobs since college, I am outnumbered at least 2:1 in the gender department. This is fine. I am used to working with men and quite frankly, find it easier most times because there isn't a lot of petty nitpicking or small talk that must be tolerated.

Anyhow, the dilemma is this: I attract fifty-year olds, plus or minus. (If I were fifty or sixty or even seventy, a fifty year old would be a great catch. But I am not fifty, yet.) As I type, I have a colleague that has asked me out to dinner or, should I refuse that wonderful offer, a ride in his personal plane, which he has taken apart and reconstructed. Now, this guy is a really nice Joe. But, I've seen his desk and his work habits. He is the most unorganized person I have ever met. Never mind that I am not interested. I would never consent to a trip in a plane that probably doesn't have all its screws due to the fact that its owner cannot find most of his own screws!

Then there's Helmut. Now Helmut is actually quite attractive for a man on the brink of being a card-carrying AARP member. He has distinguished salt and pepper hair and is quite fit. However, Helmut resides in Florida and has a son our age. Pass. I think I'll hold out hopes for a younger crowd. The bag-o'-bones, pill-toting fella with the lovely BenGay cologne just does not do it for me. I will keep you posted on the non-existent dating front, that is until the next guy comes along complete with his cane. See ya' soon. S.

SUBJECT: RE: PUSHING FIFTY

Well, I wish I could offer some advice for you here, but other than "stay away from lawyers," I'm fresh out. I have in the past encouraged my sister to volunteer at hospitals to catch the eye of some young doctor, but so far she's ignored me. It might be easier to just fake an injury and head to the ER, but volunteering might not be so bad. (You know I'm kidding, right?) Then again, would being the trophy wife of some well- heeled, distinguished older gentleman be so bad? Don't be too hasty to slam the door on middle-aged men bearing cash.

Hey, that reminds me, what's going on with Pierce? Is he out of the picture or what? Inquiring minds want to know.

Yp

CHAPTER SEVEN: MATING RITUALS

SUBJECT: PIERCE & THE DANCING QUEEN (ME!)

Hi there!

To answer your previous email: No—Pierce is not out of the picture. On the contrary, he was in Chicago. As I learn new things in this ever-evolving relationship I have been made aware of a bi-annual boys trip to Chicago. One of Pierce's good friends is a die-hard USC fan. So, every other year when USC plays Notre Dame in Chicago, the boys make their pilgrimage. And, in the true mentality of a seven-year old: "NO GIRLS ALLOWED!"

This trip is usually the third weekend in October, which usually coincides with my birthday. Since this is a relationship in its infancy, Pierce thought it would suffice if I spent the weekend with his best friend's wife in Austin while he went to Chicago. That was okay with me. I was in the mood for some female bonding and thought it would be nice to get to know Pierce's friends. So, Friday night was scheduled—girl's night out in downtown Austin. Never mind that Ashley has a six-month old to nurse at home. Justin is her third child—she knows how to do that stuff by now, I should think!

I meet Ashley at her house. She invited another friend, who invited a friend. It all works nicely because no one knows anyone. Anyway, we go to a semi-posh place for dinner. After a not-so-filling dinner, we hit the ever-popular Polly Esters. (In case you are unfamiliar, it is a throw-back club to the 70s and 80s.) I am wearing a neon lime green one-piece dress with butterflies all over it. It looks great in the disco lights and black lights. To accompany this ensemble are my "two sizes too small" lime green heels. They match perfectly and are the only size available. We dance on the 70s floor. We dance on the 80s floor. We go back to the 70s. It is great fun. I love to dance. Granted, I'm a little out of the style of bump and grind at the moment but who cares? John Travolta got groovy in Pulp Fiction, so I figure I can too. We shut the club down and hop into a cab to head home at 3:00a.m. What fun!

I crash at Ashley's place and awake the next morning to two little girls poking me in the arm. Well, it wasn't exactly morning. It is more like noon. I literally crawl down the stairs. I cannot walk. Thank you lime green shoes for crippling me for the next week anyway. Oh, and did I mention my big toe is numb? I think I must have nerve damage since the only feeling is pain. Ashley is wide awake and walking fine I might add.

Pierce is due back on Monday and it is only mid-Saturday. I decide by default that I will be spending the rest of my weekend on the couch at my apartment. I gather my lime green dress, ditch the shoes and head home. What a night! S.

SUBJECT: RE: PIERCE & THE DANCING QUEEN (ME!)

Steph,

Sounds like you had plenty of fun dancing all night, numb toes notwithstanding. I danced into the wee hours myself, coincidentally, but instead of donning a cool frock with the perfect shoes to match at a hip club with girlfriends, I wore a frumpy pink nursing gown (those flaps in the front are so snazzy!) and warm, fuzzy slippers at Club Nursery, and my dancing partner was under age, so none of the good stuff for us. But that was okay, all she wanted was milk anyway. We danced some really cool moves: the "Back to Sleep, Baby" and "Are you ever going to stop crying?" and, my favorites, the "I didn't sign up for this" and "Oh God, what have I done?" dances.

So here's a word of advice, enjoy those yummy, too-small lime green babies while you can. Once you've given birth, none of your shoes will ever fit again. In addition to providing a permanent hip spread and boob job, pregnancy does wonders to enlarge feet. Whether they need it or not.

Have a great week, dancing queen!
yp (a.k.a. "Dancing Queen Mother")

PART THREE

CHAPTER EIGHT: A WHOLE NEW WORLD

SUBJECT: SO MUCH FOR BEING PREPARED

Steph,

Howdy! You know how I've always been wired to plan for every contingency? How I'm never without preparations for the worst? I think parenting has finally short-circuited that wiring. And just when I need it most. Go figure.

Yesterday, I head to the mall with Claire in tow to pick up a few clothing basics for her. She's almost six months old and is finally outgrowing stuff. We have about eight white and five pink onesies to wear under all her winter clothing, but we're both getting a little bored with pink and white (well, I am, anyway; she probably couldn't care less). So I'm off in search of other colors in the rainbow.

Since I'm still nursing, I'm thirsty all the time and have to carry water with me everywhere I go. But I ran out of bottled water the day before and all my cups with lids are dirty, because who has time to go grocery shopping or to do dishes with a cute baby to play with all day? I adapt. I grab a great big—enormous, really—insulated tumbler of ice water and carry it into the mall with me in the stroller's nifty cup holder.

I stop in at one little mall boutique to see if they have some basic onesies and cute outfits in something other than pink and white. Not really. How is this possible?

As I head back out into the mall, I'm momentarily distracted by some outfit hanging on the wall and turn my head for just a second when one of the clothing racks jumps out and rams into my stroller. I'm sure that's what happened. Inexplicably, I hear screaming below. What on earth is wrong with her now? We've already stopped ten times for feeding, pooping, cuddling, cooing, etc. What else could she POSSIBLY need?

I race around to the front of the stroller. Either Claire has been the victim of a sudden hail storm afflicting her alone, or…a glance at the cup holder reveals that my icy cold water tumbler lies there, horizontal. And very empty. Claire is soaking wet from her little gold head to her tiny pink toes. Oh, crap.

I grab Claire and start stripping her out of her soaking outfit and blanket, right there in the middle of the store with all the other moms staring in horror at the spectacle that is us. I ignore the huge pool of water spreading out from underneath the stroller and try to comfort Claire, while simultaneously attempting to dislodge the diaper bag from under the stroller seat. Being overstuffed as it is with fifteen items I don't really need while on safari with a baby, much less on a short trip to the mall, it's wedged in there pretty good and won't budge. One of the sales clerks rushes over to aid me and, with a Herculean effort, manages to dislodge it from the stroller.

I rummage through the large bag with one free hand for a full two minutes, while hanging on for dear life to a singularly enraged infant (the screaming was my first clue, the extreme arching of the back my second), and after pulling half a Babies R' Us store from the bag, I stand there staring at it in complete disbelief. Where are the three extra outfits I carry with me at all times? Where's the extra blanket? It is January, after all.

Holy crap. I forgot to restock the bag after our last outing. How could this happen to me, of all people? The Mistress of Plan B, Miss Prepared-for-an-avalanche-on-the-Texas-prairie- in-summer? I, who have been known to carry ten diapers, the emergency medical kit, and at least five educational toys for a thirty minute grocery store outing with Claire, have not brought a single piece of clothing or extra blanket with me. WHAT COULD POSSIBLY BE WRONG WITH ME? My obsessive-compulsive reputation is ruined. It'll take months of over-packing to make up for this one.

So the sales clerk helpfully points out that, as this is a children's clothing store and all, I might buy something suitable for Claire to wear home. I certainly would never have thought of that on my own, of course. Poor, traumatized Claire is still crying and shivering, I grab the closest thing within reach: a simple, inexpensive white onesie and pink leggings. Perfect. Mission accomplished. We sure needed another white onesie and more pink leggings.

Good grief. I've lost it and will likely never get it back. yp (aka "too-stupid-to-be-a-mother")

SUBJECT: SECOND VERSE SAME AS THE FIRST

Hi there!

Get it back??? I've never had it! You think you've got problems — little Miss pink and white — take note of what a goofball I've been in just a week.

This past week I was in Florida working on my Goodyear project. To save the company money, I flew the red-eye and arrived in Orlando at 11:45 p.m. I made it to the rental agency, and subsequently to my car around midnight. The car, however, was without keys. I flagged down two employees in their personal vehicles on their way out of the parking lot to hitch a ride back to the office to start the process again. In retrospect, I do not think I would recommend this to any single female traveling alone at midnight. Anyhow, I got my car and then proceeded to the hotel.

I arrived at the hotel at half-past one to find an incredibly long line of men waiting to check in at the desk. I stood there for a good twenty minutes until it was my turn only to find out I was at the wrong hotel. I was to be at the other location, halfway across town. Second verse, just like the first. So, off I went into the night. Finally, around two in the morning, I was in a room and I crashed.

The next morning I was at the job site, meetings, etc. Mostly boring stuff for the non-initiated so I'll spare you the details. After the last meeting, I went to my car and was ready to leave the parking garage when realized I had to pay the meter. (The attendant had long gone home at this point.) I only had two dollars. So, I called my boss (in Texas) to discuss the days' work and inquire about how I might get the rental car and myself out of the garage. Needless to say, he was of no assistance. So again, I found myself flagging down some employee leaving the lot in order to barter, plead, or provide an I.O.U. to get me out of the garage. It worked and off I went.

Since I was able to get a a lower fare by departing on Saturday afternoon, I was "forced" to spend the night. But it turned out in my favor since I was traveling alone and was able to purchase a single front and center, third row seat to La Nouba, Cirque du Soliel's exclusive Florida show on Friday night. Fun.

Saturday morning I decided to head to the Island of Adventure for a quick round of roller coasters before heading to the airport. All was fun and games until it was time to leave. I do not know if you have been to this place but the parking garage is about as big as the city of Orlando.

I wandered into the sea of white rental cars and realized I had no freaking idea where my car was parked. So, (are you catching onto the song now????) third verse, same as the first. I flagged down a security guy in a golf cart with a flashing light and announced my dilemma. With an exasperated look that said you are only the 45,000th person to do this today, he drove me around while I peered into windows of rental cars looking for something familiar. At last, only two hours before I was to board the plane, I found my car.

It was a mad dash to the rental agency to dump the loaner. My wheels were screeching around the corners and, believe me, you get some pretty weird looks when you're flying through the rental car agency at mach five. I rode the transit bus to the airport, rushed through security and made it onto the plane, barely. Whew.

The flight home was the most turbulent flight I've ever experienced, with the added benefit of a leach seated next to me. At one point, I screamed "I'm going down! I'm going down!"

only to have received a smart-aleck remark from the guy seated next to me. ("You're not yet, but you certainly are welcome to.") Ugh. Thankfully, I am back home and ready for real work again!
S.

SUBJECT: RE: SECOND VERSE

Steph,

That cretin! I hope you spilled your drink on him during all that turbulence. I would laugh and say, "you goof," about losing the rental car, but that would just be the pot calling the kettle black. And I don't just have trouble finding rental cars, I can't remember where I parked my own truck half the time. I walk out of stores on a daily basis asking little Claire where we parked the truck. (At six months old, she's not too helpful in that department.) Maybe you should treat a rental car like luggage and tie a tacky looking ribbon around the radio antennae. Something big and garish and visible from 100 yards. You know, like those huge bows we wore on our prom dresses. (What were we thinking?)

Anyway, glad you made it back safe and sound. Chat with you later.

Yp

SUBJECT: EASTER PORTRAITS GIVE "CHOCOLATE BUNNY" A WHOLE NEW MEANING

Steph,

Howdy! Alert the SPCA. Claire nearly killed the Easter bunny today. It was pretty hysterical. For me, anyway. Not so much for the bunny. I took her to a studio for her eight- month portrait, and since it's Easter bunny time, I decided to kill two birds (and almost one bunny) with one stone.
We started off with just her and her Easter basket, sans bunny. The portrait gods smiled down on us, as Claire was in a darling mood and grinned and posed the whole time. ("Us, in case you're wondering, would be the photographer and myself, serving as the unpaid, overworked assistant). Things became interesting when the photographer brought out the bunny. As he placed the white fur ball in front of Claire, you could see her little mind trying to connect the dots, and then, all of a sudden — realization dawned: "Eureka! It's alive! My toy's alive!" She went nuts.

Claire screeched and squealed with delight and grabbed fistfuls of its soft white fur whenever the bunny made the mistake of getting caught too close. She loved the feel of the fur in her little hands, and as she kept pulling it out in lumps, she had plenty to study. At one point, Claire picked the pitiful creature up from his hindquarters and squeezed his back end to pieces, and then, not convinced that the bunny's pink floppy ears were permanently attached, she decided to try and remove them for closer inspection. It's a miracle the bunny survived, and that he didn't claw her to pieces. The bunny will no doubt need physical therapy and post-trauma counseling.I, on the other hand, could use a nap now. And some Tylenol. I don't understand why these photographers don't have assistants. In addition to keeping Claire sitting still and centered on the background set, not to mention keeping her happy, I had to chase down and catch the terrified bunny each time it ran—or hopped—for its life. Then I had to reposition the poor critter within the sinister baby's grasp, not an easy task when it's trying to run for cover. Claire's shrieking at the top of her lungs did little to coax the fur ball into staying on the set and contributed to, if not caused altogether, my headache. I had to chase down that bunny for at least fifteen minutes. Shouldn't I get paid for this sort of thing? I mean, I did half the work!

But there was one job I refused to do. Little bunny Foo-Foo, though frightened, was not without resources. Each time Claire nearly squeezed the life out of him (upwards of ten times, at least), he dropped a couple of brown bombs in her path, which showed up spectacularly well against the white background and Claire's beautiful, very expensive white dress. How the photographer managed to get any photos of the two of them together, sans turds, is beyond me. But the bunny's defensive tactic gave him time for his getaway while the photographer cleaned up the mess. I, naturally, draw the line at removing bunny poop. You'd think it would be worth it to the photographer to hire an official bunny pooper- scooper/chaser. All I know is, next time Claire's portrait session involves live animals, I'm conning my mom or my sister into going with me. They can chase the darn rabbit.

Anyway, I gave Claire a bath to remove all traces of "bunny," hair or otherwise, and now I'm off for that well-deserved nap.

Later. Yp

SUBJECT: RE: EASTER PORTRAITS GIVE "CHOCOLATE BUNNY " A WHOLE NEW MEANING

{Put your singing voice on...}

Lil' bunny Foo-Foo hopping through the studio; Makin' lots of poo-poo to drop on Claire's dress.

Claire squeezes Foo-Foo to make more poo-poo; Mommy scoops poo-poo and flings on photographer's head.

Photographer is blue-blue because of the poo-poo; Turns photos into a personal revenge.

Pictures of piles of Foo-Foo's poo-poo! Claire is nowhere to be seen. Ewww.

Mommy gets photos with major mojos; Goes to a different picture place instead.

It could happen...here's hoping the photos are better than my jingle! S.

Subject: RE: Re: Easter Portraits Give "Chocolate Bunny" a Whole New Meaning Steph,
You just totally made my day!!! Too funny. Thanks for the grins.
Yp

SUBJECT: THE PERFECT DAY

Steph,

You know how things go wrong so often on special occasions and you just can't believe you'll ever have an enjoyable one? I just did! Jack took me and our moms out (and a few other relatives) for lunch at this fabulous Italian restaurant. Jack was wonderful. It was practically perfect, even though Claire was with us! I'm just sitting here glowing in the memory of it.

And waiting for the sky to start falling in. You can't have this perfect of a day without something big going horribly wrong soon after. I'll just sit here and lie in wait for it. Better to be prepared, you know.
yp

SUBJECT: RE: THE PERFECT DAY

Wow! I'm still waiting for my perfect day to come. Enjoy your evening. Hopefully it will be perfect too! S.

SUBJECT: GREAT EXPECTATIONS

Steph,

Well, since Jack and I have this baby thing licked (note extreme hubris), and since it took a year and a half to acquire Claire in utero, we decided a short time ago to start working on a sibling for her. I'm not getting any younger, Claire needs a brother or sister, blah, blah, blah.

We expected this process to take some time. It didn't. We're now expecting. And given that the two munchkins will be separated by a mere eighteen months, I expect that I will not be leaving the house again after March of next year, when said baby is expected to put in an appearance.

The nausea has already hit full force. As has this amazing drop in my energy level, which I did not expect. Shouldn't I be used to this pregnancy thing by now? But I'm told that I can expect to feel this way even longer the second time around. But now I have a toddler to chase. Who hasn't celebrated her first birthday yet. I'm tired just thinking about it.

I expect I'll be tired for years to come. I expect you'll get tired of hearing about it. But I'll have two in diapers for quite a while, and by the time it's all over I will have been pregnant, nursing, or both for over three years straight (if the new baby nurses for a year like Claire, which I certainly expect).

I expect I'll need a very strong margarita afterwards.

But lest you think we are somehow displeased about this turn of events, we're not. We're very happy. I am, however, counting the days until that margarita, which I expect to taste fabulous after such a long dry spell. Have a Happy Fourth of July!

Yp

SUBJECT: SAILING THE HIGH SEAS

Hey Yvonne~

Just a quick note from the Aegean Sea! (Now I understand where they get the crayon name "Aegean Sea" because the water is the color of that crayon.) Anyhow, I can't write much since I'm at an internet café in Greece that still uses dial-up. And, you have to pay by the minute. Just wanted to let you know things are sailing along nicely with Pierce on our cruise from Greece to Italy. We have one short stopover in Turkey, which I am really looking forward to exploring.

Congratulations on baby number two! You'll have Irish twins. Are you crazy? Speaking of, we are still trying to get our family going and we are hoping this trip will get it off to a good start. Perhaps the motion of the ocean will help things along. Anyhow, hope all is well with you. I'll touch base when we return. S.

SUBJECT: I NEED AN ADVENTURE

Steph,

You're in Greece? On a cruise? And you're trying to have this man's baby? When did this happen? Did I miss an e-mail...or five? I guess well wishes are in order! And, clearly, good sex! Can't wait to hear all about it. The cruise, I mean. Not the sex.

You seem to be having a lot of adventures lately. I'm in desperate need of an adult adventure. I know you're life is full of such delights, but I'm scraping the bottom of the barrel here. You up for a joint venture with boring, preggers me?

I've been bitten by the Russell Crowe bug and I think it's going to take seeing him live to get over it. He's bringing his band to Austin to record another album, I think, and he's playing at some barbecue joint in downtown Austin. The concert's sold out, but there are tickets going up for sale on e- bay. Jack says I can spend my birthday money in advance if I'd like to fork over up to $150 to see the Aussie singing music that I'm sure I won't even like. Tickets, however, are going for quite a bit more than that, so I'll have to keep bidding. Jack refuses to go. I don't really want to go by myself. You in? I'll get two if you'll go with me (it'll have to be Dutch if the tickets are over $150 total, which they apparently will be).

Let me know! yp

SUBJECT: RE: I NEED AN ADVENTURE

Count me in! I love live music and I'm always looking for an excuse to go downtown. Let me know if you get tickets! We can be groupies! S.

SUBJECT: DID YOU REALLY DO THAT?

S,

Okay, so I can't figure out what bugs me most. That Russell Crowe's body guards pushed us away from the railing when Russell walked by? (Can you believe we were close enough to touch him? Can you believe how freaking short he is?)

Or was it that those rude idiots denied us access to the restaurant (and I'm being generous in labeling it such) and dressed me down for even trying? Or maybe it was that the blonde Amazon bimbo wearing little more than a glorified swimsuit made it through the bouncer barrier while stepping on us? I'm thinking I won't ever bother with the humiliation of serious club-hopping. Clearly, if I don't pass the "hot factor" standard applied by bouncers at a cheap barbecue joint in downtown Austin, I'll never make it past the ropes at a real club.

And you know, you'd think that when I played the pregnant bladder card, they might have had the teensiest bit of compassion. But no. Let's deny the not-hot pregnant woman access to the restroom—and let's make a show of pointing out the port-a-potties, shall we? As if I was actually going to use one of those disgusting contraptions in the dark. I mean, really. It would have been a toss-up between me fainting from asphyxia from the rank smell or from claustrophobia. And I'm so sure I want to faint in a port-a-potty.

Although, I nearly did faint anyway. Skunk weed, huh? I was too sheltered in high school, clearly. But I have to say, I'm kind of glad to have missed that unauthorized beach trip if it smelled anything like the stuff at the concert. (Nice of you to tell me about it fourteen years later, by the way—makes me wonder what else I missed.) Anyway, I just hope my poor unborn baby doesn't have an overwhelming urge to smoke a joint upon birth. I can't believe people smoke that stuff for fun. Can they not smell themselves?

But you know, it wasn't the ugly bouncers, the blond bimbo, the potty problem, the skunk weed, or even having my image of Russell as a virile, hot male dashed at seeing how incredibly short he is in person that bugged me the most. No, that would be seeing umpteen people hawking FREE tickets to this little event when I paid freaking $150 each for the privilege!!!! Am I a total sucker or what?

So what have we learned from this adventure? That Yvonne is too old for this crap. Seriously. On top of everything else, my ears are still ringing. Next time I suggest a late summer Texas outdoor concert at a joint with no bathroom access, just shoot me. Especially if I'm pregnant.

But I did have fun with you!! Just in case that wasn't perfectly clear. Thanks for hanging with me. yp

SUBJECT : CONCERT

Wow! What an amazing night-in more ways than one! I can't believe Russell Crowe is such a jerk! And, I agree—so short. Between the grumbling, grizzly voice (from the chain-smoking he has down to perfection), I think I heard the f- bomb more than the music! And, his "rope guard" that had the audacity to tell us we shouldn't be at the front of the line! He should seriously take inventory of his own life: He is a bouncer for a wannabe rock star that will never make it in the music industry. Let's hope Crowe's acting career doesn't flop because he's going to need something besides music to stay in the black!

Now that I have critiqued the show, I will say I had a great time hanging out with you! It was fun to get together and act like groupies. As for the skunk weed, I think it was apropos; after all the name of the band is "Thirty-odd Foot of Grunt." The band sounded like crap and the air smelled like crap! Let's do the concert tour again soon-but let's pick a different group to see…how about Aerosmith? Have a great week. S.

CHAPTER NINE: BABY BOOM

SUBJECT: DOCTOR'S VISIT

Hi Yvonne,

The last few weeks have been exhilarating, exhausting, and terrifying. As you now know, Pierce and I have been trying to conceive (and carry) a baby for almost a year now with no success. So after trying virtually every position in the Karma Sutra as well as being poked, prodded, and researched in more ways than I care to recount, we "move on" to the fertility doctor.

I'll spare you the many visits leading up to this particular one, but I thought I should tell you of this harrowing experience. During my baseline visit, the doctor sees a peanut-shaped "thing" which he calls out as a word I can't even retype or say. I swear it had at least thirteen letters. It must have been Latin. He sends me for more lab work and schedules a follow up appointment the next week.

I am terrified. I am convinced I am going to die. I go home and begin writing my own will. A drama queen that has been hiding out somewhere in my psyche comes to life and stages the biggest pity party I have ever witnessed. Pierce comes home to find me crying my eyes out because of this peanut that is going to kill me sooner rather than later. This, obviously, was not what we were expecting to learn at the fertility doctor. We were hoping for more joyous things, like "Have more sex!" But no, it was not so.

The entire week I moped around the house and was quiet at work. I was tired and really unhappy. The eternity of the week wore on until it was finally time for our next appointment. With trepidation, I met with the doctor in his office. This is much worse than meeting in an exam room. To me, this meant certainly that all my fears were realized. I have an incurable disease! Before the doctor could utter a word, I was already asking questions like, "Is it going to be painful?" "How long do I have?" He responded,…"About nine months and I can't tell you if it'll be painful. Your pregnant!"

Yea! Keep your fingers crossed it'll be successful! Now, I have to rest. I'm all of six weeks pregnant and really exhausted! S.

SUBJECT: RE: DOCTOR'S VISIT

Steph,

OMG!!! Congratulations and welcome to the sorority of pregnant females. How are you feeling? Your baby and mine will be really close in age. How cool is that? So when exactly are you due? What does Pierce think? Too many questions?

Oh, to answer your question to the doctor about pain, the answer is an unqualified "yes." To make it simple, I'll just issue the blanket statement that there is very little about pregnancy, childbirth, and motherhood that isn't painful. But sometimes it's really fun.

Congrats!!!! Keep me posted on your progress. Yp

SUBJECT: IT'S GONNA BE A GIRL!

Steph,

Hey! We're having another girl! We're so excited. I was secretly hoping that she'd be a girl since she's so close to Claire in age. I hope they'll be best buddies.

Sadly, I won't be saving any money on clothes here at the beginning, as Claire was a summer baby and this one will be a winter baby. And they each have to have a baby bed, so we can't reuse Claire's furniture. Having two girls is not going to help the checkbook. Jack's already complaining about all the money he'll have to shell out for prom dresses, weddings, and high maintenance personal care. I told him to chill. It'll be a few years before they're demanding highlights and the high heels. I hope.

Let me know what's up with your baby. Happy Halloween!
Yp

SUBJECT: RE: IT'S GONNA BE A GIRL!

Congratulations on the girl confirmation! Jack should stop worrying about the money and instead take note of the fact that he will be outnumbered in the house 3:1. Translation: there will not be an available bathroom in the house for the next eighteen years. Translation: Each girl in the household is entitled to ten days of hormonal imbalances; hence his entire month will be screwed as these hormonal mood swings rarely coordinate with one another. Translation: Pink and purple will become the primary colors in the household; therefore any hopes he might have of maintaining white underwear, white socks or white shirts will be dashed in the weekly laundry. Yeah, I'd say paying for two proms is the least of his concerns!

My baby is already changing my life. I am currently taking two-hour lunches because I literally cannot stay awake at work. I feel utterly stupid sleeping at my desk so I just stay home longer. One of these days, I'll probably oversleep and miss the latter half of my workday! Otherwise, things are going along relatively smoothly at this point. Thanks for asking. Take care. S.

SUBJECT: NEW YEAR — NEW YEAR!

Happy New Year!

I have been trying to catch my breath long enough to relay my New Year's Eve tale to you. It was outrageously funny at the time, but you probably had to be there to appreciate the event.

We made reservations at the ultra-conservative Driskill Hotel for the New Year's Eve party package. There was a substantial group of us in attendance. Most of us decided to arrive early to take advantage of the hotel before the festivities began. Well, this turned into the little finger that pushed the first domino in the chain of events for the night.

For starters, the couple that was shacked up next door to our room must have decided that the earth was ending in rapture and the only thing left to do was screw your way out. Needless to say, we had a nice rhythm going in our room, complete with vocals. Not wanting to listen (and the walls are thin) to this whale-calling virtuoso and her thumper husband, we decided to go down to another couple's room for drinks and socializing. When we got there, we were greeted with Vodka shots at the door. Now, since I was only three months pregnant at the time and we had not yet "announced" this little incident, refusing the Vodka shot was quite a challenge. My first response was "I'm taking antibiotics." This was answered with "The Vodka will only make it better!" Nevertheless, I managed my way into the room to visit without too many explanations. We stayed for a while, long enough for Pierce to get lit. At some point, the guys surreptitiously disappeared. When we finally realized this, we opened the door to go on a manhunt only to find them stealing apples out of the hotel display to use for a makeshift bowling alley they had set up in the hallway. Oh Lord.

After a few rounds of apple bowling, I managed to get Pierce back to the room to get ready for dinner. Thankfully, our "neighbors" had gone into orbit while we were gone and quietly landed so that our room was without drumbeats at this point. We got dressed and went down for dinner. When we arrived, I realized the majority of our group was quite inebriated. Oh, this was going to be fun.

The waiter, in his most serious demeanor, proceeded to rattle off the prix fixe menu of the evening while everyone at the table proceeded to ignore him, talking loudly. (The topics of discussion are not really repeatable either. How does that always come about?)

About halfway through the meal, I was abruptly serenaded by the ladies at the table. "Fruit salad-yummy, yummy-Fruit salad," complete with hand movements and stand-up dance motions. I was told this song was credited to the "Wiggles," four men who apparently sing and dance for small children. (Okay, am I the only one who sees something extremely odd about this arrangement? Maybe I will understand it after I have children.) I was also surprised to hear about Bob the Builder, his cat Pilchard, and his friend Wendy (whom I am convinced is his "beard"). What man has a cat named Pilchard and has tea in mid-afternoon? Gay-dar alert!!!) Then, there is Sponge Bob Squarepants and oh, I forget the third Bob...there must have been a shortage of cartoon names for kid characters... Oh, and lest I forget, did you ever put together "Chip N' Dale" when you were a kid? I didn't think so. Me neither.

The remainder of the dinner was spent discussing busty characters like Aerial and Pocahontas on the male end of the table and on the female end of the table, the hot bodies of Garçon, the sexuality of Bob the Builder, and of course whether Tinker Bell is a fairy or a slut. Yep, we were moving into real grown-up territory until the toast...

A good friend of ours, named "Bob", made the first toast. (The names of the offenders have been changed to protect the innocent, or should I say- the guilty?!) His toast started with a round of Red Snappers, a drink he used to make as a bartender. He had some really "snappy" toast filled with sexual innuendo.

Then, Pierce (no name change here) proceeded to stand up to deliver his toast. I knew then I should run, fast and far away. But no, I stayed to endure the toast. (Mind you, we are in a conservative four-star restaurant with a bunch of other couples trying to have a respectable New Year's Eve.) Pierce stands up and in his loudest voice, which he professes to be a voice modulation problem, says, "Here's to the four F's!" At first, everyone was silent trying to figure out what on earth he was referring to in this most bizarre toast. He proceeds, "Family, Fun, Friends… (Can you guess what's coming next?) Everyone at the table began to laugh, anticipating what he loudly says-- F******! I felt sheer humiliation, considering I, along with the rest of the patrons in the restaurant, was not drunk. The eleven other people at our table were not only toasted they were toasting, in unison, repeatedly Pierce's infamous New Year's Eve toast! A lovely scene. With that, we were quickly offered our check, then the clock struck twelve and we were done. After the explosive end-of-the-world shagging event, the apple bowling, the grown-up conversations and the four 'F's', I'm not so sure the hotel will ever let us come back! Happy New Year!

S.

SUBJECT: RE: NEW YEAR — NEW YEAR!

Steph,

Live audio porn, apple bowling, vodka, and R-rated toasts.
You just have all the fun, don't you?
My New Year's Eve celebration was of course very exciting. Eight months pregnant the second time around, my belly can hardly fit into the passenger seat of the truck, much less at a restaurant table. So we had a dazzling evening of movie- watching, complete with pizza and Dr. Pepper, (caffeine-free, of course). Good times, good times.
Happy New Year! Yp

SUBJECT: EMMA'S ARRIVED!

Steph,

Hey! I'm not huge and pregnant anymore! Just huge. Emma was born the evening of the 24th after having the good grace to put me through only twelve hours of labor. She weighed in at seven pounds two ounces. I think. Something like that anyway.

We've finally decided on her full name. They won't let you leave the hospital without filling out that stupid birth certificate, so clear all that up before you head to the hospital. Just giving you fair warning there. We named her "Emmaline Corinne" for when she's in trouble. It'll be "Emma" the rest of the time.

Let's see. I'm supposed to relay the birth story now, aren't I? Sanctity of womanhood and circle of life and all that. Not much to tell this time around. Emma decided to come all on her own two weeks early…

I awake Saturday morning around 8:00 a.m. with mild contractions and back pain. I know almost immediately that this is it. Convincing Jack that this is the real thing takes another hour and a half. After a bit of yelling, I finally get him to call our doula, who arrives at the house just as things start to get more painful.

The doctor on call, not mine, of course, tells me to come in immediately, so we leave before noon for the hospital, thirty minutes away, with our doula following in her own car. By the time we get to the hospital, I can see the wisdom of getting there before labor begins in earnest. That was the most uncomfortable ride of my life, every bump sending me into a new contraction. Poor Jack gets an earful. It's a wonder he's still speaking to me, in point of fact. So another word of advice: Don't wait too long to head to the hospital.

Jack drops me off at the ER entrance and tells me to hike on upstairs and check in while he parks the car. It takes a year to get to the elevator because I'm in quite a bit of discomfort and have to keep stopping to lean against the wall to get through contractions. No one tries to help me upstairs. So the whole "get her a wheelchair" thing you always see in movies and on TV when the woman in labor walks through the hospital doors? Total myth.

When I finally make it all the way down the hall to the nurse's station in Labor and Delivery, I expect to see Jack and my doula rounding the corner and barreling toward me, ready to respond to my every whim. But they are nowhere in evidence. When I manage to get a nurse's nose out of her charts long enough to pay attention to me, she asks, "Can I help you?" This is exactly the wrong thing to say to me. Yeah, hello. I'm having a baby here. Could you possibly get me in a room and find my AWOL husband? I might have been slightly more polite than that. But I kind of doubt it, because the nurse briskly escorts me to a room and starts barking all kinds of orders at me, chief among them to get naked and then put on a hospital gown. Then she leaves. Still no Jack. Still no doula. Do you know how hard it is, nine months pregnant, to change out of winter clothes and into a hospital gown with NO HELP WHATSOEVER while you're having contractions?

Meltdown time.

WHERE IN THE BLEEP ARE THEY? WHY AM I ALL

ALONE??

About the time I manage to get the gown on straight, they finally show up, trying to tell me there was absolutely nowhere to park. Labor pains have really intensified, so I am in no mood to listen to their flimsy excuses for dawdling. After all, I'VE BEEN UP HERE ALL BY MYSELF trying not to lose my balance and face-plant while doubled-over in pain and wrestling with this stupid straight jacket. My doula suggests that I should really calm down, as it can't be good for the baby to have steam coming out of my ears. We're paying her good money for her sage advice, so Jack urges me to listen. I suppose I eventually do, as I crawl into bed and settle in for the long haul.

My mom, my sister, and Jack's mom all arrive before the appointed hour to observe the spectacle of labor. Mom and sis are supportive. Jack's mom totally hacks me off. After she observes me in labor with no pain relief (yes, we're trying that again), she says, in her best Junior League voice, "Like an Indian squaw?" as if "going natural" is somehow an antiquated, unenlightened approach to childbirth that should have been abandoned after the colonial period. Jack escorts her out shortly thereafter and my blood pressure levels off. (I eventually get over it and welcome her back in the room—sort of—before it's all over.)

At some point in the afternoon, as the contractions build, I am instructed to head to the restroom. Colossal mistake. I only thought my contractions were bad before. Labor becomes super intense during the half hour (not kidding) it takes to trek across the room. I'll spare you the details of my time in the loo, but had there been a fly on the wall, it would tell you that watching a woman whose gigantic pregnant belly throws off her balance negotiate an IV pole, the straight jacket's dangling ties, and the throne itself is high entertainment, but add in a game of freeze tag, where said woman becomes completely immobilized in whatever position she's in when a contraction hits? Positively side-splitting.

By the time I'm ready to return to bed, I am so paralyzed by pain that I can't even stand up. So I resign myself to birthing my baby in the john. But Jack's not thrilled with this idea and finally rescues me from the clutches of the toilet (you don't want to know) and gets me back to bed…

Where the going gets exponentially harder. Eventually, I cry "uncle" and get the epidural. Then life is sweet. I sleep, but my doula wakes me up from time to time and tells me to turn over. I guess she wants to make sure the baby is cooking evenly on both sides. As I can't feel anything from my waist down, this effort is a little like rolling a dead pig.

The appointed hour finally arrives and its time to push. At the last possible second before the birth, and at the height of my vulnerability, Jack asks the doctor if his mom, who was standing just outside the door, could join my mom and the doula in observing the birth. The doctor says, "Sure, the more the merrier; come on in." Literally. We stop the show so his mom can be ushered in. She politely stands just inside the door, but the doctor insists that she come right over and gives her a front row seat. In fact, my mother-in-law has the best view of the birth of anyone in the room, except for the doctor. This is just fabulous, I thought. I try not to think about it at the moment but know I will be utterly mortified later. For many years to come, actually. This, I decide, is when being delirious with pain might actually be a help. But there I am, blissfully comfortable with an epidural that works like a charm, leaving me to take note of my "delicate situation."

The doctor says Emma will make her stage appearance in two pushes. It takes three, but hey, who's counting? She was, of course, all icky and very red and screaming as they put her on my deflated belly. But she's absolutely precious. And perfectly healthy. And she's got the plumpest chipmunk cheeks you've ever seen and a little bow mouth! And really bad baby acne. I have no idea what's up with that.The grandmothers were over the moon as they got to watch the nurses clean Emma up. I finally got to hold her after everyone else passed her around. And by then she refused to eat. I have discerned over the past couple of days now that this is going to be a recurring theme with her.

It was not dramatic, but still a complete miracle. I'm so glad to have had this more "normal" birth after Claire's nightmarish ordeal. And I sure as heck look better in all the photos this time around. And of course, that's what's really important, right?

Hope you have a great birth, too.
yp

SUBJECT: IN REVERSE

Hi Yvonne,

Congrats on Emma! I can't wait to meet her. I have to tell you though—what a trooper you are for allowing your mother-in-law in the room during the birth. Don't think I could go there—no matter how much I might like her!On a different note, I want to tell you there is nothing like running in reverse! Just a quickie to tell you that life is much more interesting should you find yourself "in reverse." As you know, we are expecting child numero uno in June. So naturally, that begs the question of marriage. This rite of passage we shall perform in May. Marriage begs the question of living arrangements. So naturally we'll be moving at the end of March to a more "child-friendly abode." Heaven forbid I have to live in the bachelor pad any longer. The stark white walls, lack of furniture or wall décor and the ex-girlfriend ghosts that creep up are enough to drive any person batty. Never mind what it does to a pregnant person! Oh, just so you will know, I have been banned from ladders since Pierce caught me atop one cleaning the niches at one in the morning. Thank you nesting instinct.

So much for the traditional approach! My life has always been a bit unconventional so I think it is only natural that I start off my child's life in like form. And, for the record, I don't think we have a clue what we are getting into with the whole child- rearing, relationship managing, house-running that we are about to embark upon. It should be fun! Talk to you soon. S.

SUBJECT: IN REVERSE

Steph,

Here's a newsflash that you might have missed while heading in reverse and all. Movies are fun. Amusement parks are fun. If you're a guy, anything involving a ball and a group of overly large "men" (and I use the term loosely) is fun. But taken together, marriage and childrearing are not what I'd call fun. Oh sure, there are fun times every so often. Husbands do stupid things that are sometimes funny weeks later after the rage has dissipated. Kids say and/or do the darndest things at grocery store checkout counters that occasionally might be considered humorous, though usually more so by those witnessing the incident. But the idea that childrearing while maintaining a marriage is fun? Not so much.

Gee, can you tell what kind of day I've had? Or how little sleep I've had since Princess Emma arrived? Or how helpful my husband is right now? I mean, I haven't even congratulated you on your impending nuptials yet! I'm glad everything is working out for you.

I really am happy for you. Just ignore the paragraph above. I'm postpartum and liable to say anything that comes to mind.

Good luck with that "fun" thing. Let me know how that works out for ya.
Yp

CHAPTER TEN: WEDDINGS AND MOTHER'S DAY

SUBJECT : A VERY SPECIAL MOTHER'S DAY

Steph,

Hey! I'm sending this from Mom's place. The girls and I are here visiting the doting grandparents in Lake Jackson for the week because, you know, Emma's such a great traveler and all. Note bitter sarcasm inspired by infant who refuses to nurse while traveling. Do you know how painful that is? Of course you don't. But you will. Just wait! Oops, sorry. I'm not supposed to say things like that to soon-to-be- moms, not that there's anything you can do about impending motherhood at this point. You're pretty much stuck, you know. But moving right along.

Your wedding was so much fun! I hope Emma's gassy tummy couldn't be heard up at the altar. And my sincerest apologies if the noises emanating from her diaper region drowned out the "I-do's." At least her major blowout was postponed until the ring ceremony; it was quite thoughtful of her to save the best for last. (More fun mommy stuff for you to look forward to!) BTW, you're the only person I know who can look so beautiful and so skinny eight months pregnant. You looked fabulous! Loved the beautiful pearl embroidered shawl.

After the reception, we headed back to my aunt and uncle's place outside Austin for the night. Mom kept Claire there Saturday evening during the wedding, my aunt and uncle having displayed great wisdom in hightailing it out of town before our arrival. I am told that Claire spent her evening practicing her magic act. That's the one where she makes objects (like my aunt's knickknacks) disappear, never to be seen again. They'll have to pack up and move before they find them all.

Anyway. Since Sunday was Mother's Day, it was decided that the family would lunch in style at a very nice hotel buffet. I use the term "in style" very loosely, as I don't know that wearing my dress around my neck (and only around my neck) for most of lunch is considered the height of chic. Thank God for full-length slips.

You think I'm kidding?

We cleaned, scrubbed, and vacuumed our way out the door at my aunt and uncle's. My mom thinks that a good houseguest is one that leaves not a shred of evidence for even a crime scene unit to trace. After the clean up, we headed to the hotel. Another aunt and uncle met up with us at the hotel, dragging my grandmother in kicking and screaming. She had told my mom that she wasn't about to have lunch at a hotel, and that she'd just eat by herself if we persisted in this nonsense (which was fine with us, really). She would have preferred that we wait in line for over two hours with two kids under the age of two to eat at the very posh Red Lobster. Senior logic at its best.

As this was her first time to meet Emma, you'd think she'd be happy just to see us, regardless of where we chose to eat. But not my Mawmaw. After scrutinizing Emma for all of ten seconds, she announced that Emma didn't look like anyone in the family. This is ridiculous. Even total strangers comment that she looks just like me. And that was her only remark about my sweet baby. It was my punishment, I guess, for conspiring to deprive her of hush puppies and fried fish, not that you can distinguish between the two at her favorite restaurant.

Thirteen hours later, when I finally managed to get Jack, Claire, and myself squared away at the table and down to the important job of eating, Emma started pitching a fit. This is the child who spent the weekend boycotting my milk factory, but when I tried to eat my meal-the only one that would be in my honor all year-well, suddenly she was starving and (temporarily) ended her food strike. Do they come any more contrary?

Attempts by all to pacify her failed miserably. Emma did not want a "paci." She did not want to be bounced up and down. She did not want her grandmother, her great-grandmother (no big surprise there), her great-aunt, her grandfather, or her daddy. She wanted her mommy. NOW. So much for enjoying my well-deserved Mother's Day lunch.

As I whisked her away from the table to feed her, I realized my lovely lime green frock was exactly the wrong thing to wear for nursing an infant. It's a fitted chemise with no buttons, no zippers, nada. No access to the goods. Whose brilliant idea was this? Oh. Right. That would be mine. Didn't I used to be smarter than this? I wondered.

(Sidebar: I could blame the steady decay of my brain cells over the years on my children, as most mothers do, but I think it started way before they came along. Law school apparently killed off thousands of neurons in the lobe that controls common sense so that my brain could make room for "thinking like a lawyer." Memory cells were the next to go and died horrible deaths during my first pregnancy, their demise escalating geometrically when I became pregnant again a mere ten months after giving birth. At the rate I'm going, in another five or ten years my brain will simply throw in the towel, I'm sure, and succumb to existing in a perpetual senior moment. Ironically, the very crutch I have leaned on to sustain myself these past nine years, namely umpteen thousand cans of Dr. Pepper, is likely accelerating my rapid descent into la-la land. All that aluminum can't be good for the gray matter, to say nothing of the cellulite on my thighs and backside.)

What were we talking about? Oh yeah-nursing the tyrannical infant during my special lunch on my special day.

A trip to the ladies' lounge should have solved the problem. And yet, perhaps predictably, it didn't. I attempted to disrobe, but no can do. There were no chairs to sit on, and I haven't yet sunk to nursing on a toilet. Emma was not happy. Being the resourceful person I am, however, I immediately headed to the front desk of the hotel and asked for a place to nurse privately. A hotel manager led me to an empty conference room. Aside from the fact that the big windows opened directly onto the pool area, giving unsuspecting swimmers the possibility of viewing a peep show while frolicking in the pool, it was perfect. The manager promised me that no one would disturb me and that we'd have complete privacy. Living perpetually under Murphy's Law as I do, that should have tipped me off right there. But refer back to my "Sidebar".

In light of the manager's assurances, I stripped out of my dress jacket, pulled my chemise up to my neck, maneuvered my slip out of the way, and began feeding the poor starving infant. Things were going just fine for all of five minutes. Right up until I heard the door handle turn.

A small Middle Eastern man dressed in a hotel uniform marched in and stopped right next to me, oblivious thus far to my immodest predicament. He smiled and looked down to admire the baby. If she smiles back, we're going to have an R- rated moment on our hands. And of course she smiled back And…eureka! A horrified look came across his face and I knew that he was finally connecting the dots. He beat a rapid retreat as he uttered heavily accented apologies. He might also have been sending up his thanks to heaven, for all I knew. After all, had this little scenario played out in his country of origin rather than the Lone Star State, no doubt we'd both have been stoned to death at sunrise. Three cheers for America. A place where you can flash a man and both live to tell the tale. I laughed so hard after he left that it was some time before Emma could resume nursing, it being difficult to hit a moving target and all.

By the time my fickle infant and I finally returned to the table so that I could start eating, everyone else was finishing dessert. So, that was my wonderful day to be honored for all the sacrifices I make as a mom. Isn't it great? You might as well get used to the idea of missing meals, particularly the ones in your honor and/or with really good food. Of course, the best part is, you get to play the martyr and hold this stuff over your hubby's head for years to come. It's kind of like a mileage rewards program. A few more Mother's Day outings like this, and I'll have saved up enough points for a guilt trip to the Bahamas.

At least I get to neglect my children when we're with their grandmother, but I guess I should at least peek in on them. I don't want them to get used to all this attention, you know. Plus, I can't risk Jack hearing that I did next to nothing all week. Might lose some of those martyr points. Catch you later.

yp

SUBJECT : RE: A VERY SPECIAL MOTHER'S DAY

Hi there,

I'm glad you enjoyed the wedding. I sure did. Aside from being bigger and on an emotional roller coaster, my life has not changed much—yet. It sounds as if you had a hectic Mother's Day with the nursing and all. (And, BTW you were supposed to TELL me these things in advance so that I could make an educated decision about child rearing!) The whole baby thing should be a fun adventure for the rest of my life. Oh I forgot—fun only relates to movies, etc. I can't wait. Well technically I can as I still enjoy dancing and staying up late AND possessing functioning brain cells. Anyway, have a happy rest of your week and rack up those martyr points! S.

SUBJECT: LAMAZE CLASS

Hi there!

Pierce and I are entering the final stages of babyhood. Or, maybe we are just beginning. Anyhow, now that we have made it through the entire marriage ceremony, etc. we can turn our focus to Lamaze classes. So far, we have attended two classes. There are only a total of six so it is questionable whether or not we'll conclude the series considering my due date is June 30.

It has been quite interesting. I, in true first-born fashion, am trying to learn as much as possible so that I am completely prepared for the experience. Pierce, in his true style, is making light of every possible moment. At our first class, Pierce introduced himself as "Pierce THE Jack. You know, like Jack THE

Ripper, Cedric THE Entertainer, etc." He introduced me as his wife and when it was time to tell everyone how we met he promptly announced we met at a strip bar. Well, I'd heard this line before so I was prepared and quipped back with "Yes, it was amateur night at the gay bar and Pierce was dancing." I thought it was amusing. Most of the classmates thought we were weird, which got us off to a good start. The next question of the round robin was "What do you hope to get out of this birth?" Sweat began bubbling on my skin and not because of the 95-degree Texas heat. I could only imagine Pierce's response. It wasn't too bad…. "Well, we certainly expect the baby to be bald and fat like me, unless of course the FedEx man was involved. Regardless, we are two Aggies so there is no telling what a little cross-breeding will do here." That caused our classmates and instructor to look at us and question whether we were cousins with mental issues. This is going to be a fun journey. And all that was at class numero uno!

At our second class, we were given the opportunity to handle all the medical devices that may or may not be used in our delivery. Pierce took the opportunity to make alien antennae for his head, scratched his back, or otherwise annoyed and agitated me with his silly antics. During the visualization portion of the class, Pierce started to sing "Memories" all too loud. After a glare from me hot enough to heat water, he changed his tune to "Shake your groove thang." I couldn't win. I just wanted to be delivered from my humiliation! Needless to say, I was not nearly in the mood as I was at the first class. We only have four more classes to suffer through. I am beginning to hope that this is more grueling than the delivery.

I'm out of steam, as is the case on a daily basis. So, I'll sign off for now but keep you posted as things progress. See ya. S.

SUBJECT: RE: LAMAZE CLASS

Steph,

Well, at least your marriage to Pierce will never be boring. Often humiliating, but never dull. It's a give and take thing for you, I guess. Your "classmates," on the other hand, sound very boring. You and Pierce have to liven up the place, as this birthing stuff gets way too serious. And you'll really appreciate Pierce's humor when the torture begins. I'm not referring to the ultimate torture of labor and delivery, where a husband's attempts at humor on his wailing wife put his nether regions in great peril. No, I'm talking about ice cubes here.

My gentle birthing class instructor, a wonderful lady whom I hired as my birthing assistant both times in anticipation of Jack's shortcomings as a coach (just kidding!), turned drill sergeant on us during class one night and forced all of us breeders to hold large ice cubes in our bare hands, one hand at a time. This was intended to condition our minds for labor and managing pain for the length of a contraction. We only had to hold it for a minute each time, but that was the longest minute ever. (Well, until the actual labor, that is. Those long minutes were not constrained by normal time and space, of course.) She explained that if we could mentally manage a small thing like ice for a minute, we'd be well on our way to mentally handling a contraction. Yeah, right. Whatever. Maybe if she'd given us burning needles dipped in hot coals to hold it would have come within the same solar system as labor pain. Nevertheless, I don't think I made it half a minute with that stupid ice cube. I guess that should have been my first clue that natural birth wasn't going to work out for me.

Maybe your birth instructor won't attempt mind conditioning. In the end, it probably doesn't matter. It's going to hurt like hell, and you'll scream at, hit, and possibly bite Pierce at one point or another, so he might as well just accept that now. Of course, Pierce may want to do some mental conditioning by having a pack of dogs attack him. That could be helpful.

Now watch, since I said all that, you'll be earth mama and deliver in half an hour with mere menstrual cramps. (I hope so, anyway!) Good luck. May God grant you a healthy boy, a safe delivery, and no episiotomy.

yp

SUBJECT: BABY MAXWELL

Hi there!

Baby Maxwell is here! And, as you have done previously I will do now. I must carry the torch of relaying my birthing story, although I don't remember too much. You see, I have been awake every two hours since Maxwell was born. He is refusing to eat and the doctor has ordered a feeding every two hours. Pierce and I are taking shifts. He gets the nine p.m. to one a.m. hours, I get the rest of the clock. I also get to pump in between feedings so that Pierce can have a four-hour shift! Joy, joy. Never mind that I cannot sit, walk, or otherwise maneuver without assistance. And, I'm supposed to be holding and feeding a baby? What demands!

Back to the birth story you've waited for! Maxwell was due on June 30, which is my grandmother's birthday. Instead, he was born on June 23, which is Pierce's grandmother's birthday. Precisely at 9:47 a.m., Maxwell arrived for his great-grandmother's ninetieth birthday party which started at 10:00

a.m. Of course, Pierce had the immense joy of going to the party (late of course) to announce Maxwell's arrival. Throughout the rest of the day, I had a steady stream of party goers tramping through my room to offer advice and do you know not ONE of them brought me a piece of cake! I was relegated to hospital food. Even though I had eaten a fairly decent meal the night before, I was famished. Whatever happened to "let them eat cake!"? I deserved it.

My brother and his wife were in town, so Friday night we went to dinner and then to the movies. During the movies, I noticed my water seemed to have broken--but not really. I mean, it wasn't like in the movies where the flood of the Mississippi comes gushing out. Just a steady stream, which is probably a foreshadowing of what life at seventy will be like. Anyhow, after the movie we took my brother and his wife back to my house and got everyone settled in for the night. We decided to go to the hospital just to have things checked but didn't want to wake anyone. In Romeo and Juliet style, my mom (who was visiting, too) came out on the balcony and said, "Where art thou going at ill hour?" We told her we were confirming a false alarm and would be home soon.

When we got to the hospital, however, the nurse informed us that we were not leaving. We had assumed that it was another false alarm and left our overnight bag at home. There we were at the hospital at midnight with none of the calming things we were told in the Lamaze class to bring. Oh well. That class didn't go so well anyhow.

Once the doctor on call arrived and checked everything, he was concerned that my labor had not progressed. According to him, I had been in labor since six-ish the evening before. Oops. In goes the IV after the fourth attempt and in goes the half-dose of Pitocin. (All my meds were half-doses since I am extremely sensitive to drugs!) That sent me into orbit to say the least. Maxwell didn't much care for it either as he started to show signs of distress. Out came the fetal monitor. What a cumbersome contraption. After a few hours of this, I asked for drugs. I opted to have half-doses of narcotics straight through the IV instead of an epidural. They worked magic. They also made me sleepy and slowed down my labor. So, I slept between contractions while Pierce tried to stay awake. Finally around seven in the morning,

Pierce called my mom and his sister and told them if they wanted to be around for the birth they had better hurry. Once they arrived, Pierce sent his sister in to take over for a few minutes. She asked if there was anything she could do and I offered her the position of having the baby. Soon after, my mom came in for a bit. I don't remember anything I said to her. And lastly, my sister-inla-w came in the room. Again, I don't remember what I said. (There went the brain cells!) Finally, the doctor came in to check my progress. When he left the room to grab a sandwich, I yelled that he did not have time to eat. I was deliriously thinking he was going out for a sit-down dinner which would be at least a two-hour ordeal. I had no intentions of continuing the labor for two more hours. And, since there were no windows in birthing rooms, I had no idea what time it really was outside.

At some point thereafter, the doctor ordered the nurses to "speed things up." This involved heaving me over a bar and instructing me to push while squatting. I felt more like I was in third grade attempting the monkey bars. I was already tired and weak from the labor and in no mood to strengthen my arms. I held on for dear life, however, lest my baby be born and then squashed by his own exhausted mother. Yeah—that would have gone over well.

When the bar did not work, I got to resume laying on my back. As if that were so relaxing! The doctor decided the baby would need a little help. It was episiotomy time. Imagine being told you are going to get a shot for numbing. And then, imagine seeing the four-inch needle being wielded about during the conversation. Mind you, there's no numbing for the numbing needle! Can I just go back to sleep now? OUCH! Rings of fire—true description.
The rest is boring contraction stuff with no more drugs until Maxwell arrived. (I learned too late that once you get to a certain point, narcotics are not administered for the baby's sake. A point to remember next time, I'd say!) After Maxwell's birth, the nurse began to push all remaining contents out of my floppy belly. Cool. I don't have to do any work! Gross—don't watch!

As the nurses took baby Max to the cleaning/checking station, Pierce opened the door and welcomed everyone into the room. Luckily for me, the nurse realized he had no clue that I was still being stitched up and am in no position to accept visitors. Instead of being completely tired, my body shifted into the giddy, "Hi. I'm high," mode. The drugs kicked in (again) for a repeat performance. I was feeling just fine. I made a mental note to ask for drugs to take home before I left the hospital. Fortunately (or unfortunately depending on your views), I got them as my episiotomy caused major tearing and required a C-section recovery phase. No driving. No walking. Etc., etc. But, I'll be oh so happy!

So here I am—half high, half-awake-trying to figure out how to be a mommy. I know there is not as much drama in the story; nor humor for that matter. But, there it is. And now, back to our regularly scheduled feeding. Talk to you soon. S.

SUBJECT: BABY MAXWELL

Steph,

You are superwoman! You didn't even know you were in labor? No epidural? You yelled at your doctor? (Way cool- every laboring woman's fantasy.) You rock. (Kids still say that, right?) Congratulations!
I wish I'd been there to get you some cake. That's so uncool. The insensitivity of some people (like, your whole family in this case). Make them get you one just for you. You totally deserve it.

And good for you for having Pierce help you out at night. In the hospital, I couldn't rouse Jack with a bullhorn the night after I delivered Claire. And then when we brought her home the first night, I distinctly recall yelling at him at the top of my lungs to get his behind out of bed to help me with the screaming infant. He barely lifted his head off the pillow. He had a very confused look. Well, naturally he was confused; he wouldn't open his eyes to see what was going on and vaguely suggested that I just feed the baby, which I had already done four times in three hours. Then he fell back into unconscious bliss. So helpful.
Take time to really enjoy this brief newborn stage. It pretty much all goes downhill from here.

Get some rest! And thanks for passing the torch. yp

CHAPTER ELEVEN: THEY DIDN'T LEARN THAT FROM ME

SUBJECT: CLAIRE'S NEED FOR ETIQUETTE LESSONS

Steph,

Oh my gosh. You will never believe what Claire did today.

She and I are in the post office this morning, and we have to stand in a really long line. A really long, completely silent line. The place is as quiet as a funeral home despite having about twenty impatient people crammed into its small space. No one's even talking on a cell phone. What's up with that?

Claire (who turns two in four days, which I can hardly believe) presents her usual challenges to my authority: running off, going in circles, talking loudly, picking stuff up off the floor (ewww!); and trying to pull things down off the counters. Joy. Her antics were all the more difficult to deal with today because the post office was so freaking quiet. It sounded like we were a couple of elephants with bullhorns compared to everyone else's silence.

As nothing else seemed to work, I picked Claire up and held her, still squirming and fussing as we waited in line. This did not go over so well with her. Now we were a whole herd of elephants with bullhorns and there were twenty people behind us instead of in front of us. So much fun to be the focal point of scrutinizing parents and grandparents. I could practically see their criticism of my parenting skills hanging in bubbles over their heads like cartoons comments. And no, I'm not excessively paranoid nor overly sensitive to criticism of my parenting. I'm only as paranoid and sensitive as the next mom is.

A year later, it was finally our turn. We walked up, and I set Claire down on the counter so she couldn't run off. The postal clerk appeared rather nonplussed by my presumption. I couldn't have cared less at that point. We proceeded with the transaction while Claire attempted to explore every inch of the countertop and computer. I was almost done with my transaction, thinking we might come out of this relatively unscathed after all, when Claire pierced the deafening silence with the longest, loudest burp I've ever heard in my entire life. Seriously, she could have won a frat house burping contest with it. I am not exaggerating. I don't know how a toddler can produce that much gas.

My entire body turned beet red. Claire laughed. The deafening silence continued. If the other customers had only laughed or even giggled, it would have been fine. But no, not a peep out of anyone. I was certain people two blocks down the street heard that burp, so I knew the postal patrons didn't miss it. The clerk helping me was clearly not amused. I know this because she pursed her lips, frowned ever so slightly, and sped up the transaction.

When I finally recovered, I attempted to redeem the situation by saying, in an overly loud voice, "My goodness. We say, 'Excuse me.'" My efforts to instruct Claire were rewarded with a big grin and a giggle. No "Excuse me" was forthcoming.

The torture finally came to an end, I grabbed my receipt, and with head down so as to avoid eye contact with anyone, I practically sprinted out of the post office.

Does it get any more embarrassing than this? Please don't say yes. She's a girl!!!! She's not supposed to burp at all, much less burp as loudly as any guy ever thought about doing. Does anyone offer etiquette lessons for a two-year old?

Sign me,
Too embarrassed to be seen at the post office for a while.

SUBJECT: RE: CLAIRE'S NEED FOR ETIQUETTE LESSONS

Yvonne,

Got your message. I'm easily amused and loved your tale of the belching blond-shell! Of course, my days and nights right now are filled with a burping baby that spews. I had no idea there was such a thing as projectile vomit! Or projectile poop for that matter. Just last night I was changing Maxwell's diaper and wouldn't you know the minute I got the first dirty diaper off, he proceeded to project poop everywhere. I am not talking about a little icky here and there. This was like a car running out of gas, sputtering, starting and stopping, meanwhile spewing everywhere. It was on the wall, the nightlight, everywhere. Pierce and I were delirious due to sleep deprivation. This was clearly evidenced as we both laughed hysterically during the entire event. I don't think either of us were thinking about the diaper duty cleanup afterwards. Anyway, it was pretty funny. I'll keep my eyes open for etiquette lessons. I am sure we will need them in the future as well. Take care. S.

Subject: RE: Re: Claire's need for etiquette lessons

Ewww! Projectile poop. Congratulations, you win the gross- out story for today. Your prize? Hours of bleaching the walls. Yeah. Mommyhood is so much "fun." (I did warn you about all this.)

Get some sleep! Yp

SUBJECT: APPEARANCES CAN BE DECEIVING — RIGHT?

Steph,

Jack's about to go out of town on business, so I head to the grocery store after dinner to avoid having to go with both munchkins later, an event that always ends with all three of us in tears and should be avoided at all costs. At Jack's rather strong suggestion, Claire gets in the car with me at the last possible moment. If I haven't mentioned it before, grocery shopping with Claire is a little like having an octopus in your cart. A hungry octopus, regardless of how recently she's eaten. But my list only has about 10 things on it, so I figure it can't be too bad. I calculate I'll be in and out of there in half an hour, tops. I could do this. The eternal optimist strikes again.

True to form, Claire is in eight-tentacle mode throughout the store. I think I should be forgiven for not noticing Claire's appearance, as I am just a little too busy the whole time trying to keep her from squashing the bread, eating the unwashed grapes (of which she downs at least five), opening the cheese sticks, tearing into the iced animal cookies (she only likes the elephants, the rest end up on the seat), and throwing soup cans on the floor (she apparently doesn't care for chicken and stars).

And if she isn't grabbing for this or that in the cart, she is loudly demanding this or that on the shelf. And Lord help us if I park the cart too close to the shelves (she has an amazingly long reach for a two-year old.) "No, honey, we don't really need twelve cans of green beans." Jack just can't understand why I come home with really gross stuff like canned corned beef and sardines, but then he doesn't often go grocery shopping with the terror of Aisle 9. (I have gotten a little bit wiser in my old age. After discovering three tubes of K-Y jelly in the cart while checking out with Kate at Walmart recently, I now make it a point never to go down the "family planning" aisle with her. On the upside, I won't need to replenish the K-Y for about   a decade at the rate Jack and I are going. That is an upside, right?)

So an hour later (seriously), we finally made it to the checkout. As I stood at the counter watching my grocery bill add up to an astonishingly high number for what was supposed to be a mere 10 items, I noticed the clerk looking over at Claire every so often a little uneasily. Thinking that Claire was into the animal cookies again, I finally take note of her and, as with the clerk and the people behind us in line, I am appalled. The silence grows. I can see what everyone is thinking.

Mysteriously, the shoes Claire came in with are nowhere in evidence, leaving her bare—and icky—toes dangling for all to see.

Me: What the heck did she do with her shoes?
The perfectly groomed businesswoman in line: What sort of mother doesn't put shoes on her child in the filthy grocery store? How irresponsible!

Claire's blue bow, no longer sitting on top of her little golden head, hangs down near her ear and looks like a remarkably huge earring for a toddler.

Me: If you would just stop pulling on the stupid bow, it might stay in place longer than five minutes, but that's only if you don't try to stand on your head in the cart again.

The clerk: What, you don't own a brush, Mom?

Multiple dark red spaghetti sauce stains splattered from dinner cover her pale shirt.

Me: Might as well throw that one away because those stains are NEVER coming out.

The grandmother in line behind me: How could you let her out the door in that shirt? Tacky, tacky, tacky!

Claire's forehead displays a gigantic bruise that looks, well, suspicious. (She fell off the kitchen island this week when I had my back turned to her for 1.5 seconds. We both cried for half an hour). And her little shins are covered with an unusually large assortment of bruises and scrapes.

Me: She gets her lack of coordination from her father. It's not my fault.

The clerk: Poor baby. How could you abuse such a precious little one? What is wrong with you?

To top it off, she is clutching a stuffed animal for dear life, making her look pitifully insecure.

Me: That's the fifth animal she's dragged around today, and now there's cookie icing all over it. Perfect.

Everyone around me: It's probably all she has in this world to comfort her. Poor child.

I took it all in, realizing that she appeared to everyone else to be exactly the sort of neglected and abused child that I always stop and say a prayer for (while furiously scowling at the offending parent, of course). Great. Now everyone is scowling at ME. Store alert: evil mom at checkout 4.

I desperately wanted to pick Claire up and hug and kiss on her in front of the clerk to show that I am really a great, loving parent. But would that look like I'm trying too hard to not look like the evil mom that I so obviously am? Not that I don't want to hug and kiss on Claire, sticky fingers and all. I barely suppress the urge to explain to the clerk that I was in a huge hurry to get to the store and didn't notice how she was dressed (which is mostly true). I ponder whether to mention that Claire is a very active child, that she's a notoriously messy eater, that she doesn't like shoes, and that her hair is too fine to hold a bow very well. Just wait! I can explain everything!

While I was paying for the groceries, I was so busy thinking about how not to look like an awful parent, and how to keep the store from calling CPS on me, that I didn't actually notice when Claire stood up in the seat of the cart and attempted to walk right onto the checkout counter to get to her cookies. "Oh no, sweetie. That's not safe. Your mommy should get you down and hold you," declared the clerk in the exaggerated speech of one attempting to make a point that might somehow be otherwise missed. She delivered this with a stare that clearly screamed "Child abuser!"

As I tried to wrestle an unobliging Claire off the counter and into my arms, the clerk took an inordinate amount of time recording (and no doubt memorizing for the police) my driver's license number on the check, even though it's printed right on the front. Having captured the fit-throwing toddler, I attempted to smile warmly at the clerk as Claire thrashed and screamed at the top of her lungs to be put down. With not even a hint of a smile and without a word, she handed me the receipt. I wrangled Claire and the basket and made my escape post haste.

So that's that. I went to the grocery store to take care of my family, and now I'm screwed. I guess I'll be writing to you from prison. CPS will be coming for sure.

This will teach me not to jump to conclusions about any mom whose progeny looks like the poster child for foster parenting. After all, she could be just like me: the perfect parent, framed by her toddler.

yp

SUBJECT: RE: APPEARANCES CAN BE DECEIVING—RIGHT?

Oh dear. So this is what I have to look forward to in the near future? Believe it or not, in some strange way I actually somewhat envy you for going to the grocery store. I have not been out of the house in months! Since Maxwell was born, I have been too tired to even get out of the bedroom. Everyone said that life changes dramatically once you have a child. I thought they were talking about everyone but me! Now that I do have a child who literally refuses to eat, my life has definitely taken a different direction.

Instead of getting up at 6:30 a.m. to dress myself for a proper days' work, I get up every two hours around the clock to feed Maxwell. I even have the pleasure of trying to wake him up for feedings. (Isn't there some saying about 'never wake a sleeping baby'? This will come back to haunt me in the future. I just know it.) When 6:30 rolls around, it's all I can do to just sit up in bed!

While Maxwell catches up on his 'zzz's between feedings, I try to concoct some sort of meal for breakfast out of the leftover squash in the refrigerator, the canned chicken in the pantry and V-8 juice left out from the night before. Since the grocery shopping has fallen to Pierce the last month, we eat out. Rather, he eats out and brings home one meal from the restaurant du jour for me. I don't dare send him to the grocery store as I have learned from past experience that he comes home with about $200 worth of Oreos, ice cream, tomato soup, and slice and bake cookies. Not the best diet for anyone let alone a woman who has just birthed a baby.

Pierce has suggested on more than one occasion that I 'get out of the house' for a while. I am not really sure what he is thinking as he tries to send me into the 'real' world. My hair has not been brushed in three days and I have not bathed in two. The pajamas that I am wearing could definitely walk to the laundry room on their own for the washing they so deserve. Makeup is a thing of the past as is any piece of clothing that doesn't resemble a bed sheet, tent, or otherwise 'blousy', oversized article.

Nevertheless, maybe I will take him up on the offer and head to the grocery store. Who would have thought I'd relish the day I could go to the supermarket? And, if I see the check out clerk posing in Austin, I'll just give her the little piece of my mind that I have left about chastising you! After all, the way I look she may think I'm homeless! Talk to you soon. S.

SUBJECT: RE: RE: APPEARANCES CAN BE DECEIVING — RIGHT?

Steph,

Bless your heart! I wish I could come help you. Sort of. Well, I would if I didn't have my own tyrannical children to deal with, of course. But look on the bright side: you didn't have twins!

I would say "try to get some sleep," but that just seems cruel. Hope it gets better soon.
yp

SUBJECT: EMMA THE MONSTER BABY WHO DOESN'T SLEEP

Steph,

Hey-how's it going? Is baby Max sleeping for you yet? If not, I thought this monsters' update might cheer you up. Or depress you. Depends on how willing you are to embrace your future.

The older monster, whose vocabulary had been expanding exponentially, has now regressed. Her entire lexicon can be summed up in a few choice phrases: "NO!!!" (accompanied by a fierce face and angry tone); "Stop it!!!"; Let go!!!; "No way!!!"; and, my favorite, "Don't want to!!!" She and the time out chair have spent lots of quality time together lately. She and the spanking spoon are also becoming a bit better acquainted.
Not to be outdone by her older sibling, Emma, the monster baby, offers her own challenges to parental dominance. For instance,

she refuses to sleep in her own crib now. Why we spent a fortune (or the grandparents' fortune, I should say) furnishing and decorating her room is beyond me. She doesn't even play in her room, as she much prefers Claire's abode for frolicking. I should have bought bedroom furniture for my own room instead. At least that way we could all enjoy lounging in a beautiful bed.

I say lounging rather than sleeping because, despite the fact that Emma will snooze like the dead while in my bed during nap time (or whenever her daddy is sleeping next to her), my arrival to bed, regardless of the hour, is her signal to commence hourly wakeup calls for me. We should hire her out to the local Holiday Inn for just that purpose, as she takes her job very seriously.

The only way to get her back to sleep, I've found, is for me to play my role as human pacifier, a role I somewhat grudgingly inhabited until the past two nights. Apparently, I have now been promoted from human pacifier to human teether. I can tell you that a wakeup call with teeth is significantly more effective than one without. The whole affair ends with both of us in tears, and at least once it ended with Emma flung halfway across the bed as a result of my knee-jerk reaction to being awakened in such an excruciatingly painful way. The scary thing? She only has two teeth now. There are lots more where those came from.
Don't you feel better now? It will be a few more months before Max has teeth. Enjoy the toothless grin-and toothless nursing-while it lasts!

Have a great week.
yp

SUBJECT: RE: EMMA THE MONSTER BABY WHO DOESN'T SLEEP

Thanks for the insight into the future. I, being the naïve, first-time mom that I am, still believe that I will have none of those issues to deal with in such capacity.

Of course, Maxwell is still not sleeping through the night. As you may remember, our pediatrician instructed us to wake him up every two hours for feeding the first few months of his life. I have come to realize that this pattern will be with us for a while. Although Maxwell does sleep soundly once he's down, he is like Pavlov's dog on the two-hour mark, waking to eat. I should have probably heeded my mother's advice: "Never wake a sleeping baby." But then, that would have been entirely too easy.

I am going to try to get some shut-eye before the next dinner on demand is summoned. Talk to you soon. Oh, and don't forget to vote tomorrow! S.

SUBJECT: RE: RE: EMMA

Steph,

What, there's an election tomorrow? I haven't seen any TV coverage. But then again, unless Clifford the Big Red Dog or Barney the Big Purple Freak are running for office, I wouldn't, would I? I seem to recall a distant past where I was intensely involved in elections and was even a delegate to several state party conventions. At least I think that was me. I'll have to look that up.

Oh, and you just keep believing you won't have any of my issues with your sweet baby, girlfriend. Delusions can be a good thing for a new mom. A real stress-reliever. Everything's going to be okay. Just relax. (You're ready to throw something at me, aren't you?)

yp

CHAPTER TWELVE: CAN I BLAME THIS ON THE KIDS?

SUBJECT: THE PERILS OF OVER-SCHEDULING

Steph,

Howdy! How was your day? Want to hear mine?

I had previously scheduled a client meeting to sign docs for today, not realizing that it was to be Thanksgiving Feast Day at the girls' mom's day out program, and parents were supposed to be there (which, in my opinion, sort of negates the whole purpose of the program, but whatever). When I learned of my conflict, I should have just moved my client meeting to another day. But, being the overachiever (read: hopeless scheduling optimist) that I am, I worked it ALL out.

I planned:
a) to arrive at school on time (9:15 a.m.),
b) with the girls stylishly attired (to impress the other moms at school, of course),
c) and with at least two hot side dishes for the dinner in tow.

Then I expected to:
a) help out the teachers with setting up tables for the dinner;
b) enjoy an early lunch with Emma at 11 a.m.;
c) have a later lunch with Claire at 11:30;
d) head to a 1:00 p.m. client meeting a good 30 minutes away;
e) and then zip back to the school to pick up the girls by 2:15 p.m. And I planned to do all of this while impeccably dressed in my

beautiful and professional cranberry pantsuit.

Such are the best laid plans of mice and moms . . . So I didn't get to bed this morning until 3:30 a.m., and I got less than four hours of sleep. Which probably explains a lot.

I arrived at school with the girls at 10:15, only an hour late. Not so bad. But while I appeared somewhat elegantly dressed in the aforementioned cranberry pantsuit, the girls looked like farm hand rejects in hastily thrown together overalls with mismatched shirts. I'm reasonably certain that Emma wasn't even wearing socks. So much for being stylish.

After depositing my girls in their respective classrooms, I found my way to the kitchen to offer up my one very cold side dish of mac-n-cheese. Despite only getting four hours of sleep, I somehow hadn't had time last night to make the other side dish I was supposed to bring. And because I was so late, I missed helping set up the tables and instead was assigned to transfer greasy turkeys from cooking dishes to serving platters, the very type of job I had hoped to avoid by wearing my "Can't-you-see-I'm-an-attorney?" garb. You can imagine how well my favorite cream silk blouse absorbed turkey juice, gravy, and mashed potatoes. Despite being in a stupor from lack of sleep, I did at least have the sense to take my jacket off first.

Menial labor complete, I went to join Emma for our early lunch together. The staff, however, informed me that she had, for the first time in several weeks, decided to take a morning nap. She won't do that for me at home when I really need her to, but when Mommy's supposed to spend quality time with her, she snoozes. Could they come any more contrary?

Moving right along, I joined Claire for lunch, who by this time was all decked out in a charming Indian headdress that coordinated remarkably well with the aforementioned farm hand reject clothing. As we made our way through the buffet line, Claire picked up every cherry tomato she came across and tried to put them on my plate. I don't care for tomatoes quite that much, as I tried to explain to her without any success whatsoever, and she won't eat them at all, so many tomatoes died in vain at the bottom of the trash bin today. During lunch, Claire managed to smear orange cookie icing all over herself, which looks not so bad on denim overalls but really clashes with cranberry pants, by the way. But other than that, we had a delightful repast.

I extracted myself from lunch on time (yes, amazing but true), drove alarmingly fast, and made it to my client meeting with ten minutes to spare (even more amazing as such a feat is quite unprecedented for me). I zipped through the client meeting, hoping no one noticed the orange cookie icing and gravy stains on my power suit, drove alarmingly fast again, and made it back early (yes, also amazing but true) to pick up the girls from school. So what do you know? All's well that end's well, for once.

Now, however, I'm exhausted. So ready for a nap. But my kitchen hasn't been cleaned in three days, and things are starting to walk off the counters of their own accord. So I guess I'd better quit chatting and start cleaning.
Happy Thanksgiving! yp

SUBJECT: RE: THE PERILS OF OVER-SCHEDULING

Yvonne,

Wow! I am impressed that you made it to your meeting on time and picked up the girls early. There is no way I could master that trick, with or without kids! Not to mention you saved the pantsuit from ruin!

We are staying put this Thanksgiving. Hopefully, all will be relatively calm. Have a great Thanksgiving. I will talk to you soon. S.

SUBJECT: THE GRISWORLD FAMILY CHRISTMAS TREE

Steph,

Hey! We just got back from Mom's down in Lake Jackson. I'm exhausted. As usual, it was a crazy trip, filled with crazy incidents. Like shopping for a Christmas tree.

Jack and I have always had a fake Christmas tree because of his allergies, so I love to shop for a real one for Mom. She and I took the girls to the tree lot and spent approximately 1½ hours selecting the perfect tree. Dad, cast in the mold of Scrooge when it comes to anything resembling a Christmas tradition, chose to remain at home by the warm fire. But our outing went great, especially considering it was freezing and it was bedtime when we started (I know, great planning). Emma actually fell asleep all bundled up in her stroller. Claire, on the other hand, decided that the rows of trees made excellent cover for hide and seek. The thick layer of mud beneath the trees was unfortunate, but Claire was about to outgrow those shoes anyway.

Having spent forever picking exactly the right tree with exactly the right height and exactly the right circumference and exactly the right fluffiness and exactly the right fragrance, and with exactly the wrong price, the tree lot guys then took forever carefully affixing the perfect tree to a metal stand for Mom. Then they carefully tied it to the luggage rack on top of my truck. Mom then carefully and s-l-o-w-l-y drove my truck home so as not to lose any of the perfect needles on the perfect tree. Mission accomplished, frozen fingers, toes, and other body parts notwithstanding.

In the five minutes it took to get from the tree lot to the house, it would seem that Mom forgot all about the fact that her perfect tree, which we had just spent an enormous amount of time hunting for in the freezing cold, was strapped to the top of the truck. Apparently in the throes of a senior moment, Mom drove the truck into the garage. (I confess, I was somewhat distracted by the kids and didn't really notice what she was doing. My bad, too.)

We knew there was a problem when we heard a terrible metallic-screech/huge-car-wash-brush sound over the roof of the truck. Assuming that Dad probably had not installed an automatic car wash system in the garage in the two hours we had been gone, we could come to only one possible conclusion: Mom had scalped the perfect tree with the garage door. Copious amounts of pine needles raining down on the windshield bolstered our sad conclusion.

Halfway in and halfway out of the garage, and with no way to get the tree down while it was wedged so tightly between the truck and the top of the garage door, Mom had to do the unthinkable to the perfect Christmas tree. She had to put the truck in reverse and pull back out. Much snapping and screeching ensued, and even more pine needles poured down the windows. Claire was so not happy. Mom and I, on the other hand, were laughing so hard that we couldn't speak. Yet another Griswold moment for our family history.

So Mom's tree leans a little. And the metal stand is on its last leg, literally. And one whole side of the tree looks like it's wearing a buzz cut. But otherwise, it's quite lovely. Especially since Claire took such care to decorate it all by herself. (By toddler fiat, no one else was allowed to touch the ornaments.) Claire's idea of tree trimming dictates that all the decorations must hang in a big bunch in the center of one side of the tree at exactly her eye level—and no where else. It's great. Even Scrooge likes it.

Happy tree hunting to you. yp

SUBJECT: RE: THE GRISWORLD FAMILY CHRISTMAS TREE

Hi there!

Oh, my goodness. I can just imagine the tree half-shaven with ornaments positioned two feet off the floor in a bunch! I guess everyone has a Christmas story. We will be attending the extended family celebration sometime this month. That is always an enlightening experience. Routinely, half the clan is late arriving so the other half is on the verge of steaming. After the deadbeats have shown up, we all inhale a hodgepodge of food. Usually, there is not enough sustenance but there's always an abundance of deviled eggs in different assortments and colors. My grandmother has taken deviled eggs to a new level and rainbow doesn't even begin to describe it. Next, the white elephant game is played with vengeance, sleuthing, conspiracy, and revenge. Mercy is spared to no one—not even the newcomers. And, there are always newcomers. Every year at least two different members of the clan invite some boyfriend, neighbor, gardener or a person they just met two weeks prior to the event. Why anyone would want to be subjected to our functioning dysfunctional family is beyond me. (Oh, and lest I forget, last year we also had in attendance two dogs and a bird that were in transit over the holidays.) Shortly after the cutthroat gift exchange, the clan disperses and departs. There is no leisurely visiting or lounging about the location. This group is on a mission: Eat-Play-Leave. Then, we meet again next year. And for most in the group it is the only get together during the year. If something unusual and interesting should happen this year, I'll let you know. Otherwise, have a great holiday season! I'll talk to you soon. S.

CHAPTER THIRTEEN: LIFE CYCLES

SUBJECT: BACK FROM THE TWILIGHT ZONE

Steph,

Well, I'm back from a very strange trip. As you know, my grandmother died last week. We held her funeral service in Austin at her church, but we all knew she wanted to be buried in Louisiana next to my grandfather in the family cemetery (she left little doubt as she had ordered his double headstone engraved with her own name and date of birth when he died years ago—very creepy). So shortly after the service, we all loaded up to caravan from Austin to Monroe. And when I say "all," I'm not limiting the term to merely the living among us.

My grandmother was a thrifty sort, as is her son (my uncle). Knowing this about her, he apparently decided that she wouldn't have wanted us to spend a fortune hiring the funeral home to transport her body to the out-of-state burial site. His economical solution was quite simple: to rent a van to transport her himself. Lest this detail conjure up images of the Griswold family vacation to Wally World with deceased Aunt Edna, my uncle did at least keep Mawmaw in the coffin. And he had some sort of permit. So there she was, my grandmother, making her final journey to her resting place beside her husband, appropriately attired in her favorite shade of red and safely resting in a respectable casket…being hauled in the back of a rented white cargo van with questionable shock supports. And there we were, umpteen cars following along behind.

My uncle is from East Texas, so from his perspective, the long, winding, scenic route through the Piney Woods promised a far superior traveling experience than the route I would have chosen: the incredibly direct path straight up I-35 to Dallas, and then due east on I-20 (where we all could have driven at least 70 mph the entire way and avoided those confusing one- way town square traps so favored in most of the small burgs along the way). I have never been through so many one-horse towns on a single trip in my life, and I had no idea that it could take so long to get from Texas to Louisiana, factoring in that we weren't starting out from Big Bend or Laredo, of course.

Did I mention that I had Emma with me, the breast-feeding baby who, while constantly hungry, refuses to nurse on trips and hates to travel? Who is allergic to most formulas? And did I mention that I was stuffed into Cousin Liz's minivan with said fussy baby, Liz, and my brother and his pregnant- and very nauseated-wife? (Having more sense than me for once, Jack won the argument and insisted that he and Claire remain behind at home.)

Before we ever departed Austin, my uncle decreed that, for the entirety of the trip, when one car in the caravan stopped for something, we ALL stopped for that something. Because there were so many of us on the trip (ranging from infants to septuagenarians), we quite naturally had to stop often along the way to accommodate the wide variety of bladder physiology represented in the group. As you might imagine, this "all-stop" rule greatly increased the journey's already epoch-long travel time.

Further complicating matters, none of the five cell phones in our car worked. Apparently, no mobile service has seen fit to erect cell towers anywhere in the vicinity of East Texas. We did, however, have this nifty walkie-talkie thing with us to communicate between our car and my uncle's van, but the trick was, we had to be within close range of him for it to work. Did I mention that most of the roads were single lane each way? And that they've never heard of anything remotely resembling a straight road in the Piney Woods? As a result, we spent at least a quarter of the trip playing chicken with oncoming farm trucks while trying to get close enough to the van to let my uncle know that someone on board had to pee again. Or had to have her diaper changed. Again. Or had to throw up. Or had to stop for a snack. Or had to stop and refuse to nurse…

To pass the time on this gloomy pilgrimage, I thought ahead and had acquired a murder mystery book on tape and a portable cassette player, the latter of which was necessitated by Liz's new, technologically advanced minivan, which would not condescend to feature anything so antiquated as a tape player. In retrospect, I probably chose the title poorly, as the mystery involved exhuming a grave that, in turn, brought to mind images of what happens to a body as it… well, you get the picture. Momentary lapse of judgment there. (Then again, I can't be expected to think of everything, can I? I didn't forget appropriate funeral clothes, diapers, wipes, or the baby. Surely that counts for something.)

In spite of its morbid tale, we listened to the book. (The alternative to obsessing over Mawmaw's life, death, and funeral service was not something any of us was prepared to do just yet). But at some point after the story had hooked all of us, the cassette player died and we were left hanging. As luck would have it, however, there's a Walmart in every other one of these small towns. We managed to hail my corpse-toting uncle in his makeshift hearse on the walkie-talkie before long (after yet more near misses with giant farm machinery), and it was decided that we would stop in the next town for a little shopping errand and dinner.

Well, you know when one person needs something at Walmart, everyone else thinks they need something, too. So the caravan disembarked and we all straggled in. While the occupants of our minivan obsessed over getting another tape player and batteries, the rest of the group fanned out looking for snacks, warm stockings, and forgotten toothbrushes. I had assumed that, while we all shopped, my uncle and his son would stand guard over the body of our dear grandmother in the parking lot. Thus, I was rather shocked and appalled when I ran into them on their way back from the sporting goods section and heading for the chip aisle. I inquired into who might have been left with the body while my uncle and cousin checked out shell casings and Doritos, but I earned only shrugs and a rather patronizing response for my trouble.

As it turned out, my uncle's reasoning in leaving the van-and, more importantly, my grandmother-unattended was probably correct. After all, short of encountering some weird cult with a fetish for the deceased that, coincidentally, just happened to be making its weekly Walmart run when we showed up with our dearly departed, there can't be too many car thieves who would want to make off with a van carrying an occupied coffin. Nevertheless, I couldn't help but look for the vehicle every two minutes when we later sat to have dinner at the local Applebee's, which conveniently shared the Walmart parking lot. I could just see the headline: "Thief Steals Van Carrying Grandma's Coffin from Walmart Parking Lot while Family Eats Dinner." But nobody tried to abscond with her. Good thing, too. She was so ornery, her ghost would have doubtless harangued anyone who did for all eternity.

After dinner, most everyone had to get gas and zip over here and there on odd errands, but I needed a parked vehicle to nurse Emma. Liz's van needed gas too and I was somewhat concerned there for a few moments that my uncle was going to suggest that I nurse Emma in his van with my dear grandmother, as she wasn't going anywhere at the moment. Liz saved me, however, by volunteering to hang behind in her minivan while I fed, excuse me, TRIED to feed-the princess. Does the milk taste different on trips? Does she just hate me for uprooting her from her ridiculously comfortable infant existence? What? I don't get it.

Eventually, my uncle and the recently departed got back on the road, leading the clan. Coffin undisturbed. Does it get any weirder?

Oh, nuts. Emma's awake and is starving to death, of course. Remind me to tell you about the Bates motel we all stayed in outside Monroe.
yp

SUBJECT: FUNERAL

Yvonne,

I don't know what I should say 'sorry' for more—the death of your grandmother or the trip you endured to bury her! Why is it that our families are functionally dysfunctional? I had a similar experience when my godmother died.

To make a long story short, we go to Navasota the night before the funeral because the actual service is scheduled for nine in the morning. It's only a 2½ hour drive from here, but there is no possible way we'd be able to get up, get dressed and be on-time, which is a MAJOR issue with my grandmother. So, here we are hanging out at my grandmother's house with all the antiquated relatives. It is very somber.

My grandmother, the 81-year-old ringleader of the group, mentions the daunting task of putting together "the boards" for the funeral the next day. "The boards" are those poster boards filled with pictures of the deceased that I'm sure they would've rather taken to the grave with them. Of course, she mentions this at 8:47p.m. Walmart closes at nine in Navasota. So, as a gesture, I offer to go to Walmart to pick up the necessary supplies for the boards. In doing so, I ask if anyone needs anything; again, a polite but not necessarily sincere offer on my part. My grandmother pipes up "Oh I need a bath rug. A blue one. And don't get one with flowers, I already have one like that." I guess since she is bold enough to send her daily shopping list, my great-aunt chimes in with, "I need a bottle of Clairol, my hair just looks so gray these days." (Like she's really going to have time to dye her hair tonight!

Or better, that my grandmother's deceased sister-in-law will give a flip about her bathroom rug!) By this time, it's 8:52 p.m. I race out of the door, not only to try to make it to the store but also to avoid any more requests, which from this crowd could be anything from pipe tobacco to hemorrhoid cream!

I speed through town like a bat out of hell. I am actually grateful that I get a small respite from the over-seventy crowd. It's really difficult making much more than small talk, although I have to say they do have a lot in common with Maxwell, namely, spitting up, incontinence, and babbling about nothing…

I make it to the store, buy the board goods, bath mat, and hair dye and return to the same somber houseful of people. They haven't moved from their respective chairs and positions in the house. I am wondering how much dust has settled on them in the last 20 minutes since I've been gone. As I unload the poster boards, I get this screechy-gasp from my grandmother. "Oh no. Oh no. You bought yellow boards? Clare hated yellow. Oh no." Excuse me, but isn't Clare dead? Maybe we will get the sheer pleasure of watching her roll over in her grave over yellow boards! Now won't that be fun! My short-story is turning long, so I'll spare you the comments as the boards were made, the whole hair-dyeing experience, and the sheer joy-turned-horror of a non-flowered bath mat which now has hair coloring on it. You can imagine.

We go to the funeral the next day, which was nice. Why do people say that? Nice? What's so nice about looking at a dead body with bad makeup and a hair style you know they wouldn't be caught dead in—no pun intended! Luckily, the entombment is adjacent to the church so it is just a short walk, albeit in 100-degree Texas summer weather.

The preacher says his stuff and then asks each pallbearer to recount something. Well, Pierce is a pallbearer. He is one of the few people under the age of sixty-five who could actually pick up something heavier than a remote control. And, my brother is a pallbearer. Those two together are trouble. Each pallbearer is stating something quite nice about Aunt Clare, how sweet she was, the good food she made, etc., etc. When they get to my brother he says, with a Cheshire cat grin, "Aunt Clare was always trying to teach me things. One time she took me to the horse barn to show me the horses. I was young. She turned around and when she looked back at me, she said 'Crap in one hand, wish in the other, then see which fills up faster.'"

Oh boy, tears (or sweat, as it may be in this weather) are flowing. I am dead silent. And guess who is next: Pierce. He starts off all right by saying he only met Clare a few times and she seemed easy going. So far so good. Then, comes the whopper. He says, "The time I remember the most was when I was telling her about my grandmother. She used to live in a high-rise in Austin. My brother and I used to stand on the roof and pee off the top. I told Clare about it and I never heard her laugh so hard!"

My husband and brother paint this lovely image of my godmother being a cursing sailor who has a poop fetish! Have you ever wanted to just disappear into thin air? For some reason I have become the family keeper, which means I am responsible for everyone and their actions. Needless to say, I got at least an hour-long earful from my grandmother after the whole ordeal. Thank God we don't live in the same town or I'd be listening to it to this day.

Well, I better go. Supper awaits. S.

SUBJECT: RE: FUNERAL

ROFL! Well, it's nice to know that there are weird families everywhere. Makes me feel a little less alone in the universe! yp

PART FOUR

CHAPTER FOURTEEN: AGING GRACEFULLY

SUBJECT: PIERCE DOES VEGAS

Hi there!

For a change, I thought you might enjoy this story about a man who went on a trip. This man—we'll call him Pierce*— went on a boy's trip to Vegas, ostensibly, he argued, for business and networking purposes. (All names have been changed to protect the innocent-except for Pierce— guilty as charged) (Smirk.) Excuse me! I— his wife— have proof to the contrary.

At midnight on the first night away, while his wife—the mother of his six-month-old son—lay in bed attempting to sleep, Mr. Pierce phoned home to check in. We (umm 'she') had a pleasant conversation about her day of nursing (woo- hoo) and listened patiently as he droned on about his day at the blackjack tables. "There were many deals to be had at a blackjack table." No pun intended. Ha. As the conversation drew to a close, Mr. Pierce said "goodbye," omitting one very important detail. He forgot to hang up the cell phone. Oops.

His wife was about to hang up the phone when she heard voices. She checked the receiver. Sure enough, there were voices. Two female voices, a male voice, and the din of a place that sounded like a bar rang through the receiver. She listened to the conversation about the plight of the immigrant in today's USA, yada, yada, yada, between the voices. Clearly attempting, but instead failing, (so his wife thought) to sound intellectual and sexy at the same time, Mr. Pierce held forth with his mystery companions, oblivious to the fact that he had an eavesdropper.

After approximately fifteen minutes of this droning conversation, it suddenly became very quiet. Mr. Pierce's wife strained to hear what was happening on the other end of the line and was rewarded with the sound of a steady stream of falling water. Aha! He had moved to the latrine!

His wife crept to another room so as not to awaken the sleeping infant—that's the rule, you know—and screamed into the phone as loudly as she could without disturbing said baby. After what seemed to be an eternity, Mr. Pierce put the phone to his ear. "Hello? What do you need? Is everything O.K.? Why are you calling so late?" (Never mind the fact that he had just called her a mere fifteen minutes before.)

The wife realized at this point that he was quite drunk and half-scared of what might have been heard. She promptly and diligently performed her wifely duty of interrogating him on the spot. She asked what their names were. "Who?" was his befuddled response, of course.

"The two girls you discussed the political plight of the immigrant with—never mind your devoted wife and six- month-old infant left home alone, that's who!" she replied. (She tried to use that as much as possible to pile on the guilt factor.) Mr. Pierce, fuzzy-brained and utterly confused at this point, said that there was only one girl, and he didn't even know her name (and that makes it all better, of course). It's just like a man to lie, even when caught red-handed! But, she decided to let it go as she had heard the conversation and it seemed innocent enough. Actually, it was quite dorky if he had intended to be flirtatious. She doesn't think Mr. Pierce ever figured out how she (the wife) knew about that conversation.

The next day, Mr. Pierce called home to relay an interesting postscript to the bar scene. Apparently, when he was in the bathroom (and his phone was on), two men walked in and continued to stare at him while he relieved himself. His thoughts (and words) were "Are you guys gay or what? Quit staring at me." He finished up and headed towards the room after his conversation with his wife.

Once in the elevator, the two little old ladies already inside stared at him intently and then stepped out of the elevator. This time, when Mr. Pierce looked down to get his phone (lest there be more screaming voices from the seat of his pants), he noticed the offending factor. He had forgotten to unzip! So here Mr. Pierce stood, dripping urine, smelling quite lovely. He said his shoes (new and the only pair on the trip) were soaked in pee as well.

Lucky for Mr. Pierce, it was a short business trip and he was set to return the next day. As for the lovely, talented and always watchful wife, she personally thinks it was a productive "business" trip. She'll be able to hold the "mystery" of knowing about "the conversation" to her advantage for a good while. That's good business! S.

SUBJECT: RE: PIERCE DOES VEGAS

Well, that was certainly an, um, entertaining story. Is it too late for Mr. Pierce's wife to obtain an annulment? I think she could move to dissolve the marriage on grounds of lack of personal hygiene. It seems to be a recurring theme with him.

Seriously, how drunk do you have to be to forget to unzip and whip it out?

Thanks for the grins! yp

SUBJECT: AGE VS BEAUTY

Hi there!

How are you? I am a little glum. Well, glum is not the word. I am a little weirded out. (Is that a real phrase?) I mean, I know I am "weird and out there" but right now I am just "weirded out." Let me explain.

Last weekend, the neighbor down the street called to say she had received one of those "ree" makeover promotions at Lancome. She signed the two of us up for a mini-facial and makeup makeover. It sounded quite fun.

I get dressed (for a change, but minus the makeup) and we head to the mall for our makeovers. I am going to be beautiful! I am going to be "new"!

First I have my brows done, which are in need of desperate attention. George of the Jungle may find me quite attractive but to an ordinary Joe, I am a moving mono-brow on the prowl. While enduring excruciating pain, I am chastised by the perfectly flawless attendant about waiting so long between waxes. Geez! She obviously has grown children! If not, then her perfectly arched brows have been tattooed onto her face. (And FYI, I know someone who does permanent makeup.)

Next, it is my turn for the mini-facial. I sit in the chair while the esthetician studies my youthful skin. (Well...I thought it was youthful.) She, on the other hand, proceeds to say I have wrinkles and derma-creases. Whatever she said after that is all a blur as I am still in shock from hearing the words 'you', 'wrinkles', and 'derma-creases' all in the same sentence. And, by the way, what is a derma-crease? (I ask. Big mistake. I get an entire education about the effects of age that I am not mentally prepared to hear.) So, the gal begins to quickly smear all kinds of miracle creams, not-so-miracle creams but necessary creams, and just plain creams for those little nasty words: wrinkles and derma-creases. She hands me her chart with multiple columns to take to the next station. After a quick survey of the chart, I notice there are quite a few columns to the left, and then "my" column with so much ink on it you can barely read the text. The two columns to the right are for the dead. The column to the left is titled "First Signs of Aging." I inquire as to why I am not in that column. Again, I make another big mistake. Another lesson on how incredibly old I am, blah, blah, blah. I move to the next station with numb brows and a numb brain.

After my makeup makeover, most of the aestheticians are really amazed at the difference a LOT of makeup can do for me. I can tell by the pure astonishment on their faces that they are truly amazed that someone so old could look so good after gorging on gallons of cream! This makeup takes no less than

45 minutes to apply-each and every day. Well now I am beginning to feel a bit better as everyone hands out compliments left and right about my gorgeous face!

I saunter up to the counter, with almost a spring in my step, to acquire only the necessities since the products are quite pricey for someone who spends a whopping five minutes a day on her face. The clerk said that the one thing I absolutely must have is the relaxing cream. "Botox in a bottle" she says. "They even wrote an article about it in Ladies Home Journal." Am I a sucker? (Don't even go there!) O.k.-I am a sucker. I figured if it didn't relax my face I'd try it on my nerves. Just for laughs, I ask the clerk how old she estimates the aesthetician to be. "Oh, around twenty-eight or so," she replied in a cheery voice. Just when I thought I may be able to compete with Miss Flawless, I realize I have no less than ten years (plus or minus) on the girl. At this point I figure if I am going to compete I need most, no all, of what was on my list. After that hefty credit card swipe, I am now considering permanent makeup. I think it would be much more economical and definitely more time- efficient.

Afterwards, the neighbor down the street and I head home, hoping we look like twenty-eight-year-olds, sporting our purchases and big credit card bills. And I regress to my weirded-out phase. Again, what is a derma-crease? Until, I feel younger…S.

SUBJECT: RE: AGE VS BEAUTY

Steph,

I can totally relate. One wonders how young we might look today without all those sleep-free nights spent with demanding infants…but that ship has sailed, of course. So here's an idea:

instead of contributing to a college fund, we should be investing in a future-face-lift fund.

Good luck with the new beauty regimen! Yp

SUBJECT: DISASTER ZONE

Steph,

It's time to call FEMA. By approximately 7:30pm EVERY day, my home is a complete disaster zone. Why, you ask?

Because my husband's idea of putting things away is to shove them under the bed, in a drawer (no need to find the correct one, any drawer will do), or in a pile on my closet floor. Because our dogs shed and salivate indiscriminately and track dirt and leaves all over the floor (the latter of which is a minor mystery given that we have no trees in the back yard). Because I have two kids in diapers at once (one of whom is not the least bit interested in the potty but nevertheless enjoys taking her diaper off all by herself before she has to pee and after she poops). And because I have no domestic help to speak of.

Except, of course, for the fairies, elves, and kitchen gods.

The only time my house resembles a home, as opposed to the laundromat/unlicensed daycare center/grease pit/kennel that it actually is, would be from about midnight to around 7:00 a.m. (while said husband, kids, and dogs are all in bed, obviously). During that time, my house usually undergoes at least a partial miraculous transformation, which no one but me ever sees, of course.

Little pink fairies come in each night and pick up all the dirty laundry scattered around the house while Jack and the girls slumber peacefully. Ditto for the piles of clean laundry that sit on the dining room table all day long for every visitor to see but mysteriously disappear before the sun rises, only to be discovered in the correct drawers and closets, neatly folded or hung, the next morning. The toy elves account for why the vast array of infant and toddler toys strewn over every square inch of carpet at bedtime magically return to their proper places for the start of each day-to be ransacked anew at the leisure of two monster munchkins.

But best of all, the kitchen dish gods swoop in every night to finally get around to putting away dinner and unloading the dishwasher that I can't get to all day, and then they hide the mountain of dirty dishes, which has been threatening to topple over onto the floor for most of the evening, into the dishwasher. I, of course, am sitting on the sofa half the night eating bonbons and reading trashy romance novels while supervising all these creatures busy at work, which clearly explains my ever-expanding hips and the dark circles perpetually evident under my eyes.

With so much fey help, my house should be perfect, no (at least until everyone wakes up)? Not quite. I can't figure out why the housecleaning brownies don't show up with the others. Every night, I keep watch and wait for them to arrive to do the dusting, vacuuming, sweeping, mopping, and toilet scrubbing. I can only conclude that I'm not making the proper offerings on the appropriate altars. I'm willing to sacrifice most anything short of my first-born. And maybe Emma. I'm getting desperate here.

I mean, it's got to be months since any magical creatures dropped by to clean the kitchen floor. In fact, I am no longer certain of its original color. Obscuring the tile are any number of layers of finger-paint, oatmeal, ground-up, soggy Cheerios, and multi-hued Jell-O (among many other things) that have hardened into a plaque of some sort with a staying power on the order of super glue. In centuries to come, archeologists and anthropologists unearthing my home will be able to analyze the sedimentary layers of my kitchen floor and no doubt come to the mistaken conclusion that it served as the dining area of a low-rent frat house. (They may be somewhat thrown by the conspicuous absence of beer residue, but surely the scientists will shore up their conclusion by arguing that the large number of Jell-O deposits clearly evidences gelatinous wrestling matches with a similarly low-rent sorority.)

What am I supposed to do about this? The brownies are no-shows, and despite my best efforts to put Kaiser the Wonder Dog to good use, the furry culinary snob will only eat meat and dairy products that fall to the floor. He turns up his nose at the things I really need him to vacuum up (like the previously mentioned Jell-O, oatmeal, finger-paint, etc.). So it appears I might have to actually mop the kitchen floor myself to get the gook off. I don't even know where we keep the mop. Assuming we actually own one. And assuming a mere mop would even work.

You know, I think a better plan, in lieu of my seemingly pointless vigil for the truant housecleaning brownies, might be to pick up a few five-gallon buckets of acid, some steel-toed boots, and a really cheap mop. I wonder if I could order acid on the Internet and have it delivered? But would that then get me on an FBI watch list? It'd be really embarrassing if they stormed my house with a search warrant anytime before midnight--a dawn raid might be ok so long as they don't look at the kitchen floor.

Of course, if those darn brownies would just show up for work once in a while to clean the floors (and the toilets--but those are in such bad shape I can't even talk to you about them), I wouldn't be forced to consider taking such drastic measures.

Or we could just try calling FEMA. If they declare the house a disaster zone, I get a clean, new house somewhere else, right? yp

SUBJECT: RE: DISASTER ZONE

Hi there,

Ditto. Pierce also thinks that any drawer, cabinet, space unseen by the average eye will do for storage and clean up of various items. Just the other day, I found the hammer in the refrigerator. Now I know I have been just a little loopy since my first born, but I do not think I have lost it all just yet.

Our floor monitor would be our son. Since he is on all fours now and occasionally cruising under the furniture, he is privy to all droppings of food or other items. Unlike your dog, however, he has not learned the art of discrimination and will readily put any and everything into his mouth. I keep thinking that while he's busy scooting about I should put some handy socks on his hands and scrubber kneepads on so he could double as a cleaning agent. Do you think I'll get locked up for that?

In all his unsuspecting efforts to assist with the daily cleaning, he does do his part to ensure the house remains a disaster zone. While changing his diaper, he does his best to have a projectile poop moment. Mind you, the diaper is off so we invariably wind up having to scrub the walls, floor, lamp, changing table and any other unsuspecting guests who think it might be fun to witness a diaper change. One step forward, two back I think might be the appropriate advice at the changing table.

Anyhow, my grandmother always says you have to let the house go and not work too hard. This comes from a woman whose floor you could eat off of on any given day. But I'm still taking the advice. I like being given permission to be a slob every now and then! See ya. S.

SUBJECT: ER TRIP

Stephanie,

Well, we've had an interesting day. The girls and I headed to the park a little before noon to join my friend Lauren and her boys for a picnic. We were there for all of two minutes (possibly less) when Claire fell and split her forehead open on the playground equipment. Blood everywhere, screaming, weeping and gnashing of teeth, etc., etc. Lauren, a former elementary schoolteacher and a fabulous mom I try very hard (but fail) to emulate, is much more experienced in matters pertaining to screaming, bloody, wounded children, and she informed me that I needed to take Claire to the ER immediately, so of course I did. I had been playing up our picnic at the park all morning, so Claire was far more distressed about having to leave the park before the picnic began than about her gushing head injury. Poor baby.

Jack joined me at the ER and, after waiting the requisite six hours to see a doctor (which time period must be mandated by some ER law to which we, the mere public, are not privy), we requested a plastic surgeon to stitch her wound. We want her to still love us when she turns 16, and she most definitely wouldn't if we had let just any doctor stitch it closed, allowing her scar over her eyebrow to triple in size over the next decade. We thought it was a reasonable request. Apparently the hospital did not. They seemed to think it perfectly normal to wrap a child in a straight jacket, tie her to a stretcher, and let whatever adolescent ER doctor who showed up for work today take a needle to her face.

I don't think so.

Fortunately, Jack's brother does a little plastic surgery. So after leaving the ER, Jack took a quick trip to his brother's office in Tyler and, eight stitches later, she's almost good as new. Jack reported that Claire was positively loopy afterwards from the I.V. sedation (no straight jacket for my baby!), and that she kept giggling. Like her mama on too much rum were his exact words, I think. Wish I could have seen her! Anyway, I can't wait for them to get back to see the finished product.

Oh, and did I mention that we're scheduled for portraits with the Easter bunnies next week? Isn't that great? Let's see, so far we've had a black eye (just in time for fall pictures at mother's day out and lasting all the way through Christmas portraits), a bloody nose, and now stitches on the face. Is she her daddy's girl or what? Never a dull moment here.

On a totally unrelated but also-as-fun-as-pulling-teeth topic, I'm thinking of taking a trip down to Corpus to see my cousins and show off my precious little cherubs. (I can't even type that last part with a straight face.) Maybe I can stop in Austin for a visit on the way down there and share a little bit of my traveling hell with you. I'll be sure to give you plenty of warning as to the possible dates of this trip so that you can be prepared to leave the country. I have no idea when I might find time for such a trip down south (or for the psychotherapy I'm bound to need afterwards), but I'm thinking about it. I'm also thinking about writing a novel, losing 40 pounds, and having my legs waxed. Not necessarily in that order.

Well, I have to go. I haven't had more than 3-4 hours of consecutive sleep in days and days, or nights and nights, rather. I've got to get some shut-eye so I can avoid committing sleep-deprivation-induced malpractice tomorrow on some client work. yp

SUBJECT: RE: ER TRIP

Yvonne,

Isn't Tyler like four or five hours away from you? How is Claire doing? I'm not sure I could have maintained my composure after a six-hour ER visit, but it sounds like you did it.

Get some sleep. You obviously have forgotten about your last trip to Corpus to see your family, when you had only one child. Check your memory bank before embarking on a day-long journey with now two cherubs! Good night. S.

SUBJECT: EASTER SURVIVAL

Hi there!

How is your Easter holiday going? We've been inundated with relatives for the Easter holiday. This includes my mother and grandmother, the two of which do not get along. Of course, they both stayed at our house so the tension was at a very steady level orange the entire weekend. Defcon Five and the "red button" were just words away. Add to that the same crappy weather you have, and we had a stinky indoor hunt as well. I'll be finding rotten eggs for the next two weeks in the most precarious places I'm sure. Please remind me of the virtues of plastic eggs next year.

For Easter brunch, we went to the local country club with sixteen of our relatives and 'closest' friends. (I use the term "closest" loosely.) Two relatives showed up with coughs/colds and another with walking pneumonia swearing they were on antibiotics; interpret: not contagious. Well, as you might expect Max (who just recovered from a 3 month cold) now has a new cold and I am losing my voice. Lovely.

Add to that my frustrations with Pierce. It seems he has lost all manners in the course of our marriage. This is especially true when it comes to dining at restaurants. The things he used to sneer at, like letting kids run amuck or men ordering before women, have become commonplace in his psyche. And those are the politer crimes. Think of various noises one might consider making in a restaurant with their armpits to amuse the children. Since when did this become gentleman- like behavior? I won't bore you with the details, as I am sure every woman must deal with the same situations at one time or another. All men seem to regress to cavemen behavior at some time and it is only in a few years' work that it will take to domesticate them again.

I have to go. I have been swarmed upon by my family so there is not another second of time that I can actually think, type, and write. Multi-tasking disappeared during the birth of my firstborn. Talk to you soon. S.

SUBJECT: RE: EASTER SURVIVAL

Steph,

Multi-tasking is highly overrated! But you survived Easter guests and inconsiderate family carrying communicable diseases, so that's something. Sorry Pierce is going through a second childhood. Now you have two children—on the plus side, you only had to give birth once! Have a good week!
yp

SUBJECT: WHITE TRASH MAMA

Steph,

Hey! How's your day been? Less embarrassing than mine, I hope. In my journey from serious career girl to Supermom (that would be your cue to laugh), I have apparently hit a bump in the road. I'm calling it my "redneck/white trash" detour. I'm reasonably certain it's a temporary thing, lasting only as long as the duration of my children's inability to shod their own feet and to eat without wearing their food. Couldn't be more than ten years from now. Anyway.

I took the girls to the mall today with only two goals in mind: successful completion of a portrait session at a photo studio to mark Claire's third birthday (success being defined here as at least one shot of Claire looking directly at the camera sans brooding stare, protruding tongue, or visible tonsils); and the purchase of a pair or two of shoes for Emma. Pretty ambitious for me, I know, but Emma's feet apparently hit a huge growth spurt this week, and I literally cannot get them into a single pair of her shoes. And so I'm forced to take her out in public without shoes. Like, literally.

We arrive at the mall just in time for our session, which actually goes quite well, to my utter astonishment. In fact, it goes so smoothly that we take portraits of Emma, too (enormous drool stains and all).

So I am feeling rather confident in my parenting abilities at this point and decide to treat the girls to cherry slushees and chocolate chip cookies in the food court before hunting for Emma's new shoes. I believe the Greeks have a word for this: hubris. Loosely translated, it means "How stupid could she possibly be? Tragedy to follow."

In less than 12.5 seconds after sitting down at the table, Emma spills her slushee all over her adorable portrait outfit. Very nice. The red stains do, however, beautifully mask the enormous drool spot running down the entire front of her top that will no doubt show up in all the photos. Emma doesn't like to be very wet. Or cold. The slushee all over her outfit exhibits both qualities. Great howling ensues. So less than a minute into our refreshment, I reload the stroller and head to the family restroom, at which point Claire joins in the howling in protest at my taking up the goodies and leaving the fun booth (a virtual jungle gym to Claire).

Further upsetting them both, I hastily bypass the mall carousel, which just happens to be located directly in front of the restroom area. Only a man with no small children could have designed that setup. Do you know how hard it is to get a kid to go potty at the mall when you haven't hit the carousel yet? Great fun, especially when Claire has to tinkle so badly that she's holding herself, yet she keeps insisting that she doesn't need to go and should definitely ride the carousel first. Good grief.

Location notwithstanding, the mall's family restroom marks our most successful foray into potty training. Claire gets excited about relieving herself in the little toilet that's "just my size." The little potty conveniently sits right next to the "mommy" potty, so Claire just loves it if we can sit on the two potties simultaneously and hold hands. A hallmark moment. (Now any time we go there Claire performs right on cue. But why she can't perform in her little potty at home that's "just my size," I don't know. I guess I need to move into the mall for a week to potty train her.)

As you well know, I am a "plan B" person and always carry spare clothes and diapers for both children in the diaper bag. So while Claire spends ten minutes on her wee throne extolling the virtues of the little potty, I change Emma into her extra outfit. However, her outfit happens to be about two sizes too small. Belatedly, I realize that her freak growth spurt in shoe size is perhaps not unrelated to a general full-body growth spurt. The extra clothes fit just fine three weeks ago   back when I put them in the bag. At this moment, however, well… let's just say that I hadn't actually planned on Emma baring her belly to the world quite yet, as I think perhaps we should save such immodest displays for her Britney Spears-retro phase sometime in the far distant future.

So, fifteen minutes later, we head back to the booth with hopelessly melted slushees and unhappy munchkins, the latter due to my once again diverting us away from the so- close-you-can-touch-it carousel. Back at the table, Claire proceeds to spill her quite-liquefied slushee down her mostly white shirt. After evaluating the situation, I decide to forego yet another exciting trip to the family restroom in favor of letting Claire run around with a now very red "white" shirt. Emma, not to be outdone by her big sis, dribbles copious amounts of red liquid all over her too-small, very white (what was I thinking?) outfit. Enough. I toss the slushees and break out the cookies. Oh, yeah. This is an improvement. By the time we head back downstairs to shop, the girls' white tops exhibit cherry and chocolate stains in quantities sufficient to qualify them as entries in a modern art showcase. Jackson Pollack would be impressed. If he weren't dead and all. Anyway. To top it all off, Emma's hair hangs down all over her face, her hair bow nowhere to be found. Whatever. No matter. We are on a mission for shoes. Downstairs.

The elevator for the stroller conveniently lets out straight into the mall's play area. It just keeps getting better. The girls insist on playing, and since I vetoed the carousel ride, I decide to acquiesce to their demands. Claire immediately strips off her shoes and jumps in. Emma beats her in, because she, of course, isn't wearing any shoes, a fact I hope no one has noticed. Another fifteen minutes later, I round them up. Claire jumps in the stroller (after throwing a hissy fit about leaving the play area) and refuses to put her shoes back on. Fine. Whatever. She's staying in the stroller anyway. Right?

We head to the nearest children's shoe store. Our last stop. While the sales lady measures Emma's foot and attempts to find her some shoes, I hand Claire a notebook and pen from my purse so she can draw instead of trying to exit the stroller without my permission and run wild in the store. My ploy works for all of three minutes. Then Claire leaps out of the stroller without permission and runs wild around the store.

We strike out on finding shoes for Emma. They don't have anything cute in her size. How is that possible? The sales lady is very sorry and asks if I would like to try visiting one of their other stores in the Dallas metroplex. Because, you know, shopping with my girls is such a wonderful, bonding experience. I don't think so.

Instead, I buy Claire shoes, despite the fact that she doesn't need them. Why? Because in the relatively short time we are in the store, Claire has knocked over several displays, written in pen on the chairs, pulled out her hair bow, and in general made such a nuisance of herself that I feel I sort of owe it to the saleslady to buy something.

My glorious parenting triumph at the photo shoot has by now been completely supplanted by exhaustion, impatience, and a marked lack of clear thinking, as evidenced by my next missteps. On the way back out of the mall, I remember that I want to check out some tourist guides for our upcoming trip to Ireland (have I told you about that?). The bookstore beckons. Do I dare? I wonder. The girls are both quiet for the moment, ensconced in the stroller with their sippee cups of water. Curiously, both girls are covered in ink marks (face, hands, arms, clothes-pretty much everything). Where is my notebook and pen? Both still have bare feet (this despite the fact that Claire has not one, but now two, pairs of shoes sitting in the stroller basket).

So I head into the bookstore with admonitions to the girls to be patient while Mommy does some shopping. After showing approximately four minutes of forbearance (possibly a record), the girls start yammering loudly to head to the children's section, which unfortunately is quite visible from our current location in the travel section. As the store does not appear particularly crowded, I sternly warn them not to run wild and allow them to disembark from the stroller as I grab about six different guides and follow them. Only a handful of other people are milling around in the children's section, so I let the girls explore the area (within my peripheral vision, of course) while I cram my large hindquarters onto one of those itty-bitty kiddy chairs and pour over the guides.

Absorbed in my "research," some time passes before I look up to see what the girls are doing. I take in the three or four stylish moms sitting at tables, quietly reading brightly illustrated books to their perfectly behaved, attentive cherubs. I observe how lovely all the children look in their Gymboree and Baby Gap outfits with matching socks and hair accessories. How nice. Idyllic, even, in a yuppie, commercialized sort of way. Who are these people? Who are these children? I briefly contemplate searching out a copy of The Stepford Wives.

And then, I notice two ragtag children running amuck through the racks of books, pulling down a wide assortment of children's literature and dumping shiny new books on the floor after mere cursory glances at them. Their clothes are covered in stains and ill fitting, their hair hanging in their faces, in need of a good brushing, and they both need a bath. Where are their shoes? More importantly, where is their mother? These poor children clearly need attention and supervision.

Like a blurry picture slowly coming into focus through a lens, it gradually dawns on me that these ragamuffins belong to me. And that perhaps they shouldn't be roaming freely through the children's section on what is clearly a search and destroy mission. I conclude that perhaps I should beat a hasty retreat to the car before a client walks in and recognizes me, swearing never to trust such an obviously unobservant, neglectful mother with their private legal matters again.

It is then that I experience an epiphany, of sorts. I have turned into the redneck and/or white trash parent I always accused my dad of being. Of course, it would have been a totally different story if the girls had had their shoes on. Then I could only have been accused of being a redneck parent.

They call me: White Trash Mama.

SUBJECT: RE: WHITE TRASH MAMA

Yvonne,

Ha! That's too funny. If memory serves, I think you just described my childhood (and occasionally my adult) appearance on a good day! I wouldn't sweat the small stuff. Case in point, nine times out of ten when I'm out with Maxwell, someone will approach me with some horrific questions about his eye. Not only do the bystanders think that I am a ruthless child beater but a magnificent liar as well when I attempt to explain that "Herman" is a birthmark. The most blatant, idiotic clerk at Costco asked just yesterday 'What happened to its eye?' "It," I explain, "is my son." But I gave no explanation of Herman, as I doubted her salt-sized brain could comprehend a hemangioma, seeing as she couldn't figure out what a baby looked like. If in one day there are a plethora of questions about Max's eye, I have a tendency to ignore the person(s). I just pretend I'm deaf. It usually works! Oh, and he never has on shoes. What's the point in 100-degree heat? I don't wear shoes half the time myself! Better luck at the mall next time. S

SUBJECT: MARATHONS

Hi there!

I hope you are doing well. Now that I am through with my six months of physical therapy for knee rehabilitation, I am writing to give you a very important piece of knowledge: DO NOT, UNDER ANY CIRCUMSTANCES, THINK THAT A MARATHON IS A WALK IN THE PARK. (Pun intended!) I know that you are training for a marathon in Ireland. I should have paid attention and booked a better location for my first (and probably only) half-marathon.

After three whole months of running through the park while pushing Maxwell in a jogger, I attempted a half-marathon. (Mind you, the longest mileage to date that I've put on my tennis shoes in one outing has not yet reached double digits.) Why wouldn't I think I was ready? After all, what is an extra four miles?

I arrived before the rooster crowed in the freezing rain to get my chip, number, and the 'look', which in retrospect I now know was not meant as encouragement but pity for my poor soul. Naïvely, I headed to the starting line. I was so excited about the race. I had psyched myself up even more by blasting Aerosmith in the car on the way to the race. Now, it was starting time. The race sponsors were playing Aerosmith at the gate. It must be fate! (Or so I thought.) I ran (but not too fast). You have to conserve, you know.

About one-third of the way, I realized this must be the most difficult half-marathon around. There were hills and valleys and not much flat land in between. One saving grace was the competition of the bands every few miles. Each group would dress in a theme and try to get the most 'votes' from the runners. Here I was dragging my over-worked, under-trained body up Mt. Olympus. Naturally, I readily took the opportunity to stop and vote. After all, it is a democratic nation that we must support!

About halfway into the race, my enthusiasm waned. I had seen Elvis, the groovy chicks of the sixties, some American making an embarrassing attempt at French, and a band that should not have been allowed entry. The upcoming (and last) band was somewhat cynical in their presentation. All dressed in funeral shrouds, they play somber funeral music as they marched back in forth in time. Great. So much for Aerosmith; I was on my way to the Dead. I had seen many, many, many people go before me. But, there were still those behind me and I was not going to be last!

So I kept going. (Note, I did not say I ran; jogged is more like it; well, if you call bouncing when you walk jogging.) I was at the last two miles when Pierce and Maxwell showed up to cheer me on. Of course, they brought friends who were visiting from California. Great. It was just what I needed. I wanted to look good in my running gear for my husband. Instead, I looked more like a marine in training with full jungle camouflage face paint that is commanded to run in the rain. I wanted to look strong for my son so that he would know that his mother finishes what she starts. Oh, what the heck does a toddler know anyway? And then there were the visiting guests. Of course, I couldn't make a fool of myself in front of them. (In hindsight, I was probably already looking quite like the fool, limping along like someone who got up in the middle of the night but didn't turn on the light because it would hurt their eyes and stubbed their toe on the corner of the bed because they could not see.) Nevertheless, after many "you can do it" encouragements, I was almost there. I responded to their cheers with glares of anger and coy smirks of hate. If they only knew…this is why I am forewarning you! Don't do it!

I finished, only second to last and behind the seventy year old with headphones. Our coach in high school was correct. Her grandmother can run faster than me.

So, best of luck in your marathon. I wish you good knees and at least a handful of people behind you for a dignified finish! S.

SUBJECT: RE: MARATHONS

Steph,

So your warning came a little late. We had already bought the plane tickets to Ireland for the Dublin marathon. And, after all, I had actually gotten up before dawn almost every morning for six months to train for it (with my friend Lauren, who despite doing most of the same training did not get a fun trip to Ireland out of the deal). And I had already raised the money for charity and couldn't figure out how to gracefully get it back from the charity and into the hands of my donors, so...Jack and I went.

Poor Jack. This was a full 26.2 miles, and he hadn't trained at all for it. His role was to drive around and encourage me at various points along the way, but due to all the road closures for the race, he ended up walking half a marathon himself just to meet up with me from time to time and cheer me on. He was such a trooper.

I managed to stay ahead of the pacer, but given that he wore an enormous, heavy-looking green leprechaun hat and full costume and didn't look particularly fit, I'm not sure that's saying much. So you are in good company in being slower than your grandmother; I was slower than both of our grandmothers. But I did manage to finish within the time limit. Barely. They were sort of taking down the racing barriers that kept the crowds out of the way by the time I neared the finish line. Had to dodge a few cars and groups of tourists. But I crossed the line! Not much of a crowd left to cheer me on as I finished, but Jack was there--he kept pace with me the last mile and then ran ahead to take pictures of me falling over the line…isn't he great?

The next day we crammed our very sore selves into our teeny, tiny Barbie-sized rental car (have these people never heard of mid-size sedans?) and started off on our week-long adventure through the south of Ireland. My muscles kept freezing up in the tight confines of our clown car, so getting in and out to stop and admire the beautiful vistas was quite a challenge. For both of us actually. Poor Jack had to drive hunched over the whole week, his head jammed up against the roof.

I let Jack plan this tour, which is to say that it wasn't planned at all. He likes to be spontaneous. We'd pull into a town at dusk, figure out where to spend the night, and hope for the best. Worked out well sometimes, other times, not so much (I can't really recommend sleeping above a backwater village pub in twin beds whose sheets were last changed during the Nixon administration).But we had fun. Jack would tell you that the highlight of the trip occurred while driving the Ring of Kerry. I might have a different take on that outing.

We parked the car on the roadside and climbed a big hill littered with grazing sheep to take in the beautiful vista looking out to sea. The sheep didn't seem to mind us being there, but I think that only because we (or more specifically, I) provided them with high entertainment.

On the hike back down the hill, I slipped. In sheep dung. Twice. By the time I got to the bottom, my entire backside was covered. So much so that it soaked through to my undergarments. Fortunately for me, our suitcases were crammed into what I'll generously call the back seat (Jack's golf clubs took up the entire trunk), so I pulled out a complete change of clothes. Problem solved? Not exactly.

This particular stretch of bucolic countryside offered no buildings of any kind. No tall grass or big rocks to hide behind. Nada. And we weren't the only people who had stopped on the side of the road to admire the view. As I couldn't possibly sit in the car, covered as I was from neck to feet in odiferous sheep poo, I had no choice but to crouch on the road by the car, sandwiched between Jack and the open car door, and strip naked. And I do mean naked. Jack was laughing too hard to hold his coat steady enough to offer much in the way of a privacy curtain, so the cars and trucks driving by, along with some curious tourists a few yards off, got quite a peep show. I'm just hoping I don't end up in someone's photobook.

Once out of the icky clothes, I tumbled into the passenger seat of the miniature car to wrestle with getting my fresh ones on. If you can imagine trying to get dressed in an area a third the size of an airplane lavatory, but with clear windows all around for the other plane passengers to watch you through, you get the idea. But I got some friendly honks from truckers passing by. So that was nice.

It was three days before Jack could think about our hike without doubling over, howling in laughter. As I said, the highlight of his trip.

But the best part is, I got two things knocked off the bucket list this trip: finishing a marathon and stripping in public for my husband (technically, the stripping thing was on his bucket list, not mine, but I'm counting it).
Yp

SUBJECT: THANKSGIVING DAY

Hi there!

How was your Thanksgiving? Mine was chaotic. I wish I could say through no fault of my own, but I cannot. Nope. Thanks to my brilliant idea of being everywhere on one single day, I was on the late end of the bloom all day long. My Thanksgiving Day schedule was ludicrous. Even a superhero would not have been able to pull yesterday off in a timely fashion.

I was up at dawn preparing dressing and green bean casserole for my friend who had a baby just three days ago. She was set to come home from the hospital on Thanksgiving Day and Lord knows she wasn't going to cook. So, I suggested I would bring over 'the meal'. I had to pick up the turkey and other trimmings before nine in the morning and deliver the meal by 10:00a.m. so that we could go to the next agenda item of the day. By 9:30a.m. I was running out of the house with a soupy green bean casserole and burnt dressing to fetch the bird.

After delivering the promised turkey dinner at 10:45a.m., Pierce, Maxwell and I drove to my grandmother's house in Navasota for our Thanksgiving meal. Whoopee. We were supposed to be there by 11:30a.m. It's a two-hour trip. We arrived at 1:00p.m. We were only an hour and a half late. Needless to say, that did not go over well. We sat in the garage at a card table drinking tea that was curiously strong. The plan was to leave my grandmother's house by 3:00p.m. so that we could be home by 5:00p.m. That way, we would have an hour or so before we were set to be at the neighbor's house for another Thanksgiving meal. (Don't ask me why we agreed to eat Thanksgiving dinner twice in one day. In retrospect, this was a very bad idea.)

Since we had only arrived in Navasota at 1:00pm, we were not able to graciously leave until 4-ish. This put us back in our driveway at 6:30p.m.-precisely the time we were to be at the neighbor's house. We jumped out of the car, rushed inside to change Maxwell, and then ran next door. Mind you, my grandmother's dressing has this unique ability to "grow" three times its normal size after you consume it. We were stuffed from lunch and expected to eat again. We arrived at 7:00p.m. to do so.

I don't think I have ever been so full, or tired. Finally at 10:00pm we walked back home. What a day. The only thing we wanted to do was sleep. However, that was not going to happen. It was the tea. Not only could Pierce and I not sleep, Maxwell was like a ping-pong ball in a shoebox. His eyes were darting about while he wiggled and giggled deliriously. No more caffeinated tea from grandmother's for the nursing mom of an infant. No more scheduling three dinners in one day for me! (I am just thankful I only had to eat two of them!) See ya! S.

SUBJECT: RE: THANKSGIVING DAY

Steph,

Good grief! You took a page right out of my "Here's How to Drive Yourself Crazy Over the Holidays" book, to be published early next year. You can write the foreword.

We had a rather quiet Thanksgiving with my brother and my mom. My sister-in-law fixed a fabulous meal for all of us. Although, the pecan pie was something of a disappointment. She apparently went through six pecan pies before she finally figured out that her grandmother had forgotten to write "eggs" on her hastily scribbled recipe card. Personally, I'd have given up after one or two failed pies, but my sis-in-law is rather tenacious that way. Can you imagine how much sugar and flour—not to mention pecans?—went into the garbage can before she called her grandmother, who finally fixed the recipe? I'm still laughing about it.

Happy Thanksgiving! yp

SUBJECT: FAMILY PORTRAITS—PRESERVING FOND MEMORIES

Dear Steph,

Howdy. Christmas greetings to you. Done with your shopping yet? Please say no. I am so tired of all these smug, suburban moms who had their Christmas shopping all done "months ago." And now their presents are all wrapped and under the tree. Who are these people? They clearly have way too much time on their hands if they're out shopping for Christmas in July and can wrap gifts in November.

In any event, it would be a total waste of time for me to shop and wrap ahead. Claire and Emma, in their little egocentric universe, think that any gift that's wrapped and under the tree must surely belong to them, and so they open it, post haste. So, really, I'm saving myself lots of re-wrapping time by waiting until three days before Christmas to shop and then holding off until my traditional Christmas Eve midnight madness wrapping party to package my gifts. Besides, when else am I going to get to watch A Christmas Story five times in a row on TNT?

I did, however, get a head start on one Christmas gift this season. As a surprise to my mom, my siblings and I decided to have group portraits made. One gift, split three ways, no gift receipts to deal with, can't be returned; seems like the perfect gift. So, of course, it isn't.

My siblings and I agreed on a low-rent mall photo studio for the portraits due to universal budget constraints. We arrived right on time for our appointment, which is quite the miracle for five adults and three children, the latter all under the age of 3½, but had to search around for our "photographer," a term I employ here very loosely. During

the busy Christmas card portrait season, the mall studio apparently finds it makes good business sense to limit their studio to one employee. Clever, don't you think?

When we did finally locate her, after the girls have had plenty of time to run amuck, the "photographer" was largely non-communicative to us live subjects. She didn't seem to know what to do or where to put us. She did inform us, however, that the studio's cameras max out at seven people in one shot, so she wasn't sure if the eight of us would all show up in the portrait. Someone might actually get cut out. Dumbfounded silence followed. "Okaaaaaaay… seeing as how we're already here, and we're all decked out in our holiday finery, how's about we just give it a try?" someone suggested. She shrugged, clearly noncommittal.

We did the little ones first and hoped that all three did, in fact, appear in the portrait. Emma (almost 2) was thoroughly put out by this whole affair. She didn't want to keep her spiffy black patent-leather shoes on, she insisted on flashing her underwear at the camera, she kept taking her beautiful black velvet bow out of her hair, and her incessant squirming caused her stockings to bunch up at her ankles-just like Mommy's! She also wanted to hold her baby cousin who, at not quite five months, seemed rather annoyed with Emma's constant cuddling. My baby nephew refused to smile for the camera, or for anyone else for that matter.

Claire, being the eldest at 3½, was of course her normal, smiling, very cooperative and compliant self. And helpful, too. As my sister and I attempted to straighten Emma and Claire out between shots, baby nephew just fell right over and off the blanket-covered seat he and Emma were sharing. (Why the "photographer" chose to put a poor, innocent five- month old who can't sit up yet on a bench with a wiggling twenty-one month-old is beyond me.) But for one reason or another (read: Emma's fussing and squirming), we didn't happen to notice the baby's tumble until Claire tried to get our attention. "Look at the baby! Look at the baby!" she yelled, over and over again. Her words finally registered with us, and it's then that we noticed that my poor nephew was lying face-down in the fake snow that covered the table. He was rescued from his dire predicament post haste, and since he wasn't hurt, and didn't cry, the situation struck my sister and me as absolutely hilarious. His mommy? Not so much.

The situation went downhill from there, surprisingly enough. Tension abounded while sis and I tried to keep from howling with laughter. Jack got a migraine from all the camera flashes.

Matters were not helped by the fact that the "photographer" kept disappearing for 4-5 minutes at a time between every 2-3 shots. It seemed that, in addition to actually taking portraits, the "photographer" had to hand out finished portraits to other customers who arrived during our appointment time. Also, she had to answer the phone each and every time it rang to schedule other appointments, even though, interestingly enough, I always got the answering machine when I called the studio.

We got so tired of waiting, and the children got so restless-that my brother finally took the clicker thing on the camera and shot a couple of photos of the kids himself. Couldn't be any worse, right? As it turned out, these shots were actually better than those the "photographer" took, but she was annoyed with our initiative and erased them when she finally made it back into our portrait cubicle. Half an hour later, we finally came up with a whopping four shots of the kids. In the first, Emma's flashing the camera again. In the second, Claire and Emma appear to be viewing a UFO on the ceiling, their eyes turned upward and mouths agape in wonder. In the third, the girls look great, but baby nephew doesn't, so his mother nixes that one. That left us with the final shot: Claire's mouth is wide open in laughter, the baby isn't smiling, and Emma looks poised to either laugh or cry, not sure which. That's a wrap, folks.

It was time to move on to the family shot. The "photographer" wasn't kidding when she said somebody might be cut out of the shot. In the worst composition I've ever seen from someone purporting to be a photographer, the kids barely made it in the picture. Here is the result:

Jack and my brother, like all the adults, are wearing black, and are seated side by side. Their shoulders are huge, so right smack in the middle of the photo there's this enormous black gap between their heads. The "photographer" could have stood Claire or Emma in the middle behind them to break up the black blob, but instead, she placed my black- garbed bean pole of a sister in between them, with my sister-in-law and I-the much shorter, plus-sized branch of the family-flanking her on either side. You can barely see my double chin above Jack's enormous skull, and my brother's shiny, reflective shaved head cuts off part of his wife's double chin and neck. And despite being lined up in a row, the three women are all standing at vastly different angles. To top it off, the whole lot of us are off-center to the

When you look at the picture your might ask, "Where are the kids?" They're at the bottom of the picture, as if they're peeking up from below the edge of the portrait. Emma and Claire share Jack's lap, and Claire gets pretty good coverage along the edge (and I do mean the edge) of the picture. You can see one of her shoulders and the top of her chest, anyway. Emma, on the other hand, appears to be decapitated; if she were just an inch or two shorter, you would barely see the tops of her shoulders. You can, however, clearly observe her blond hair hanging in her scrunched up face because she finally succeeded in removing the offending bow. But my poor nephew... Sitting in his father's lap and wearing a similarly dark color, it appears that the baby's head, which dangles a mere millimeter above the edge of the photo, is a disembodied, floating orb. No neck, no arms. Just an unsmiling, disembodied, floating orb. It's perfect. Mom will just love it.

Word of advice? Just buy your mom the slippers and robe. Much less painless. Trust me.

Well, gotta go. We're supposed to visit Santa at the mall tonight. Last year, Emma screamed her head off at the sight of Santa. Very entertaining. Maybe we'll get a repeat performance this year. Bye. Yp

SUBJECT: RE: FAMILY PORTRAITS — PRESERVING FOND MEMORIES

Hi there,

I want a picture of the family picture! Just the floating orbs and black abyss should be a hoot. This is a good warning for me not to attempt this with our family. Our biggest effort at a family picture to date is the mall photo with Santa. We decided last year that we would make it an annual tradition. Each and every year, Santa looks at Pierce and me like we are some kind of smiley, weird hippie parents who want to be in the photo with the screaming child. But hey, that's what a good $10/hour job will get you! (And, OK — we are smiling, weird hippie parents.) At least we are not the hyper- fastidious parents who neatly arrange their neat children next to Santa's neat beard.   Neither are we the ones who bring our young to test the validity of Santa's beard while chewing gum and popping bubbles dangerously close to the old fella's whiskers. So, I think we are pretty good customers- albeit a six foot four man, a five foot four woman, and a two footer, makes it a bit tricky to get us all in the frame. I'll send you one when I get around to the cards this year, right after I get around to the presents. Happy Holidays! S.

PART FIVE

CHAPTER FIFTEEN: LEARNING FROM OUR CHILDREN

SUBJECT: CLAIRE'S THEORY OF RELATIVITY

Steph,

I think Claire's going to be a theoretical physicist or something equally as esoteric. She has interesting ideas about reality. The other day, she piled up every toy she could find on the rug in her room. It was a huge pile. When I asked her what she was doing, she replied that she was building a fire. I thought this was rather inventive, so I decided to encourage her creativity and went along with it, telling her that she was going to have an awfully big fire.

A bit later, after Claire became bored with her campfire and moved on to something else, I reminded her of her room and the enormous pile of toys on the floor. I very kindly instructed her to put her toys away. Her immediate and unequivocal response was, "I can't, Mama. They're all burned up!" No amount of discussion on the subject could move her from this position. I finally had to threaten a time-out if she failed to pick up. This did the trick, but she was quite upset with me for interfering. As you can imagine, it's somewhat difficult to argue and/or reason with a child who often operates on a different plane of existence.

I knew Claire had a unique way of ordering her universe from a very young age. She used to like to line all of her animals up. She still does occasionally. She'll put all of the dinosaurs in a long line facing off against the zoo mammals or even the farm animals. Tragically, but perhaps predictably, the prehistoric creatures slaughter the mammals every time. But Claire has to group each subset of dinosaurs together by type, and she does the same with all of her other animals.

Then again, sometimes she decides to line up her animals by color. All the brown ones over here, all the green ones over there. And occasionally she gets it in her head that she's going to have a "green party." I have no idea where that concept originated, but she recently gathered up every green item in three rooms and piled them all together. And I mean every green thing. I could not discern a purpose for the green party, but she did this several days in a row. At least she knows her colors, I guess. Maybe her choice of green means she's going to be an environmentalist, rather than a theoretical physicist. I am convinced that her favorite color is green because we painted her nursery light green. It makes me wonder if she'd be more amenable to "girl" stuff had we painted her room lavender like we did Emma's—or maybe even pink. There's a theory for you. Not only does every word you say and every gesture you make impact your child, for better or worse, from a very tender age, but the very colors you choose for his or her room impact personality, preferences, and proclivities. Wow. There are just so many ways we parents can screw them up, aren't there? Have a great day, Mom!
yp

SUBJECT: RE: CLAIRE'S THEORY OF RELATIVITY

Hi there,

I suggested "blue" as a topic for my photography class. So, I can totally relate to having a 'green party.' I guess that confirms I have the mindset of a --how old is Claire now?— four-year old.

I guess it makes me weird, immature and unusual. However, I'd prefer to be called interesting, curious, and eclectic! I think Claire will do just fine in the grown-up world. If nothing else, she can hang out with me; albeit I'll be as old as her mother!

On another note, Pierce and I found out that we are expecting baby number two! We are really excited. Of course, nothing is simple with us. Tomorrow I leave for Italy with nine female family members who have no clue we are even working on a second child. It will be a challenge for me to sidestep the many of offers of wine I will receive in that country. Wish me well! S.

SUBJECT: THE CASE OF THE MISSING AZALEAS

Steph,

Let's see. You're leaving for the idyllic vistas of Tuscany. And oh, wow. I've just returned from a fun-filled weekend trip to Oklahoma. Who got the better deal here, I wonder? But I'm so excited for you!!! Pregnant!!! And Italy!!! I think I still hate you, but I wish you all the best.

So, in case you're the least bit interested in what I was doing in the very exciting state of Oklahoma, my cousin Liz has this great photographer who meets you at a Tulsa park, which is in full bloom with azaleas, takes two rolls of film, hands them to you, and only charges $50. We don't really have azaleas in Frisco that I've seen, so I was looking forward to getting some beautiful portraits of the girls amid Tulsa's colorful blooms.

I don't know why I put myself through these things.

First of all, Jack bails on me. Last minute work commitment. Never mind that the company is laying off all and sundry and no doubt we're on the hit list in the near future, so what could possibly be the point? Anyway, the girls and I arrive Friday night right before a terrible deluge hits. Lightning and sheets of rain everywhere. And I have yet to get the girls their dresses for the portrait session. Because, you know, I've only been planning this for a month. I had thought I'd just quickly run to the mall and grab something for them upon arrival at Liz's. Hadn't really planned on needing an ark to get there.

But out into the gale I go. I only have time for one big mall store before closing (or flooding, whichever comes first), and it has nothing in the way of matching dresses in my girls' disparate sizes. Of course. After scrutinizing every dress at least three times, I finally settle on about 6 distinct designs to take back to Liz's. After much weeping and gnashing of teeth, I get the girls to try them all on and, due to fitting issues, itchiness issues, and flat out "I-don't-want-to-wear-that" issues, I'm left with only two blue dresses that are vastly different in pattern, length, formality, and basic quality. Perfect.

We arrive late, of course, to the park the next morning. Having overlooked the purchase of shoes in the mad shopping dash the previous evening, the girls must go barefoot for the shoot. Fine, whatever. It will be cute to see their pink toes. Except…the deluge from the night before is everywhere in evidence at the park in the form of mud. Lots of thick, black mud. So much for cute pink toes.

Claire's incessant leaping about in her overly long sundress causes her to stumble and nearly fall umpteen times. That we managed to get through the session with her dress relatively unscathed by mud or rips is a minor miracle. I am near tears (and the girls are in tears) as we try to wrap up the interminable, muddy session. After pleading, cajoling, wheeling and dealing, and, ultimately, threatening the girls to cooperate in even the smallest measure with the photographer, I think we may have gotten a few good ones! The eternal optimist…

We drop off the film at the local Walmart to be developed. When we pick it up, after talking with several of Liz's acquaintances in the store who now are standing just in front of where I am trying out the new-fangled, self-service check out register, I try to pay with my check card. A while back, our credit union had sent out a notice that our banking institution's check cards would no longer be accepted at Walmart. I've no idea why. Not remembering this, of course, I am shocked and appalled as the computerized register voice announces to the store—and everyone in a three-block radius—that my payment form is declined. "Please try another form of payment" reverberates through the front of the store like it's on the PA system. "Attention Walmart shoppers! Idiot trying to pay with bad credit card on register 19."

Not content to humiliate myself just once, I gamely try again, thinking this must be some sort of mistake. No dice. If anything, the second such announcement is even louder. Or, at least, it seems that way as I take in the stares of the nearby shoppers, some sympathetic, others appalled. Belatedly, I recall the letter from the credit union and prattle on about it at length in an attempt to explain away my "bad" card to the checkout lady I have to crawl over to for payment. She just looks at me as if she's heard it all before. With my tail tucked between my legs, I manage to make it out of the store with the prints.

So was it all worth it? I guess so. We got a sweet shot of Claire bending down to her sister, who is smiling with hands clasped together. Very precious. And the bow perched on Claire's head looks like a dove ready to take flight, adding an odd amount of charm to the photo. But most delightful are the seriously muddy toes, which really stand out beneath the mismatched dresses.

And the azaleas I trekked all the way up to Tulsa for? Notably absent from the portraits. Actually, there are no flowers of any kind whatsoever in ANY of the portraits. But there are lots of nice, grey rocks in the background. Which we never would have found in our local parks here. Sigh…
Yp

SUBJECT: RE: MISSING AZALEAS

Hi there,

After all that, it sounds like you need a relaxing moment (or two). Try going outside after the kids are in bed and have a glass of wine. (Red is supposed to have heart healthy additives so it's reputed to improve health. Or so the French say.) Enjoy the cool night air-or at least pretend it's cool and try not to get swarmed by mosquitoes. If that doesn't work, lock yourself in the bathroom with a good book, a bubbly tub, a great smelling candle, and another nice glass of wine. Soak up the aroma and wallow in the suds. If that doesn't work, try putting on some music in the living room, have a third glass of wine and engage Jack in one of those 'theoretical' conversations like "If you could go anywhere in the world…" If that doesn't work, go to bed and pass out. You should be on your way to quite drunk after three glasses of wine and when you wake up in the morning it will all be a foggy memory anyway. Good luck and good night! S.

SUBJECT: MAY DAY!! MAY DAY!!

May Day! May Day! Breaker One-niner, we have incoming! S-O-S! Sending out all calls for help. We have a code red!! Alert! Headline: Deranged Man Buys Hotel: No Experience.

It is true. At the IRS auction last month, my husband took temporary leave of his sanity and bought a dilapidated hotel in a backwoods town. Before entering the auction room, we decided on a pre-determined amount that would be the limit of our bidding. Unfortunately, Pierce had the bidding paddle and I, standing behind him and being a full foot shorter than him, was nowhere to be seen. I did my best to remind him of our maximum amount by gently tapping his shoulder when the auctioneer called the next highest bid. When the paddle in Pierce's hand went up, I knew the tapping was imperceptible on his part. So, I very strongly patted him on the back as the next friendly reminder of our pre-determined amount. He coughed and shifted forward as if a hairball were stuck in his throat. Again, the paddle went into the air as perhaps an involuntary reflex of my stern 'pat'. Pierce obviously was having an out-of-body experience, as he did not respond to any of my 'hints.' The paddle was going up and down as if there were an invisible string attached yanking it to and fro. At this point (and well over our limit), I was ready to whack him upside the head with a ruler, pull a wedgie, and bounce up and down like a scene from Mutt & Jeff to get him to stop bidding. Luckily, I did not resort to that as no one else counter bid. As good as that may sound, it was not so fortuitous for us as we — ahem, he just bought a hotel — with no experience in the hospitality industry.

Plan A was to refurbish the hotel and hopefully be open by Memorial Day weekend. It seemed realistic at the auction. A little demolishing here, a little paint there — how hard can it be? After further inspection on site, however, Plan A seemed a little ambitious. The structure was intact. The interiors were not. It seems high school boredom and vagrancy had moved into the hotel and hence the inn had become a new form of 'art school' to be polite. Further, in a meeting with the City Manager, it was determined that the good ol' boy system is very much alive and prospering in this town. This will inevitably cause a delay considering the plumber 'we are to use' is also a city councilman who is occupied right now in a run-off election.

On to Plan B — remodel and be open for July 4th weekend. It seems much more doable. While Dad and Pierce head off to begin the construction end of things, Mom and I head to Ross and Costco for the furnishings. As we did not have enough time to order hotel linens and supplies from hotel vendors, we improvised. Costco provided us with all the bed sheets, towels, and paper goods while Ross provided us with comforter sets. As we made rounds throughout Austin and San Antonio buying every matching set we could, I realized I had totally forgotten the personalities of my parents. Since they lived overseas for the past eight years, all my time spent with them in person was quite enjoyable as it was vacation for them and catch-up for me. Now, after spending a large volume of high-stress time with both my parents I remember how incredibly detail-oriented and methodical they are, not to mention advance-planners. Although I share those same traits, I have the ability to go with the flow, improvise, and otherwise shrug off almost anything. My parents don't have that uncanny knack and as a result the refurbishing and opening of the hotel will surely be performed at high stress levels.

So folks, here we have it. Headlines read: "Hotel in the Making: Divorce Contemplated". I'll let you know how it turns out. In the meantime, keep your radio tuned for "tests of the emergency broadcast system" or sheer cries for help as the case may be! S.

SUBJECT: RE: MAY DAY!! MAY DAY!!

Steph,

So to recap where we are, you have a toddler and are now pregnant with baby number two. Pierce, who already has his hands full with a successful commercial real estate business, wakes up one morning and decides it would be a really good idea to buy—and run—a dilapidated hotel. You con your parents, whose help you're desperately going to need when that second baby arrives, into helping you refurbish and open it. So, in short, y'all are nuts.

Have I missed anything?

Send photos of the hotel!! yp

CHAPTER SIXTEEN: IT'S A TRIP

Subject: I am not responsible for my behavior. I'm under the influence of paint fumes.

Hey! I couldn't open the attachment you sent. Probably your pics from yet another exotic beach, I'm guessing. Or the hotel refurbishment? No clue how to open them. Could probably ask Jack, but that would be an admission of weakness and might convey the notion that I actually need him for something.

We're currently operating under a cease-fire agreement, but mounting tensions could give way to an outbreak of hostilities at any time if we actually speak to one another. To avoid an all-out firefight, I find it's just easier to miss out on all the lame jokes, insipid stories, dancing presidents, and exotic beach pics that everyone sends me in these stupid attachments that, for some reason, I can never open. No offense.

I guess you've been super busy with the hotel remodel. How's the pregnancy going?

I haven't been up to much, really. Mostly lounging around the house eating bonbons all day. But in between sugar highs and long naps (and skirmishes with my husband), I've been working on a couple of things. In fact, this past week has been somewhat more eventful than usual.

SUNDAY, JULY 13:

I spent all day priming the walls in anticipation of my handyman/yard-guy/painter coming tomorrow morning to paint the living/dining/hall/foyer areas. The more I get done today, the less I have to pay him tomorrow. Congratulate me for getting ahead of the game for once. But primer is not particularly attractive. Glowing white splotches are everywhere. Really looking forward to the walls being painted a warm gold (or "macaroni-and-cheese," as my brother's wife opined yesterday). By someone other than me. Obviously.

MONDAY, JULY 14-10 A.M

Painter fails to report for duty. Numerous calls to his home, his cell phone, and his wife's cell phone yield nothing but endless rings followed by voice mail. Not going to panic. Glowing white walls are not closing in on me. I keep calling and leaving messages. He has to answer or return my call, eventually.

MONDAY, JULY 14-NOON

Apparently not. His refusal to return my umpteen phone calls inquiring into his whereabouts could mean only one thing. He's AWOL. And I'm SOL. (Did I say that out loud?) He's not coming. What exactly am I supposed to do now?

Had I not already primed ALL the walls, I would drop the whole thing. But no. I just had to try to get ahead of the game. I could live with glowing white walls for a while until I find someone else to paint them, except for a teensy-weeny problem. I have previously agreed to let my brother and his wife host my nephew's first birthday bash this coming Saturday at my house.

Five days from now. Over 40 people have already received their invitations and will attend, and many of these guests are neither related to me nor personal friends of mine and cannot, therefore, be counted upon to dismiss my glowing, splotchy white walls with a laugh and a wave and an "Oh, that's Yvonne for you," should I not get around to painting them.

MONDAY, JULY 14-THURSDAY, JULY 17

So I paint. Twice, actually. Because contrary to the assurances of EVERY guy in the paint department at the home improvement store (including Joe Shmoe, who doesn't even work there and would therefore appear to have no vested interest in selling me primer), a single coat of paint does NOT—I repeat, does NOT—in fact, cover primer. It takes a minimum of two coats. Three, really, but who has time for that?

Jack gets a number of migraines and backaches during this hell week and spends hours in bed after getting home from work, so not much relief from that quarter. Thankfully, though, my brother's wife comes over to help me paint some, so I'm not completely on my own. And Mom hires a guy to come paint the top half of our 50-story foyer. I think she saw me teetering on the top step of the ladder one too many times and decided that maybe I needed professional help. Painting, I mean.

Fortune smiles on me (or grins wickedly, depending on one's perspective), as Claire is spending the week in Mississippi with my sister and Emma is rotating among various relatives. So at least no munchkins are under foot. But when I stop to think about the missed opportunities here, I nearly lose it. No meals to fix or baths to give or stories to read for a whole week. But instead of movie-going, lunching, shopping, reading, writing, or somehow thawing the cold war with my other half long enough to engage in activities that require very little communication or clothing, I spend these golden, solitary hours PAINTING THE DARN WALLS. Clearly, I do need professional help.

FRIDAY AFTERNOON, JULY 18:

Less than twenty hours to go until my house is swarming with strangers and children celebrating my adorable nephew's first birthday. Still have HOURS of painting to go. And then I actually have to clean the house. Oh, lookie here. We have an invitation to a friend's wedding tonight. Forgot all about that. Who gets married on a Friday night? Somehow going to have to scrub all the gold paint off of my skin and out of my hair, don a dress and hose in 100+ degree weather, and dash down to some country club in Dallas for this wedding, then haul a** back and finish painting. No sweat. I always work well under the pressure of a looming deadline. Just ask my moot court partner from law school. That would be the one who had his half of the paper done a week before deadline. I would be the one who started her half of the paper at 10:30
p.m. the night before the 8:00 a.m. deadline. And got it done, of course (and my score was only 2 points less than his). "This? This is nothing." (My favorite line. Dustin Hoffman. Wag the Dog.)

I manage to talk Jack into escorting me to the wedding despite the migraine that's threatening. The anticipated camera flashes at the wedding virtually guarantee a massive headache. Looks like I'll be on my own painting again when we get back. Wow. What fun. And, oh yes, poor Jack. (Compassion is my gift, you know.)

FRIDAY EVENING, JULY 18:-WEDDING CHECKLIST

—Arrive at ceremony seconds before bridal party actually walks down the aisle? Check.
—While being hastily seated by usher under scornful gaze of all wedding guests, notice that Jack is only man in entire room NOT wearing a dark suit or tie and that I am only woman in entire room NOT wearing sequined cocktail dress? Check.
—Make mental note to chew out best friend who recently told me that summer weddings in Dallas have become ridiculously casual? Check.
—Manage to sit through whole ceremony without obviously gagging on minister's words extolling the virtues and joys of the marriage relationship? Check.
—Telepathically attempt to ask the bride if she has a clue what she's in for? Check.
—Fake a smile and clap along with everyone else at the rapturous sight of two lovers bound in chains forever? Check.
—Sign the guest book? Check.
—Deposit wedding gift on overflowing gift table? Oops. Forgot gift. Shocker.
—Leave before pictures are done to avoid having to offer obligatory and utterly false congratulations to the bride and her new husband? Check.
—Jack's migraine explodes in full force on the way home? Check. All righty then. All done.

SATURDAY, JULY 19— THE WEE HOURS OF THE MORNING:

It's four in the morning. I'm on my hands and knees using six-year old, highly noxious semi-glossy white paint (i.e., not the kind that washes off with soap and water) that I found lurking in the garage to cover all the gold speckles, dirt, and spider webs on the baseboards. Because, you know, people are going to be inspecting the baseboards during the party. I'm sure of it.

I just love the wee hours of the morning. It's a good time to think. To question one's existence in the universe. At the moment, I'm asking myself some really deep questions. Like, how the heck did I get myself into this mess? How am I going to get all the pictures re-hung? What am I going to do with all the painting paraphernalia littering the house? What if my guests faint over the paint fumes? Am I going to get any sleep before the party? And most importantly, how am I going to get this non-washable white paint out of my hair? These are the questions that plague women's souls at four in the morning.

SATURDAY EVEING

Against all odds, I survive the painting, the party, and the day. Having had only three hours of sleep, if that much, I bow out of going to the baseball game planned for this evening. My sister takes my place with Jack, who, although plagued with a migraine all day such that he had to hide out in the bedroom during most of the party, is now thankfully much-recovered and able to attend a ball game. Leaving me, the exhausted mommy, with the over-tired children.

At this point, I'm reasonably certain that I will never pick up a paintbrush again. And that I deserve a trip to Mexico. Wouldn't you agree?

yp

SUBJECT: RE: I AM NOT RESPONSIBLE FOR MY BEHAVIOR. I'M UNDER THE INFLUENCE OF PAINT FUMES

Yvonne,

Should I sign you up for the Betty Ford Clinic for detox of the paint fumes; marriage counseling; or, the mental institute for the hopelessly insane? What were you thinking, you crazy woman? I hold the title of "All Unreasonable Requests Fulfilled at Any Given Moment's Notice." As of late (and while six months pregnant), I have been putting up wallpaper in the soon to arrive baby's room. This room, of course, will most likely not be inhabited until her fourth or fifth year of life as we expect she'll follow in her brother's shoes of being a "bed-dweller." (That's my bed she'll be dwelling in for a while.) Anyhow, as you know any self-respecting mother cannot have the nursery painted three different colors with a wallpaper overlay and border to match and NOT paper the closet as well. Naturally, the bathroom will have to be redone to coordinate, as every infant is certain to be domestically fashion conscious. As the eyes would have it, I also noticed the adjoining bedroom, which had been somewhat put aside for the last three years, and decided to paper in there as well. After all, I might as well do it since I'm knee deep in wallpaper glue as it is.

Now, in keeping with my Insanity title I also undertook baking a cake for my grandmother's birthday. She will be eighty-two and we (of course) will be driving round trip five hours to celebrate for an hour or two. I'll take the cake (and eat it too) before I return to finish the wallpaper job. Did I mention we are having house guests this weekend? Yes. So see? As demonstrated in my abbreviated narrative, you have a ways to go to secure the title from me! Take care. S.

SUBJECT: WHO CAME UP WITH THIS SCHEDULE, ANYWAY?

Steph,

Heads up: I'm venting. You'll recall in my last e-mail (in which I was also venting) that I had just finished painting the house and hosting my nephew's birthday party. I got an average of about three hours of sleep a night that whole week, so I had plenty of energy reserves to deal with the following:

Last week:
Claire had Vacation Bible School from nine to noon Monday through Friday, so I had to entertain Emma for 15 hours in Claire's absence (no small feat) and had to keep several other children of desperate friends as well;
—On Tuesday, I had to go to the grocery store and run numerous other errands, and so of course, Jack had to work late so I had to drag the kids along with me;
—On Wednesday, I had my regular two-hour hair appointment (some of us take longer to get beautiful than others), and then took the girls to the library, which sounds innocuous enough, but...

...The girls are still unclear on the concept of whispering or even using an "inside voice," so every 30 seconds or so I have to strongly admonish them to keep it quiet; of course, if I fail to, then the librarians (or even better, some other mom) will helpfully step in to remind them to pipe down. That always makes me feel like I'm totally on top of this mom thing.

If I'm not working on keeping the girls quiet, then I'm trying to make them understand that we'll save climbing for the park's jungle gym and that mommy will be happy to grab whatever colorful books they think they might want on the top shelf (and why, after all, do we even need ladders in the stacks if children aren't supposed to be on them? If even I can reach the top shelf, they can't really be that necessary).

My favorite part of library time is thinning the girls' selections from 20 "absolutely-must-haves" to only 5 books each. And if that sounds a bit short-sighted for a mom trying to raise voracious readers, keep in mind I have a limited amount of time in my schedule to hunt all over the house for missing library books.

This tear-filled winnowing exercise is followed immediately by the interminable checkout process. If I make it through the ordeal without either of the girls' escaping the library, whose automatic sliding glass exit doors are conveniently located RIGHT NEXT to the checkout desk and are VERY FUN to run through if you're a preschooler or a toddler, I reward myself with a Dr. Pepper and chocolate upon returning home (full disclosure: if they escape and I have to chase them down in the lobby of the civic building, usually running into several policemen who frown at me rather sternly for losing my children, then I later console myself with a

Dr. Pepper and a double dose of chocolate). —ON THURSDAY NIGHT, there's a bible study Jack and I go to that I have to spend several hours preparing for (and which is particularly meaningful and effective given that we can't stand to be in the same room together right now);
—ON FRIDAY, JACK'S BIRTHDAY, he took the day off, but due to our ongoing hostilities, this time off from work did not benefit me in any way;
—ON SATURDAY, I prepped for and hosted not one but two more birthday parties: a family lunch for about 25 people at the house celebrating the birthdays of Jack, Claire, and Jack's mom; and later that afternoon, Claire's big friends' party at a crazy bounce-house party place with 22 kids in attendance, plus parents.

THIS WEEK

—I have three client meetings (one in a hospital way down in south Dallas for an ill client, and I don't do well in hospitals);
—I have a pediatric consult for Emma;
—Claire's in nature camp Tuesday and Thursday from nine to noon, so I have to entertain Emma again;
—Claire has her four-year checkup at the pediatrician this week, which I understand involves at least four needles and lots of screaming;
—There's yet another birthday party to go to this Saturday;— I'm still trying to catch up on housework, laundry, sleep, and exercise from the past two weeks;
—And through it all, Jack and I have barely been speaking to one another.)
I don't even want to think about next week. So far, we have scheduled a combined total of six doctor, dentist, and eye

appointments between the four of us; x-rays of Emma's bladder at the hospital (using a catheter and dye-should be fun); a trip to a water park (why?); two baseball games; library time; a client meeting; and a viewing of a partridge in a pear tree.

Not, perhaps, as exhausting as revitalizing a hotel while pregnant, but a little busy. As my dear Mamaw used to say, it's just life, and look at the alternative. I hope you're doing well and taking it easy for you and your baby's sake. Let me know what's up!

yp

SUBJECT: RE: WHO CAME UP WITH THIS SCHEDULE, ANYWAY?

Hi there,

Dare I say you came up with the schedule? I'm one to talk. But, being in the bold mood that I am in, I (again) dare to say, "Now things will be different!" Although it has been quite busy around here with wallpapering, house guests, and birthday parties I am turning over a new leaf. Part of this is not by choice but demand.

While wallpapering baby girl's room, I put up all the pieces that were in the chair rail vicinity and up to five feet high. Then, I broke out the ladder and finished off the room. It was easy enough as it is a wide-open space with carpeting. However when moving into the bathroom, which is a bit cozier, I was standing atop the counter when Pierce decided that was not such a good idea for a pregnant lady. I was ordered to hire wallpaper specialists to finish the job. Oh boohoo. (Detect a sense of sarcasm here?)

As for the birthday trip, Maxwell did not do well in the car for some strange reason. He fussed most of the way to my grandmother's and then boycotted the entire song-singing, cake-eating frenzy. On the way home, he screamed, cried and otherwise tormented Pierce and me because he did not get any cake. Pierce verbally (which makes it official) declared 'no more birthday trips or parties until next year'. Boo-hoo- hoo. My life moving towards utter boredom. (Again, insert sarcasm.)

Finally, our house guests, while pleasant and virtually undetectable, seemed to put me on the edge. I think I am just getting closer to the realization that our family is expanding and we'll no longer be a quiet household. Truth be told, we're not that quiet now so I'm more in the mode of preparing during the calm before the storm. "Herewith, there shall be no more houseguest, lodgers, or interlopers of any sort until aft the birthing of the daughter!" (A pregnant lady can get away with declaring this sort of thing, especially in her worst attempt at Shakespearean language.)

Worker bees for me. Boredom. Peace and Quiet. My life for at least the next week or two. Talk to you soon. S.

SUBJECT: OF EGGS AND BOOBS

Steph,

Thought you might enjoy Claire's latest observations of her world. There are a great number of ducks near my mom's residence, and some have nests of eggs right now. Claire observed these recently and said, "Look Mommy, the mama duck pooped out her eggs!" "Yeeess . . . okaaaay," was my enlightened response.

Claire is figuring out her body and similarities and differences to others. So the other day we're getting dressed in my bathroom, and Claire is wearing only underwear, and I'm wearing only a bra and panties. She looks at my chest, then she looks at hers. Then she looks at my chest again, runs over to me, grabs my boobs, then points to her own chest and exclaims, "Look, Mama! I have some of those, too!" My response? "Um . . . yes. Yes, you do. That's because you're a girl and I'm a girl." Claire then corrected me, "No, Mama. I'm a boy. Not a girl. I don't like girl stuff."

I see therapy in our future. Lots of therapy. yp

SUBJECT: THERAPY

Hi there!,

In response to your latest e-mail about Claire's denial of sexual self, I have two words: Group Therapy. I bet we can get a discount if we sign two kids up for the same type of counseling. I'm sure Claire does not want to be a girl any more than Maxwell wants to be a boy right now.

What does every little boy (o.k. -maybe just Maxwell) want to do every morning while he watches me do my hair and makeup? His hair and makeup, of course. I am constantly barraged with questions about what eye shadow does, how to apply it, and of course, can I have some? Every morning we do our hair—

complete with blow dry and hairspray. Never mind that his dad is piping up in the background with subtle directions like "Boys don't wear hairspray." No wonder it takes me twice as long to get dressed as it did before I had children. I am now "dressing" two people simultaneously, albeit I try fervently to sidestep the lipstick until I get in the car or out of sight!

Every time Pierce and I go out on a date and I am at the accessory stage, I am again deluged with statements regarding Maxwell's requirements for necklaces and purses. (Mind you, there are no questions at this point. He knows about accessories and by George, he knows how to use them!) He is picking out stiletto shoes (and wearing them, too) while parading around the house with his hair spiked to high heaven, eyebrows perfectly brushed, and multiple gaudy Mardi Gras toy bead necklaces draped about his person. And the ensemble would not be complete lest he don the pinkest purse he can find.

If you ask Maxwell what his favorite color is, the answer will always be "pink." And what does every boy dream of driving when they get big? A pink truck. (At least it is a truck, right?) So, don't despair. The way I see it, we have a few options. Either the two kiddos grow out of this phase and ultimately accept their God-given genders. Option number two: The two can try counseling in efforts to accomplish the first option. Or, (the most radical option) the two marry each other. Then, Claire can be the boy and Maxwell can be the girl! Time will tell! See ya'. S.

CHAPTER SEVENTEEN: AM I LOSING MY MIND?

SUBJECT: MEMORY FAILURE

Dear Yvonne,

That is your name, right? I have to tell you, lest I forget, that my memory is going fast. I can't remember two days ago much less two years ago. There you have it— my very legitimate excuse for forgetting your birthday on the 24th!

So I got you a card (and there's a little story there), but since I can't seem to remember to buy stamps to mail you the card, let me just quote it to you.

"I'm standing in the line to buy you a freakin' birthday card, and the line is like seventeen billion people long 'cause the only thing the dumb teenage boy at the register is thinking about is the dumb teenage girl at the other register."

Meanwhile, I'm checking out the teenage boy thinking, You can call me Ms. Robinson anytime, which, of course, leads to: What? Am I some kind of middle-aged pervy woman now that's drooling over a kid that could be my kid? But boy is he ever cute!

Back to your card..."And then, some dumb lady is turning her purse inside out to come up with 'exact change,' like she's gonna win some kind of 'exact change trophy' or something."
To add to the scene, some idiot (as if on cue) starts up with "This item was marked with the sale price" crap so I decide to finally

move to the self-service check out lane in order to not only expedite my eternal grocery store visit, but also to keep the drool in my mouth instead of all over the counter over the check-out guy whose name tag should read "I'm not the check-out guy, but the check-me-out guy."

This being my first attempt at using the self-service lane I, in less than three minutes flat, completely lock up the register. The computerized voice is screaming at me, "Please place your item in the baggage area!" — which I do, only to have the voice scream, "Item not recognized. Please remove from bagging area." This goes back and forth several times until I'm screaming at the monitor "Make up your mind lady! Do you want it in or out? There's only two ways to do this!" Of course, after this yelling match I realize my words are easily and completely misconstrued by the umpteen-thousand patrons who are waiting in line behind me. Just put Clayton Williams and me together — we'll win every election for sure!

So I'm half-expecting the computer to start screaming back at me with some smart-aleck remark like "Computer illiterate needs immediate help, redneck de-briefing and anger management course on checkout five." Instead, the computer "silently" summons the helper to the scene for assistance; there must be some under-the counter alarm button like they have in banks to alert the police. Does this officially put me in the wacko category? Guess who shows up?

Hottie Number Two! Is there some job requirement at the grocery store that all male cashiers and baggers must look like models for Abercrombie and Fitch? Here I am, a middle-aged momma, looking at Mr. Pearly White, Tall-Drink of Water- Perfect for assistance with a stubborn computer. After much babbling and stuttering (since when did I have this problem?), we (and I use the term "we" loosely) reprogram Ms. Computer Voice, and I'm on my merry way with the groceries (among other things) checked out.

And lastly, to quote your card, which describes my literal actions, "And so, I just really hope you like your card 'cause I stole it."

Not intentional of course, but I'd like to offer the two hotties at the grocery store as definite distractions and my lack of memory as my defense. (Off the record, I didn't even have my kids as distractions on the premises. Shameful!)

My wish for your birthday is that you don't have to go to the grocery store more than once during your birthday week. And, if you're in my shoes, that you don't get printed or have your mug shot taken because your brain has turned to mush and you've become a kleptomaniac!

Happy Birthday. S.

SUBJECT: RE: MEMORY FAILURE

Stephanie,

I cannot believe you stole my birthday card--I laughed so hard. I can totally relate to distractions and memory loss.

I cannot believe I'm thirty-four tomorrow!!!! Lately, I have taken to examining all the plastic surgery and micro-dermabrasion ads I get in the mail. You know you're getting old when you sit and compare prices for laser vein removal.

How are you? Other than on the lam, I mean. You know, shoplifting is a "very serious offense"! Thanks for remembering my birthday. I just hope you don't get arrested for your thoughtfulness!
yp

SUBJECT: THE VALUE OF A FOREIGN LANGUAGE

Dear Yvonne,

Why didn't I pay more attention in high school during our foreign language classes? I have always wanted to be fluent in multiple languages but have never quite gotten over the shyness to speak to others without really botching up their language. That being said, I have determined (much to my detriment) that my children should be fluent—in a language- perhaps even more than one!

As you know, we have Maria who works for us two days a week. She is from Venezuela. I have asked her to speak to the kids only in Spanish. This is really paying off. Maxwell now understands more than I do, and the two of them converse regularly. As you might expect, Maxwell also uses his second language to 'talk' to me. (Albeit, I only understand about half of it!)

Under Maria's careful tutelage, Maxwell has already learned the verbal attributes necessary to become a road rage driver. In two languages. Just the other day, I was driving Maxwell to music class and the traffic slowed to a snail's pace. Maxwell started yelling at the drivers around us, "Arriba! Arriba! Vamanos! Nosotros no tiene el tiempo!" I was quite impressed with his vocabulary and diction. Clearly, I was right to insist that he acquire a bilingual education. Right now, I'm enjoying good thoughts about furthering his education, wondering what other linguistic skills he will have already-mastered upon entering Kindergarten. Perhaps he'll be able to tell potty jokes in Spanish by then. Dare I hope?

We arrived downtown at music class, got out of the car, and fed the parking meter. Then we proceeded inside, where everything went relatively smoothly until the end of class when Maxwell announced he had to go to the bathroom. Since we are in serious potty-training mode, I quickly gathered up our things and anxiously waited for Max to put his instruments away.

During this brief transition, Maxwell demonstrated what I like to call "The Mexican Potty Dance." It's similar to "The Mexican Hat Dance," I suppose, except that it involves a lot of squirming and requires the participant to yell things like, "Vamanos! Yo me voy!" I probably shouldn't have spent so much time worrying about being polite and having Max put away his stupid instruments, as we didn't even make it out of the room before we had an accident. I knew this because Max started crying, "Mis pantelones son con tinkle!" (I guess he hasn't learned the Spanish word for "tinkle" yet.) So of course, we had to cut music class a bit short.

As we headed back to the car, Max stopped in the middle of the parking lot and proceeded to strip and moon the next class of kids on their way into music. I guess he just couldn't take the wet pants anymore. It took quite a bit of persuasion on my part (you know, yelling, gesturing wildly, freaking out) to get him to see reason and pull them back on until we could make it to the car.

As we approached the car, I noticed a little yellow envelope under the wiper. — Translation: parking ticket. Great. This day was shaping up quite nicely. At this point, Maxwell, clearly lacking in both common sense and wisdom regarding his mother's now frazzled mental state, proceeded to point out this minor infraction in the loudest possible volume his little body could muster. "Mi madre tiene una boletta! Mi madre tiene una boletta!" "Be quiet," I admonished, only to hear, "Tu no me hablas. Tu no eres mi jefe. Yo soy la que habla." Wonderful. Now my toddler has mastered talking back in two languages. I think Maria and I need to have a long talk. In English.

I just want to call it a day and be done with it. Talk to you soon. Adios. S.

SUBJECT: RE: THE VALUE OF A FOREIGN LANGUAGE

Steph,

Well, I'm impressed with Max's Spanish. And forewarned. Maybe I'll hold off on those preschool French lessons I've been thinking about for my girls. But I wouldn't be too worried about Max. At least, not until he starts translating Maria's Spanish soap operas for you. Then, maybe worry.

Buenas tardes, mi amiga. yp

SUBJECT: MY ENCROACHING SENILITY

Steph,

It's official. I'm losing it. I had a client meeting tonight to sign a couple's wills, powers of attorney, etc. These are people that I've met with at great length at least two times previously and talked with over the phone and thru email multiple times. I've typed their names in at least 12 documents, plus invoices, agreements, etc. They served as witnesses for prior clients, and those prior clients served as my witnesses tonight. Bottom line: I know all of these people. Been with them multiple times. I know all kinds of intimate details about their lives. At a bare minimum, I know their names.

Nevertheless, we're in the middle of signing the wills and I'm asking the clients to swear to this and swear to that, using their names in my questions. I then get to the point where I'm supposed to start asking the witnesses questions. Let's call the clients John Doe and Jane Doe, and call the witnesses Mutt and Jeff. I turn to the witnesses and I'm supposed to say, "Do you Mutt and Jeff swear that John and Jane have asked you to serve as witnesses?" Instead, I say the following, verbatim:

"Do you . . . ah . . ."
[feverishly trying to think of WITNESSES' names but failing miserably]
" . . . Ah . . . wit-ness-es"
[saying the previous word as slowly as is humanly possible]
" . . . swear that . . . um . . ."
[desperately trying to think of CLIENTS' names but drawing a complete and utter blank and saying instead:]

"...Um..."

[really long pause during which I stare intently at my clients' faces, as if their names might magically appear on their foreheads, and then, in total frustration, I SHOUT at them:]

"...OH. MY. GOSH. WHAT ON EARTH ARE YOUR NAMES?!!!"

Yep. That went well. Really well. Going to get a lot of referrals there, aren't I? That's me, Yvonne M. Parks, ace attorney, at your service.

I gotta get a new career. Sign me: Over the hill at 34.

SUBJECT: RE: MY ENCROACHING SENILITY

Hi there,

Oh yeah. There will be a lot of referrals coming your way. I see the headlines already. "Lawyer Forgets Law: Incriminates Self." Better be careful there!

On a slightly different note, I just celebrated my birthday with Ashley. She celebrated her anniversary with me. We went to dinner downtown for a brief outing. Being very pregnant, I wasn't up for much. Pierce and Ashley's husband Rick celebrated together in Chicago at the USC vs. Notre Dame game weekend. What a relationship. Oh, and let's hope baby

#2 isn't early! Her due date is in two weeks. Priorities you know. S.

SUBJECT: FROM UTAH TO ROSE BLOSSOM

Hi Yvonne,

I'm still exhausted but am in need of a little normalcy so naturally I turn to the Internet! Our second child has arrived on her due date—November 12 at 12:31pm. I find her numbers very reassuring—1-2-3 all the way around. (In case I have never told you, I have this thing about numbers. For example, her birthday is 11-12-03 (1-2-3) at 12:31pm (1-2-3). It's just a quirky thing, but something that grabs my attention.)

Anyway, we found out in March that we were expecting number two. Since we've had problems in the past, we did not want to tell everyone right away so we devised a code. Baby would be called "Utah". (It was determined that Utah was her state of conception.) So, in mixed company or around family we'd discuss Utah as needed. "How are things in Utah today?" Etcetera. This proved to be handy for us although we did get some weird looks from bystanders.

As Utah grew, so did my sense of smell and my cravings. I craved anything ethnic, especially Hot and Sour soup. I could smell things I never knew existed. A heightened sense of smell is quite a cool trait to have at times. And, at other times, not. Changing Maxwell's poopy diapers definitely falls into one of those 'not' times.

Additionally, during this pregnancy, I contracted poison ivy three times. Needless to say, this was not a fun thing to have while pregnant. I guess that's what I get for working in our yard. A yard that, at the time, could easily hide a small Toyota truck in the weeds!

The day of Rose's birth was quite busy. That morning, Pierce, Maxwell and I were getting dressed and my sixth sense told me today was the day. I, however, chose to ignore that thought because I was not really sure I was ready for a second dependent considering the first child can be incredibly demanding! So, we went to the car wash! Yep! My contractions were only seven minutes apart and the doctor said we should call at five minutes, so we headed to the car wash to get the oil changed and car washed. That was at 10:00 a.m.

At 11:00 a.m., I called the doctor, who said I should stop by the office for a quick peek at the goods. So, we headed to Chick-fil-A to get lunch for Maxwell and Pierce. Then, we took Maxwell to Pierce's mom's house-for safe measure just in case we were having a baby. We got to the doctor's office at 11:30 a.m. He said we should head to the hospital. Immediately, if not sooner. So we did.

For the first time ever, Pierce drove the speed limit. My contractions were about five minutes apart at this point and I had no patience for slow driving! Pierce got an earful about how I wished I was at the wheel since I am an avid follower of Mario Andretti's style. We arrived at the hospital and drove around looking for a parking space. And around and around and around. It wasn't until we got to the third floor of the garage that I realized I had better hop out and go inside. After all my minor procrastinations, it finally dawned on me that "ready or not," Utah was on the way. So, Pierce dropped me off at the elevator and I proceeded to the labor and delivery area on my own. (Well, there was this janitor who followed me from the elevator to the nurse's station to make sure I didn't fall over or deliver somewhere weird.)

I got to the room at 12:06. The nursed checked me and discovered I was at the magic ten centimeters. She freaked. And hastily paged the doctor. The nurse was in such a hurry that she forgot to turn off the intercom. That was actually pretty cool because I got to hear lots of stuff that ordinarily would be kept private. For instance, my doctor while en route to the hospital asked if he had time to change. The answer was "no" so he just showed up, tucked his tie in and delivered our baby girl! At 12:31 p.m. (Did I mention this was sans drugs? Clearly, no time for that, not even for an IV. Just like in the olden days, except I didn't have a stick to bite on or even a shot of whiskey!)

We decided to name her Rose Blossom. Rose is a family name and Pierce liked Blossom. Plus, when you put the names together, you get Rose Blossom. We think she'll be beautiful with all that spring brings (even though it's fall) and, luck notwithstanding, will already have a stage name should she choose to be a stripper (albeit a full-figured stripper considering she came into this world at 8 pounds, 6 ounces)!

Speaking of the princess, she's hungry, so I have to go. It was good to 'visit' via e-mail. I'll touch base again once I get some sleep! S.

SUBJECT: RE: FROM UTAH TO ROSE BLOSSOM

Steph,

Holy crap! Talk about a drive-thru delivery! I cannot believe you gave birth in half an hour with no drugs. You are Superwoman!

Love the name. And yes, Rose Blossom will work nicely for her future stage name. And in the event that she becomes really famous, it was quite far-sighted and considerate of you to give her a name that the tabloids can have fun with.

Can't wait to see pics of her. Try and get some rest. I know sleep is quite beyond any new mom, but rest might be doable.

Congratulations!!! yp

PART SIX

CHAPTER EIGHTEEN: ON THE ROAD AGAIN

SUBJECT: FLORIDA TRIP

Yvonne,

We just returned from our "runaway to Florida" trip. As is par for the course, we let everyday pressures boil to an uncontrollable level and then, at the point of spillover, decide to go on a trip. I'll recount our vacation but with fair warning as it will probably take several emails to convey it.

Three days before we leave, my day starts as usual. I'm awakened at 6:00 a.m. by a hungry little girl who calls not by crying, but by slamming her legs onto the crib, which sounds like you have a construction worker with a jackhammer right next to your bed. Wham! Wham! Wham! This, in turn, wakes up her sleeping brother (who happens to have taken up residence in our bed) so that he is screaming at the top of his lungs "Mommy, I want milk!" Rose is now wailing at the highest pitch you can fathom with sympathy cries.

Pierce is feigning sleep; I know this because the snoring has stopped. This fuels my already bug-eyed, crazy-lady state of mind. So I do the only logical thing in the situation—I start yelling along with the kids. Naturally, Pierce is the target. I am yelling at Pierce about my lack of sleep, my inability to get anything done, and my loss of independent "me" time. For good measure, I throw in a few relics of the past, like the time he forgot me at a bar in California three years ago. (That's a whole different story.)

Anyway, on this particular morning, the entire family is wide-eyed and bushy tailed by 6:15 a.m. With two kids screaming in bed for food, a bear of a husband yelling about even being awake at 6:15 a.m., and me ranting on at decibels too loud to measure, we decide by an overwhelmingly loud vote, "We need a vacation!"

"Fine. Let's go to Florida. We'll do Disney." "Fine. Disney it is." And so the story goes... As you might expect, now in addition to the 'normal' daily events I have to deal with, I also have the added responsibilities of finding flights, hotel rooms, cars, etc., which seems to be a lot easier than expected. Thank God for the Internet!

As the Routh family mantra dictates, "we" (that would be me and the mouse in my pocket) do not start packing until the day we leave. (It is hard work going somewhere with two kids! I had no idea the volume of stuff you have to take along.) Of course, I am packing for two little people who cannot function without every baby gadget and toy known to mankind. As I pack the diapers, wipes, and three outfits for each kid per day, etc., Max promptly removes everything I manage to get into the suitcase. He feels the only items necessary are the beach shovels and every matchbox car he owns. Now mind you, it is roughly 3:00 p.m., and we have to leave the house at 4:00 p.m. in order to get to the airport 1½ hours in advance. And then lo and behold...the doorbell rings. We have visitors!

Pierce's sister arrives with her youngest daughter Penny in tow. Now don't get me wrong—Penny and Max get along fabulously. But, if there is anyone who can wind him up tighter than an 8-

day clock, it's her. With one hour to go, I am on a marathon mission of packing for four people, entertaining guests, providing crowd control for screaming banshee Indians—I mean children—and sending out an APB for a husband who is MIA. (Oh, I guess I forgot to mention that Pierce conveniently has to "run down the street for a few minutes" to take care of some work stuff before we leave. That was about five hours ago.)

For some reason, I just had this image of Mrs. Cleaver in this situation. She'd be in her nicely pressed business suit and heels, pouring martini's, all the while gently encouraging the boys to calm down as she ever-so efficiently packs neatly folded clothes into the one and only suitcase necessary. Afterwards, she even has time to pull a drag on a Cool Menthol Light in the bathroom. (I'm sure she had at least one closet vice!) I digress…or wish.

Somehow, I manage to get our four suitcases, two car seats, and two kids into the car. I beg Pierce's sister to lock up the house while wishing I had a bullhorn to use on Pierce. Can't you just see it? I'm driving down the street with a bullhorn attached to the roof (just like a political protester's van) screaming non-stop with a very clear message to all other husbands within earshot—"Don't desert your wife on packing day or you'll endure the same embarrassing scolding your neighbor is currently receiving!"

I finally find Pierce, and we somehow manage to get out of the house and arrive at the airport the requisite 1½ hours in advance only to learn our flight has been delayed by two hours. Well, I figure, at least we'll have time to eat. I'll have to e-mail you the continuation of the saga later…Max is calling. S.

SUBJECT: RE: FLORIDA TRIP

Okay. So you're stressed out and decide to unwind on vacation. Good for you. But at Disney? Hello? Are you nuts? You need a vacation FROM the kids, not WITH the kids. And sure as heck not at Disney! I really cannot wait to hear how this ends. I'm guessing in a straight jacket in a padded room.
yp

SUBJECT: PART 2 OF THE FLORIDA TRIP: GETTING OUT OF TEXAS

Yvonne,

You'll be glad to know I survived Disney without a single trip to the insane asylum. Came close, but…see for yourself. Part II.

The Austin International airport is not nearly as cosmopolitan and sophisticated as the "international" in its title suggests. Everything—and I mean everything—closes at 6:00 p.m. It is now 5:45 p.m., and we are starving. To death. And we haven't made it through security yet.

We eye the security checkpoints and make our best guess as to which one is going to let us through the fastest. Chute number three has a grandmotherly sort waving people through, and so we choose her. I'm sure I don't need to tell you that she turns out to be the Gestapo of airport security. "Undress to your skivvies!" No, not really, but we do have to remove shoes, belts, coats, watches, and basically every article of clothing short of exposing our private parts. And for a minute there, I'm not sure that Rose will be allowed to keep her diaper on. She might be packing heat, you know. After a ten-minute search of our belongings, we emerge from the security line and make a mad dash for the closest food vendor, carrying shoes, belts, phones, diaper bags, car seats and toys in hand. I think I would have forgotten Rose had she not been strapped to my chest in the Snugli!

We order our food and wait while the slowest counter help in the universe prepares it with painstaking detail. It's airport food for crying out loud! As we make our way to the table and unload for what will no doubt be an unnaturally long dinner, I notice Max has an extra bag of chips in hand. "I got these for you, mama." Of course he did—right off the rack. Now, however, it is well past six and the shop is closed. Well, as we both know this is not the first klepto experience we've had. I guess the apple didn't fall very far from the tree, huh?

Fast forward to our flight. The plane is full, so we are quite crowded, especially since we didn't buy a seat for Rose. Pierce and I agree to take turns holding her. Not fifteen minutes into the flight, we hear a delightful sound. -Pbbbttt. Yes, you guessed it. The biggest motherload of a diaper full you can imagine! What do you know? Rose is packing after all.

Pierce and I bust out laughing. Rose squirms all over the place as we do our best to keep her diaper contents from spilling out onto our clothes while we prepare to clean her up. Pierce holds her up. I retrieve a stack of wipes and away we go. I wipe, she wiggles, and we all giggle. We get her put back together. Yeah us! Survived a close one.

But wait, there's more! Not five minutes later, she does it again!

So, here goes round two of the wipe-wiggle-giggle routine. We're thinking this is too funny. Why? I don't know. Because it's laugh or cry? In any event, we are amused. This is a good thing since Rose proceeds to poop yet again not ten minutes later. After round three, we seriously hope that there are no further incidents because we are out of diapers and out of wipes. And only two and half more hours in the sky to go!

But alas, our hopes are in vain. We should crown the child the Queen of Poop today. Incident number four happens. Well, this time there is nothing we can do except laugh and wait. Luckily, Rose is a good sport about it all. The man behind us, poor guy, gags (loudly) and shifts in his seat throughout the entire flight. I guess it just goes to show you even your nose adjusts to certain things during parenthood!

I'll finish telling you about the rest of the trip later. Gotta run. S.

SUBJECT: RE: PART 2 OF THE FLORIDA TRIP: GETTING OUT OF TEXAS

Steph,

Oh, my gosh. Poor Rose! Poor you! Poor guy with the overactive gag reflex! I'd say, "Poor Pierce," but since he abandoned you in your hour of packing need, I think he deserved the poopy diapers. At least y'all could laugh about it.

And now that Max is well on his way to becoming jailbait, are you going to instruct him in the finer points of shoplifting, or just let him sort it all out on his own? I don't handle criminal cases, you know, but I guess I should start brushing up, huh? Can't wait to hear the rest of this one.

Yp

SUBJECT: DISNEYWORLD DEBACLE

Yvonne,

Here is—as Paul Harvey would say—"the rest of the story."

As you may remember from my last e-mail, just getting to Florida for this Disney/beach vacation was a mess. It should have been a warning to me not to hold any hopes out for a respectable family vacation. But alas, I did not pay attention to the glaring red flags that were not merely waving but slapping me in the face saying, "Welcome to your vacation! You'll need a vacation when you return."

We get to the Magic Kingdom on Saturday around 3:00 p.m. First mistake. Don't ever go on a weekend if you can avoid it—there are throngs of people. It's a mucky day, the weather a cross between drizzle and a light sprinkle. The fog just hovers, waiting to engulf any small child who strays too far from his keeper. Pierce and I immediately start searching for a kid leash—you know the kind that is very similar to a dog leash but supposedly more humane. We get some very weird stares when asking at the counters for these contraptions. Am I the only person who knows about these? I should market them to Disney. I could be a billionaire. A kid leash would be a hot commodity in a sea of parents screaming at kids, trying desperately not to get separated. Believe me, even the righteous, perfect-parent types would be scrambling to get one after an hour of trying to corral a three-year-old in Mecca. I digress. (I do that often!)

The first thing we do when we arrive is head straight for the "It's a Small World" attraction. Mistake number two. Apparently, this is still a very popular ride and not only with the seven and under crowd. I can't tell you how many same- sex couples stand in line around us for this ride. And, being all of two years old and highly curious, Maxwell blurts out "Where's she mommy? Is that she mommy? Why is she holding she hand?" I do my best, with Rose strapped to my chest, to get down on his level and quietly explain that the two lovey-dovey women in front of us are very good friends, and that it is not polite to talk about people. I guess I do a good job (or for once Max is listening) because he then starts tugging on the lady's pants in front of me asking, "Is she you mommy? Is she your friend? Are you a bobo?" (That is his new word meaning absolutely nothing.) I try, ever so politely, to explain (this time to the ladies) that he is two and that 'bobo' means absolutely nothing.

Fortunately, I am rescued by a seventeen-year-old screaming at me, "Lady, get in the boat. You're holding up the line." So much for that renowned Disney customer service. The sound of squeaky, nasal-toned voices singing "It's a small world after all" never sounded so good.

Next on our adventure itinerary is having our picture taken with Mickey. We have, after our one and only ride of the day, seen other characters (not all of them Disney employees, mind you). However, Maxwell is terrified of any over-sized bear, dog, or ant coming at him for a nice photo-op. A larger-than- life rat, on the other hand, appears to be perfectly acceptable to him. So, we head off in search of Mickey.

We pull out our trusty, and by this time crusty, map of the Magic Kingdom, which indicates that Mickey plans to make his appearance at spot "X" on the map between 5:30 p.m. and 6:30 p.m., just before the fireworks show. We, of course, are at spot "Y," which is not even in the same universe as spot "X." And the time is now 5:29 p.m. Therefore, we must make a mad dash to the Mickey photo site or risk losing the opportunity of a lifetime to get a portrait of our precious children mugging with a giant rat. We get there just in time to stand in a line a mile long. We wait…forever.

After much cajoling and several lengthy discussions with Max about the importance of standing quietly in line, why having a picture taken with Mickey will be really cool, and so forth and so on, it is finally, finally our turn. Max has grown at least two inches in the time we've waited. All four of us march up to Mickey for "the picture." The mouse silently fusses over Rose, clearly overcome with awe in the presence of such a beautiful baby—because, you know, he sure doesn't see those every day walking all over Disneyworld.

Then Mickey turns to Max. Out of the blue, Max points his finger at the oversized rat and yells—in a voice not to be missed by even the near-deaf, much less our fellow Mickey admirers standing all around us—"Mickey's got boogers!"

Snap.

And that's our picture: Max with his fingers as far up Mickey's plastic nose as possible; me with a look of sheer horror, mouth agape; Pierce with a Cheshire grin that clearly conveys his "That's my boy!" attitude; and Rose, my beautiful baby, with a scrunched up red face, obviously caught in mid- grunt as she reloads her diaper for the third time today. That's one photo I know I'll cherish forever. In fact, I think I'll send it out with our Christmas cards this year. Good grief!

So far, we've had quite a day: one ride and one photo. We are beat and start heading back to the hotel. But before we get out of the park, a gentle voice comes over the loud speaker to announce that the fireworks show starts in only three minutes. "The voice" also says to stay where you are and "Do not attempt to move about while the lights are dim." Okay. We think this could be a nice finishing touch to our one and only visit to Disneyworld on this particular vacation. (We made that decision right about the time we almost fell into the water canal getting off the "It's a Small World" ride. Events since that moment have only confirmed how brilliant we are.)

The music starts and everyone is filled with anticipation. BOOM! BOOM! BOOM! Maxwell begins screaming like his arm has been shot off. Obviously, the fireworks are not doing it for him. It's time to go.

We do our best to find our way out of the park, going against literally thousands of people staring up at the sky, all trying to see through the heavy fog some glimmer of light that should be accompanying the sonic booms overheard. Maxwell is still screaming, and then Rose chimes in with sympathy wails, both of them overwhelming the grandiose music. Pierce pushes through the swarming masses like a bull. We are not going to win any popularity awards with this crowd.

Nevertheless, we persevere to the gates with Pierce receiving only minor umbrella stabbings. (Because he's so tall, he leads the way. But, because he is so tall, everyone's umbrellas reach him right around eye level.) It is a minor price to pay to get out of children Mecca — a.k.a. Parent Hell, especially since it's not my eyes in jeopardy!

And that was our trip to Disney. We'll treasure the memories forever. In fact, I think we should be in a commercial for Disney:
— A family four-pack of two-day passes to Disney World, used for all of four hours: $400.00
— Cost of purchasing and acquiring photo with Mickey: $22.00
— Explaining gay public displays of affection to your two-year old, preserving on film for all time the same two-year old picking Mickey Mouse's nose, and running for dear life in terror from invisible fireworks display: Priceless.

I've got to run. I have to pick Maxwell up from Mother's Day out. I think they should consider a Mother's Week out every now and then, don't you? I could really use a vacation. Talk to you soon.
S.

SUBJECT: RE: DISNEYWORLD DEBACLE

Steph,

OMG. You know, I'm starting to totally rethink our Disney vacation we have planned for two years from now (some of us need a little more than three days' notice on a Disney trip). Maybe I should wait until the girls are teenagers. Do they make leashes for teenagers?

I hate to say, "I told you so," but... I'll just say that I hope you'll recover from your "vacation" soon! (See, I can be diplomatic — bordering on empathetic, even — sometimes.)

yp

SUBJECT: MUSIC CLASS

Just a hello email on this April Fool's Day. Overall, we're doing okay. Max, Rose and I all have cough/cold du jour. Max is still potty training, and so far it hasn't been very successful. Today at music class, we had to rush to the bathroom (leaving Rose behind in class!) only to have our own "April Fool's no show." Being the unprepared mother that I am, I let Max go commando for the rest of the class. What could go wrong in fifteen minutes? Well, you guessed it: During the last song, he came walking towards me with his legs half-cocked and proudly announces to me and the class, "Mommy, I went tinkle in my pants!" So, we rushed out to the parking lot just in time for Max to drop his drawers and moon the patrons of the next music class. Again. I'm going to get kicked out of the music school for indecent exposure by my children on more than one occasion! I get him in the car, only to get the diaper on backwards. I figure I can at least get him home in his semi-put together state. Rose was blissfully asleep during all this.

When we get home I decide to take care of Max and then bathe Rose, who has not had a bath in three days, much less a change of clothing. I get her all squeaky clean and then, you guessed it, the motherload of all poopy diapers. I have to start over again.

Take care and keep it together. Talk to you soon. Keep in touch!

S.

SUBJECT: RE: MUSIC CLASS

Steph,

Um…did we not learn anything from the airplane ride? Did we not learn anything from the first potty-training mishap with Maxwell at music school back in October? Plan B, Mom, plan B! (that would be to carry around a pair of underwear and a pull-up at all times in your purse—like I do! And don't worry, you'll eventually get over the embarrassment of retrieving a pair of undies on the end of your pen as you pull it out to write a check at the grocery store.)

Poor you! Don't you just hate it when you have to do something as difficult as bathing a wiggling infant twice in a half-hour?
yp

CHAPTER NINETEEN: I'LL TAKE ALL THE HELP I CAN GET

SUBJECT: CAN RELATE

1. Have laryngitis. No more drugs. Expect two to three week recovery. $100 Doctor bill.
2. Husband is sex-starved. Requests servicing often. Deep six that. Too darn tired.
3. Maxwell can draw circle. Happy face to be exact. On the wall. With permanent marker.
4. Rose is now super-pooper. Need diapers. Otherwise, just me, poo and you-know-who.
5. Sugar to be eliminated from MY diet. Too many deposits on hips. Too much ADD behavior.
6. Monsters destroying house. Monster spray on order. Bulk quantity.
7. End of transmission. S.

SUBJECT: THANK YOU, DISNEY

Steph,

I've come to believe that TV is a parent's best friend. I am so thankful to studios like Disney and Dream Works for producing such wonderful children's fare to instruct my girls and to occupy their time. My girls have learned so much from their movies.

For example, from the movie, Spirit, Claire now knows how to respond to me when I repeatedly ask her to do something she doesn't want to do: "Get off of my back!" There's even a catchy song about it that she knows by heart and can sing anytime she likes. Thank you, Dream Works, for giving my daughter the ability to articulate so well her rebellion.

Emma has learned to communicate through movement from her favorite movie, The Little Mermaid. Apparently, the evil octopus exhorts Ariel to use her "body language" to communicate. So Emma, taking this advice to heart, has taken to wiggling her bare bottom in my face during bath time while saying in her sexiest three-year-ldo voice: "Bo -dy lan-guage," complete with appropriate emphasis and perfect wiggling rhythm. Thank you, Disney, for encouraging my child to learn the fine art of exotic dancing.

Claire can give voice to her dissatisfaction with her family now that she's seen "Lady and the Tramp 2: Scamp's Adventure." Every time she receives a reprimand, she, like Scamp the dog, declares, "I don't want to be in this family anymore. I'm a wild dog [child]." Thank you, Disney, for teaching my child to express herself and for giving her hope that she can ditch us for a better family when things don't go her way.

The film Pocahontas taught Claire to wield a bow and arrow and hunt down her sister. She has become so proficient at producing makeshift bows and arrows out of plastic hangers and Lincoln logs that we finally had to buy her a plastic toy bow with Styrofoam arrows so that she wouldn't harm her sister when going in for the kill. Thank you, Disney, for teaching such important offensive weapons skills and for encouraging healthy sibling rivalry.

Claire reminds me from time to time that we can never truly be sure of anything in this life and that we should always question the truth of others' words. When she queries the veracity of one of my statements with, "Are you sure, Mom?" I invariably reassure her with, "I'm positive." But as Claire learned from Fern Gully, "Only fools are positive." She also shares this sense of doubt with her preschool teacher whenever her teacher is positive about something. Thank you, producers of Fern Gully, for reminding us that you can't rely on anyone's words.

From Disney's many "princess" movies, Emma learned to express her true self through role-playing. She no longer feels the need to be Emma and to wear children's clothing, as princess costumes tell others who she really is: Cinderella; Snow White; Ariel; Belle, the "Booty"; or even Rose, the Sleeping "Booty." When the costumes themselves become tiresome, Emma simply parades around as a half-naked princess in her panties, showing us how comfortable and in tune she is with her body. Thank you, Disney, for creating in children the capacity to become someone they are not and will never be. And thanks for showing us how beautiful we all should strive to be.

From Brother Bear, Claire learned the truth about what she has always secretly suspected and hoped for: humans can turn into animals. So Claire now spends hours at a time as a real bear, growling at, clawing, and sometimes even biting her little sister. Thank you, Disney, for encouraging my daughter to further loosen her tenuous grasp of reality, which, of course, can be so limiting to a child, by believing that she's a bear. And thanks for giving Emma a healthy fear of bears.

Also courtesy of Brother Bear, Claire and Emma have learned the proper way to end a conversation when they are tired of listening to one other. Claire: "You shut up, stupid." Emma: "You shut up, stupid." Claire: "You shut up, stupid." Emma: "You shut up, stupid." And on and on and on, ad nauseum. Thank you, Disney, for encouraging directness over politeness and decorum in our children's speech.

From Finding Nemo, Claire learned how to handle her little sister's pestering and constant shadowing: "You want a piece of me? Huh, huh, huh? Do ya? Do ya?" Thank you, Disney, for encouraging my children to draw and enforce appropriate relationship boundaries when conflict arises.

And from Aladdin, my girls learned something I am truly thankful for: "Group hug!" Thanks, Disney, Dreamworks. Thanks for the memories.

SUBJECT: RE: THANK YOU, DISNEY

Hi there,

I have to say I have yet to see even one of the films you cite. We were going to attempt Finding Nemo but were warned of a certain barracuda. We passed on the video, as Maxwell is still easily frightened. We are not without mass media influences, however.

Maxwell has watched Bob the Builder so many times that even I walk around humming little tidbits from the video. And, lest we feel alienated, the Bob the Builder video also has a Spanish version. Needless to say, we have watched Bob Construjer many times as well. The Wiggles are a mainstay and occasionally SpongeBob makes an appearance.

Maxwell's aunt has dutifully purchased and presented him with many videos that are, at this point, quite scary to him. For example, we have yet to make it past the first few scenes in 101 Dalmatians or Aladdin or Beauty and the Beast or…well, the list is quite long. When he's ready, we'll have enough viewing hours to insure he is ADHD! I better run. Speaking of the tele, Maxwell is turning it on now. S.

SUBJECT: PRESCHOOL MOTHER'S DAY PROGRAM

Steph,

There are moments in every mom's life when she looks at her little darling and thinks to herself, "What a wonderful world," as the song plays in her head and she beams with pride over the accomplishments of her offspring. Then there are those moments when a mom thinks to herself, "How can I grab the kid and slink out of here without any of the other parents noticing, and could I then disappear for two weeks until all this blows over?" Guess which kind of moment I had today.

Before school this morning, my friend Lauren said to me, "Take your Kleenex. You'll cry during the whole Mother's Day program at preschool-it's so special!" Well she was right about one thing: I did need a tissue for all the tears that threatened. Seventy kids took to the stage this morning to sing over a dozen songs to us moms, recite pledges and verses, and in general ooze charm and, ultimately, justify the ridiculous amount of tuition we pay for a mere nine hours of instruction each week. Sixty-nine kids did just that. One, however, decided to give an entirely different performance. That would be my daughter, Claire, of course.

Showing an amazing lack of foresight, the music teachers placed Claire front and center, for all to see. Literally, she was smack-dab in the middle, under the brightest of the spotlights. Couldn't miss her, particularly since she's taller than half the school and since I had topped off her standout, spun-gold hair with an enormous blue bow. And if the lighting, her location, her height, and her gold hair and bow didn't draw your attention, then you couldn't possibly miss her outstretched arms over her head or the fierce grimaces and severe neck rotations she applied to observe the many pretty lights. She apparently thought that the morning's activities included vigorous upper-body calisthenics. No one else seemed to be laboring under that misapprehension.

When she wasn't exercising and grimacing, she adopted a deer-in-the-headlights gaze of terror and fiddled with her frock. Most bothersome to her was the sash on her beautiful, smocked dress. Inexplicably, said sash sat tied in a huge knot in the front of her dress, rather than in the bow I had tied at her back when I dressed her this morning. Seriously, this knot was worthy of a Boy Scout. Claire spent a good portion of the 45-minute performance attempting to untie the knot and, failing to accomplish that, she engaged in gymnastic maneuvers to wiggle the sash all the way down to her ankles and step out of it. Unfortunately, the sash was still knotted in back, too, so this proved an impossible task. Thank God she didn't roll down the steps head over heels as she tried to step out of it. Then again, that might have shortened the misery for all of us.

When she wasn't fiddling with that darn dress, she stuck her tongue out and wagged it from side to side, catching it in her fingers and pulling on it, as if it was supposed to dislodge or something. Eventually, Claire became bored with her dress and her tongue, so she then focused on covering up her eyes from the lights. At one point, she even felt it necessary to lift her dress up over her head to protect her eyes, revealing her lovely little Dora the Explorer panties for all to see and record on video for posterity. Everyone else, mind you, was deeply engaged in singing their little hearts out for their mommies. Not my Claire!

During the latter part of the program, twenty-six kids lined up behind the group at large and went down the line reciting Bible verses that correlated with a letter of the alphabet. The rest of the kids sat on the stage steps during this group torture. Claire couldn't sit still, of course, so she had to investigate the nearest thing she could lay her hands on-the vibrating sound system monitor speaker/amplifier, which some idiot left in the middle of the stage steps. She found it fascinating to put her hand inside its grooves and feel its vibrations, and being the sweet, giving child that she is, she had to share her discovery with the two boys sitting closest to her. Thus, one of the teachers and the director of the preschool had to come over to her at least twice during the Bible verses to tell her to cease and desist. In front of at least 200 parents and grandparents. Many of whom know me.

You know that ad for Southwest Airlines that ran a while back? The one where they ask, "Need to get out of town in a hurry?" after the object of the commercial suffers some public humiliation? That was me today. I should get paid to do a commercial for Southwest. Or at least to write it.

To be fair, Claire suffers from sensory integration dysfunction. Her little brain doesn't process stimuli the way yours and mine (and 90 percent of other children's) do, and so the bombardment of stimulus inherent in public appearances always makes such occasions crapshoots. You never know how she's going to react to the lighting, the noise, the crowds, etc. I wanted so much to run down there today and grab her off the stage and put her-and me-out of our misery. But I didn't. And, as luck would have it, I was rewarded somewhat for sticking it out until the bitter end.

The last song the children sang was "God Bless America," a tune that Claire sings quite well-and in a perfectly normal fashion-on a daily basis around the house. Having completely ignored the fact that she was a participant in a music program up to this point, she decided at long last to join in the fun. So with affectations worthy of Shirley Temple herself, she put her whole heart into singing about the mountains and the prairies and the oceans. I honestly thought she was going to raise her arms up over her head in true diva fashion and belt out the last part while beating on her chest. Eat your heart out, Celine Dion.

The final insult to injury came in the bathroom after the "performance." A woman looked at Claire, laughed, and said to me, "I sure hope you were videotaping her. There's always one in every bunch who's looking around at the lights with their tongues hanging out." What was I supposed to say to that? Wanted to slap the woman. But hugged Claire instead and let her know she did an awesome job singing that last song.

So, how was your day? yp

SUBJECT: RE: PRESCHOOL MOTHER'S DAY PROGRAM

Hi there,

I once saw a Steve Martin movie with a scene very similar to the one you just described. At the end of the preschool performance, the wife says something along the lines of life being a roller coaster and how she loves the ride. I'd say you are in for the ride of your life! Hopefully, you enjoy roller coasters. Otherwise, I should suspect you'll be burying your head in a trash can quite often for the inevitable puking that goes along with the thrills! Oh-and Happy Mother's Day. S.

CHAPTER TWENTY: ROAD TRIP

SUBJECT: CAL -I-FORN-YA-HERE I COME!

Yvonne,

We've just returned from our 'runaway' trip to California. Pierce and I both have been working on major projects for the last month and we both need a break. So, (show tunes, please) 'CAL-i-forn-ya—here I come; da-da-da'. Or rather, here we come, the Routh family household, kids in tow. And I do mean 'household..' (Please refer to the amount of crap I told you we lugged to Florida and just "ditto that.")

Our flight to San Jose was fine, if you excuse Maxwell from throwing up fifteen minutes into the flight. I do not care. I was in that "I'm on vacation, no worries" mode. Never mind that I didn't pack extra clothes for the bloke. Why would I? Everyone knows that three-year-olds don't get sick—ever--in mid-flight. So, after a three-hour plane ride we deplaned— shirtless. Yeah, we got the stares and the 'what happened to your shirt?' questions. But, again, I did not care. I was on vacation.

After deplaning, we navigated through the "currently under renovation" San Jose airport with all the agility of an elephant trying to corral her hyperactive young. Imagine her trunk flailing about, screeching and roaring, stomping non-stop accompanied by the occasional spewing. (That is Max's role- the spewing.)

We loaded the rental car and were off to the sunny California coast. Only, it was foggy and cold. Never mind the weather — we are on vacation! We drove down "the 1". (Why Californians call their highways "The 1" or "The 405" is beyond me. It's as if the road is an object of their affection.) Anyway, it was a beautiful drive. Maxwell mysteriously stopped spewing, thank God, and Rose was sacked out in her car seat. All was well with the world. The houses we saw are so quaint, tucked into the hillsides. The waves were knocking ever so gently on the shore. People were out enjoying the coast...

POW!! Pierce was sightseeing while driving, or not driving as the case may be. He turned the corner just a little too sharply blowing out a tire. Literally. It was a rental car after all. Max was now screaming 'Daddy, don't do that!' Rose was wailing at the top of her lungs. I was jumping out of the car on a hillside to survey the damage and Pierce was yelling at me to get back in so he could drive further UP the hill to stop. He did. He got out but forgot he was on a hill and didn't set the brake. Down the hill we went, backwards, lolly-gagging along on a lopsided tire. Max started screaming again. Rose was still wailing. By this time, I was laughing hysterically. We got the car stopped only to realize all we had was a rim— no tire. It was okay, I was on vacation! Albeit, it was turning into a National Lampoon's movie in the making.

Knowing that I am a better handyman than Pierce, I immediately picked up the phone to call roadside assistance. No cell service. Pierce boldly proclaimed, "I know how to change a tire." Oh no. With all the determination of a man to prove his worth, Pierce ensued on an all-out manhunt for the jack. This is a man, mind you, who has left the cabinet door in the kitchen hanging on one hinge for over a year because of a lack of skill, knowledge or desire to put in one measly screw. And now, he wanted to change a tire—with five lug nuts! He's nuts! As luck would have it, our rental car had no jack.

But, Pierce having an equal amount of bad and good luck, flagged down the one and only car that passed us on this residential street. Well, the guy didn't have much choice but to stop. After all, a six-foot-four, two hundred plus pound guy was standing in the middle of the road waving his arms like he was at a rock concert feeling the love. Personally, I don't know that I would've stopped. I guess the guy figured since there were three suitcases, a wife, a baby and a hyper three-year-old on the curb he was safe. Luckily, the man had a jack and, an added bonus, two kids the same age as Max. We were all occupied for the next hour and a half. Did I mention this was still the first day of vacation?

All in all the vacation was good. I'll have to tell you about the San Francisco sidebar later. I have a mountain of laundry waiting and two kids who are still on California time and need to go to bed. Talk to you soon. S.

SUBJECT: RE: CAL -I-FORN-YA-HERE I COME!

Steph,

RE: your poor, shirtless son: HAVE WE LEARNED NOTHING FROM THE TRIP TO FLORIDA AND THE MUSIC CLASS DEBACLE????

RE: the tire mishap: Don't you just love rental car companies and cell phone services? They're always there when you need them. So reliable.

Glad you had a good time regardless! yp

SUBJECT: SAN FRANCISCO SIDEBAR

Yvonne,

The laundry is almost done and the kids are napping so I have just a moment to tell you about the San Francisco portion of our trip. It is the last day of our vacation before we returned on Friday. We decide to head to San Francisco, not wanting to venture to far from San Jose. (We have a history of getting lost.) I have been there before and wanted to show Pierce all the "touristy" things—and then some. We had less than twenty-four hours to do it all. It is only forty-nine square miles after all.

When we got into San Fran proper, we parked the car ($28) down at Pier 39 and head to Fisherman's Wharf for a cup of chowder with clams right off the dock ($8). Next, we made a side trip to Payless for socks for the little princess ($8). (She has a habit of wanting to be footloose and fancy free.) Back at Pier 39, we rode the carousel with Max ($2), watched the magic show ($5), bought the token streetcar souvenir ornament ($14) and then headed back to the car and dashed full-speed ahead to Chinatown. We parked the car (got lucky this time-no meters) and off we went into the markets and street shops. Sixty-five dollars, a pair of booties for toddler Rose, and a watercolor painting later we are up the stairs to the Pearl for dinner. Aside from being seated in the corner away from the adult diners, spilling one drink and scattering rice all over the floor, it was forty-five dollars worth of good. Which, for dinner, isn't bad.

Now, we had to find a hotel. Well, there was the Westin St. Francis at Union Square. Only $219/night plus $39 parking plus $20 property fee. So we splurged. Besides, we got to kill one bird with two stones by sleeping and seeing a tourist destination all at once. (Okay, sleeping and seeing at once are not really conducive to one another, so let's say we experienced Union Square via osmosis.) That was, of course, after a total meltdown by one tired Maxwell because we were out of soy milk. You'd think everyone in California would drink soy, but no. This high-brow hotel did not have a drop. So, Pierce got to see a little more in his jaunt around two blocks searching for soy milk. He came back empty-handed.

The next morning, we ate at Lauren's ($40) while sitting right next to Keith Johnson. (Do you know who he is? I hadn't a clue, but Pierce informed me he is THE baseball pitcher of our time.) Back at the hotel, we locked and loaded and headed back to the Cannery. We parked ($15-a deal) and stopped at In & Out for a soda ($4) while we waited for the fire engine tour ($90).

The tour started and boy was this a hum dinger. We got to ride in an open-air, 1955 fire engine while dressed in fireman jackets. Our tour guides (husband and wife) were big on the sing alongs, so we were belting out show tunes while crossing the Golden Gate Bridge. (Check off another tourist destination as well as Sausalito, the Presidio, and the Palace of Fine Arts.) It was actually quite fun!

Back at the Cannery, we walked down to Ghiradelli Square where Maxwell lifted a chocolate bar (free). (We are going to have to work on that.) The line at the restaurant was too long, so we headed up the street to eat at Buena Vistas for a late lunch (another $40). While there, this nice gentleman commented on what beautiful children we have and how lucky we are to have two sons that are so close in age. I guess he didn't notice Rose's pink and purple dress. Or maybe he did. We were, after all, in San Francisco!

Lastly, we headed to the historic trolley, turned around to stand in line for a jaunt up to Powell Street($6) and went back down($6). Back to the car and we hit the road. We stopped for a few bucks of gas ($30)--$4.64 per gallon—and left our hearts (and our wallets--$689 to be more exact) in San Francisco! (Darn show tunes!) S.

SUBJECT: RE: SAN FRANCISCO SIDEBAR

Steph,

Sounds like you had a lot of fun. Expensive fun, too! Doesn't get any better than that, does it? But you know, you're really causing me to rethink this whole "dying-to-travel" thing I've had in my head for some time now. We're headed to my sister's wedding in Mississippi next week with the girls, so we'll see if we fare any better than y'all in transit. I'm not sure I could handle spewing in such close quarters. I'll rephrase. I KNOW I couldn't handle the spewing. You're my hero.
Yp

SUBJECT: MY SISTER'S WEDDING

Steph,

Well, my baby sister's hitched and we somehow survived the trip. Here's the scoop:

We left Thursday afternoon, hoping to get into Jackson around 9 pm. In an effort to reduce the cost of the trip and to avoid yet more burgers and fries (we've had way too many this week), we decided to bring a picnic dinner to eat on the way. I packed fruit, snacks, peanut butter, cheese, lunchmeat, etc., for sandwiches. After hearing interminable cries of "I'm hungry," from the little people in back, we started looking for places to stop for our picnic on the highway as we got closer to the Louisiana border. Hmm. Where were all the rest stops we remembered being here? Nowhere to be found. The hue and cry of the starving increased dramatically. And someone had to go potty.

Oh, salvation. The Louisiana border rest stop with picnic tables and bathrooms was just a few miles ahead. We were going to live.

Oh, damnation. The rest stop was closed to traffic. Naturally. No stopping allowed. Of course. It would be, wouldn't it? The children were, according to them, about to expire from hunger and someone still needed to really go potty. With the food situated way in the back and with no safe place to pull over, we were forced to listen to their howls for what felt like a century.

We were surprised to find that it was actually only twenty minutes when we finally pulled into Monroe at Jack's favorite stop, The Cracker Barrel. He just loves this place. He especially enjoys chasing the kids around the store trying to keep their little hands off all the toys and candy. He was very happy right about then.

We found a parking spot in the back with all the RV's and decide to have a "tailgate party" right there. Very classy, I know. After two trips to the ladies room that each took an eon, at least (because certain little munchkins swear that they don't need to go and then change their minds when you're almost all the way back to the truck), I discovered that I couldn't make the peanut butter and jelly sandwiches I'd been promising the girls because I have, inexplicably, forgotten to bring a spreading knife. And jelly.

So Jack headed into the restaurant to get some jelly and a knife. About 10 minutes, $5, and a jelly jar later (because they won't pass out their free breakfast jelly in those convenient little plastic containers unless you actually order breakfast), I now had the tools to feed these starving kids. I made the PB&J sandwiches, placing one up front for Claire and one in the back for Emma. Problem solved. Everyone was happy as Claire crawled over the seats up front to look for her sandwich and … splat. She stepped right on it. Great.

Explaining to her that we could not eat sandwiches bearing shoe prints, she headed all the way back to the rear over the seats again to get another sandwich from me, whereupon she immediately stepped on the ham, lettuce, and tomato sandwich I had just made for myself. Oy!

I attempted to make another footprint-free sandwich for each of us, but discovered that we were now out of bread because, while

I was experiencing the nightmare of taking two little girls through a store filled with goodies to go potty, Jack was helping himself to multiple sandwiches, not calculating the possibility that Claire might stomp on our evening meal. In the meantime, I dropped half the chips on the ground, Claire knocked quite a few cookies onto the parking lot asphalt, and at least two drinks fell out of the truck, rolling underneath it.

Clearly, the picnic gods were not with us. We gave up, packed it all in, and headed to McDonald's. Five minutes, a Big Mac, and two happy meals later, all was right with the universe. And it cost us a whopping $8 for dinner. Wow. We really saved ourselves quite a bit of time and money by packing that picnic, now didn't we? (For the record, the darn jelly costs more than the happy meals.)

Then we slogged through hours of Louisiana highway with tired and grumpy kids. After umpteen stops with children who refused to fall asleep until five minutes before we arrived, we got there around midnight (only three hours overdue) to find that we'd been kicked out of our hotel that we had reserved months ago for a guaranteed late arrival. Perfect. They sent us to the Hilton across the street. Cool, we thought. Nicer digs. Wrong. The room we had reserved was a one bedroom suite with living room and kitchen. The room at the Hilton was just that—a plain double room. Fabulous. Now we had a smaller space and had to unload everything twice when we switched hotels the next morning. On the upside, we didn't have to pay for the room that night.

Well, fast forward to the wedding Saturday afternoon. The bride was radiant. Having acquired the tall, thin genes in the family (which completely bypassed me, of course), my sister evoked Audrey Hepburn in her beautifully tailored, custom-made ivory silk gown. Her very soon-to-be husband looked quite handsome in a dark suit. My two daughters, resplendent in icy blue silk dupioni dresses that matched their eyes, their hair wreathed in baby's breath halos and satin ribbons, looked like little golden cherubs as they waltzed around the back of the wedding chapel carrying tiny baskets of ivory and pink roses. The scene was just too perfect.

So, naturally, I was quite terrified.

The girls' instructions were very simple: walk slowly down the aisle — a beautiful hardwood floor — in the small chapel just prior to the bride's entrance and sit beside us in the front row. Emma went first, Miss Priss the entire way down the aisle, smiling and blushing and tossing her ringlets about her head just so. Perfect. She sat down beside me and looked up expectantly, wanting to hear how well she has done. I, of course, obliged her. Then she asked for gum. Repeatedly. "Not now," I had to say fifteen times during the ceremony.

It was Claire's turn. Claire's strappy shoes had quite a heel on them. (Why? Because bridal stores don't think little girls should actually look like little girls anymore? You tell me. I expect Manolos will be out for five-year olds any day now.) Anyway, her heels clomped noisily on the hardwood floor as she practically ran down the aisle, covering her eyes with her one free hand as she went, apparently laboring under the misapprehension that if she couldn't see us, we couldn't see her. Aside from a near-miss with a chair on the aisle edge as she blindly wobbled off course, Claire managed to make it to her seat without falling down or bumping into anyone. We whispered our praises to her as well. We won't be able to see her lovely blue eyes, or any other part of her face, for that matter, in the wedding photos, but hey, she made it down the aisle as per instructions.

The ceremony goes well, except for when my sister-in-law's camera suddenly—and loudly—rewound automatically in the middle of the vows. She frantically tried to silence it by covering it up with her skirt, but it audibly backtracked the whole 24 frames, clicked off at the end of the roll to boot. In the meantime, Jack had been videotaping the ceremony at various points, turning the camera on and off from time to time, sounding a charming little bell tone each time he hit the record button which, in the confines of this nearly silent chapel, sounded like the bells of St. Paul's. I kept giving him "cease and desist" looks from the corner of my eye, several of which we later learn he caught on film inadvertently from his lap. (Note: I can say categorically that one never wants to be captured on film from an angle below one's nasal cavity. As a rule, nostrils do not contribute to the aesthetic of a good wedding video). My nostrils aside, the wedding was quite lovely.

The trip home…not so much. More fighting, complaining, whining, starving, and general griping for nine hours. We just love to travel together as a family. We yell. We scream. We whine. We bond.

yp

SUBJECT: RE: MY SISTER'S WEDDING

Hi there,

I cannot believe your sister is married. She just doesn't seem old enough. I'd like to wax on about how she's just so young, blah, blah, blah. But really, it's more about me feeling quite old at this point. I can't believe we are at this station in life: married, with kids!

Today, I am working on arrangements for Maxwell's birthday party. We are having his entire preschool class plus children of our friends come to the house for a big bash. I have the required SpongeBob jumpy thing, which should help promote at least one stubbed toe upon exit and/or skinned knee. I've ordered the cake with two pounds of icing in a myriad of colors in order that everyone's tongues will be an interesting part of the party and their clothes will acquire a rainbow of stains that are virtually impossible to remove. I have even managed to convince the local firefighters to drive the fire truck to our house for an all-out WOW factor. (I tried to get them to let us have the party at the station, but 'for insurance purposes' that is not allowed. I think they are just wise to the idea of having no less than 40 three-year-olds running amuck on a sugar high as a 'not so desirable' situation.) Anyhow, I don't have much time to chat between feeding the little one who is always hungry and keeping Maxwell on an even keel. I'll catch up soon. Wish me luck! S.

CHAPTER TWENTY-ONE: THEY GROW UP SO FAST

SUBJECT: JAMAICA MON

Yvonne,

When am I ever going to learn? We just returned from a trip to Jamaica. It was a last minute decision to go, literally two days before departure. Several of our friends were headed there, so after much deliberation, we decided to join them. Of course, Pierce in his infinite wisdom, gave me the rundown on what he'd heard about Jamaica. "There are guards with machine guns manning the perimeters of all resorts. You cannot leave the resort, even attended, so we'll be stuck eating the same food for a week. There are no reasonably decent medical facilities on the entire island, should something happen—God forbid." Coupled with my own research, which yielded a U.S. directive against travel in Kingston, we decided to load up the kids and go. Adventure awaits us!

Our flight to Jamaica is uneventful and we have a wonderful time while there. I do manage to leave the resort, not once but three times, while there. Once, I took a trip ALL BY MYSELF (read: no kids) on a tour to the local villages, across the mountains and into the heart of marijuana country. Quite an enlightening trip, although I don't see any doobies! Bummer. The vacation overall is great and the only embarrassing antic is Maxwell announcing to me in his most serious voice (and with concern) that "The lady's hair looks like noodles!" at the craft market. I cannot help but to laugh and kiss his innocent little face.

The return trip, however, leaves much to be desired. We depart the hotel happily and make our way to the airport. We are ready to be home. We board the plane only five minutes before scheduled takeoff since they had a gate change and failed to notify the passengers. (Mind you, every single clock in Jamaica is stopped on any given hour. They literally do not work so even if we were paying attention, we would have thought it to be eleven-thirty — for the entire day.) We taxi out to the runway and then the daily thunderstorm begins. Both kids are blissfully asleep and I am a wreck. I hate flying in the rain. We get to the end of the runway and the pilot announces we will not be able to take off from this end of the runway due to the rain so he is going to "drive" to the other end to see about taking off from there. Does this make sense to you? The runway is only a couple hundred yards long. If it is raining at one end, it seems obvious that it will be raining at the other. Now, my confidence in our pilot has waned. Obviously he is not a brain surgeon. But is he even a pilot? Needless to say, we get to the other end of the runway where we cannot depart due to rain. Duh.

Then, the wannabe brain surgeon announces "Fourteen of our planes have been struck by lightning in the last seven days, so we will clear the runway and wait on the apron until the storm passes." Again, does it not make sense that if you could be struck on the runway while sitting in a metal tube (a.k.a lightning rod turned horizontally) that you could also be a target not fifty feet away on the apron?

An hour passes. At last, the storm passes. We take off. By now, the children are bright-eyed, bushy-tailed, wet and hungry.

Lovely. For the next three hours, we do the normal parenting routine of changing diapers, feeding, and diffusing meltdowns. We arrive safely in Memphis exactly one hour late and one hour before our connecting flight. We run through immigration, rush through customs, claim and recheck our bags, and then speed to the next security checkpoint. The official government worker/security checker decides to cram the stroller through the x-ray machine. It gets stuck. Now, not only are we really stressing about getting to our gate, there are about thirty other angry, stressed-out passengers trying to wring our necks for holding up the line. They too have connections to make. After much struggling, pushing and pulling, the stroller comes flying out of the x-ray machine. Leftover food, spoons, sippee cups with milk all come flying out spewing all over anyone within arms reach. We grab the stroller and get the heck out of there. Connection or not, we don't want to be lynched by the mob behind us.

We literally run across the airport to the other terminal. To the last gate, of course. We get to our connection at 7:07; the plane is scheduled to leave at 7:10p.m. However, today the plane is departing early, precisely at 7:07p.m. We wave to it as it backs away from the gate. Lovely. No bags, a cranky kid, fussy baby and no baby food, no other flights out that night. We are relegated to the closest hotel to wait until morning. Needless to say, there is a small crowd waiting for the airport shuttle as they too had missed their connections. We aren't very popular on that bus.

We try our best to sleep, au natural, kids and all, but what the airport attendants failed to convey to us was that Memphis is a Fed Ex hub. Therefore, from midnight until four in the morning planes depart every five minutes. Imagine sleeping only several hundred yards from the runway. Whoosh. Whoosh. Whoosh. Jet planes landing and departing in your room. Backwash from the planes eerily seeping into the room. Lampshades vibrating with every takeoff. No, there is no sleeping. Just four naked people staring at the ceiling wondering if driving to Texas-naked-at o'dark thirty was an option.

On Friday, we finally arrive in Austin still in our stinky clothes from 48 hours prior. No bags. Still. And, since the computers were down in Jamaica when we left, we only have handwritten bag tags. Read: no record of our bags anywhere. It's Tuesday. It looks like a shopping spree is right around the corner because our bags are not! S.

SUBJECT: RE: JAMAICA MON

Steph,

First of all, how is it you get to go to Jamaica and I get to go to the grocery store? And, please tell me, why in the heck would you take two kids to romance central? Are you nuts? Even so, I'm jealous. Well, maybe not over the actual traveling portion of the vacation (talk about the trip back from hell), and certainly not over a trip with kids in tow, but the beach…oh, to be on a beach right now. I hate you, you know. Glad you got back safely. Yp

SUBJECT: TODAY'S TOPIC: BIRTHDAY PARTIES—FAMILY FUN OR SADISTIC TORTURE? YOU DECIDE.

Dear Steph,

Is it the Mormons that refuse to celebrate birthdays? Or maybe the Jehovah's Witnesses? Or is it both? I can never remember. Anyway, whoever they are, those people are way smarter than we are. And how, you ask, could a Southern Baptist-raised girl come to such a heretical conclusion? Read on.

It's Saturday. The girls have two birthday parties to attend today, back to back, starting at 12:30. Have we bought any gifts for these parties? Three guesses. So at 12:05 we pull out of the driveway like Batman on speed and head all the way to the other end of town to the toy store.

I'm pretty sure I know what I want to get each little friend (that would be four such little friends, as we have two more parties next week. Please congratulate me on thinking ahead: I calculate that the girls and I could be in and out of the toy store in less than 15 minutes and be only slightly late to the first party, "slightly late" being only 15 minutes, max. After issuing stern warnings to the girls all the way to the store, which include, "do not wander off," "no grabbing toys off the shelf," "we're in a huge hurry," "don't dawdle," and "if you ignore me, dire consequences will follow," etc., I confidently and swiftly stride into the toy Mecca with my munchkins running to keep up with me (they sort of have to run, because I am holding their hands tightly on either side of me.) But it takes five minutes longer than I had estimated to get to the store, so we now have ten minutes to shop and still be only "slightly late" to the party.

I am thrilled to report that, a mere 25 minutes later, we are standing at the checkout counter with three of the four birthday gifts we need to purchase. Oh, we get a free gift with our Barbie purchases, I am told, since Claire and Emma each picked out a special Barbie princess for today's birthday girl, (this despite my assurances that one would suffice). Do we want the pink Barbie boat or the blue Barbie car? To the delight of all the shoppers standing in line behind us, Emma and Claire take a full two minutes to deliberate over this important decision that apparently could affect the rest of their tender young lives. Sensing a riot beginning behind us, I deliver the verdict without further consulting the jurors. A pink car it is. And where is it? The back of the store, of course. Our checker can send an "associate" to the back to retrieve it for us? While all of the nice people in line start looking for tiki torches and pitchforks? Great. We'll wait, I said.

And we wait. And wait. Well, I wait. Claire and Emma make much better use of their time…as superheroes. They pull bags to the ground faster than a speeding bullet! They are more powerful than a locomotive, or at least they pretend to be as they knock over multiple signs posted around the checkout! They leap tall counters in a single bound! And look, everyone, Mommy has superpowers, too. She can make steam pour from her ears and nostrils.

You know that "monster mom" that you see in stores occasionally? The type who locks her jaw and moves only her lips as she threatens her children to within an inch of their poor, pitiful lives while grabbing them by the elbows and dragging them around? You know who I'm talking about. When you run across them, you cast a sad gaze in their direction, you shake your head at the senseless cruelty of a world where a mother could act so harshly toward her own flesh and blood, and then you utter a prayer for those wretched, misbegotten children, hoping against hope that they won't turn into the serial killers that they're so obviously destined to be without the love and nurturing of a good mother.

If you are standing in line behind me at that moment, then you are praying for my children because, yes, I am Monster Mom. In the flesh.

This, of course, is in stark contrast to the model behavior I exhibited earlier throughout the store. Behavior such as whacking a little girl in the head with a toy (accidentally) and telling her "You're okay," without apologizing before realizing that she was not, in fact, my little Emma; mowing down Claire with the cart while attempting to get her out of the Play-doh aisle for the third time; running over Emma and knocking her down with the cart as I backed up because the stupid "Associate" didn't bother telling me to "come to the other side, ma'am," until I was at the wrong side of the register--and he saw me coming the whole time!! Apparently no longer capable of recognizing my own offspring during this outing, I falsely imprisoned a child that I, again, mistook for Emma by holding onto her shoulder as her parents instructed her to come to them and get away from that crazed woman. Congratulations to me. I get the Mom of the Year Award and the Model Citizen Award.

It is at this point that I am thinking of converting to whatever religion doesn't involve celebrating birthdays. And we haven't even made it to the first party yet.

Shockingly enough, we arrive at the first party over half an hour late, (in case you're keeping score). The birthday boy had selected Pump-It-Up as the location for his party. It's a Mecca of bounce house fun and games, ear-drum splitting music, and migraine-inducing strobe lights designed to render children over-stimulated and uncontrollable, (a real plus for parents who just adore going to birthday parties). Of course, in this case, I think it's fair to say that this is mere payback. We held Claire's party there last year.

Anywho. Despite the fact that Jack bails on me and I have to take the girls by myself, the party goes relatively well for us…until the end. In the last 15 minutes before the cake and gifts debacle, Emma gets her feelings hurt and pouts dramatically because someone wouldn't share a toy with her. Claire injures her head by tackling one of the dads in the stomach (why? I have no idea) and cries to go home, and Emma climbs the stairs of the giant slide for the umpteenth time and, also for the umpteenth time, refuses to go down the slide and backs all the way down the stairs, running into everyone else climbing up. But it could have been worse.

Actually, it does get worse. Claire cries almost the whole time the cake is being served and while the gifts are opened; she still wants to go home. You see, she doesn't have a napkin. And can't find her fork. Then she can't get her straw in her juice pouch. And she doesn't want chocolate cake. And she doesn't want to sit by that boy. Can we possibly leave now without appearing terribly rude? No. Darn.

Finally, the torture ends, we prepare to depart, and . . . that's when we notice the deluge outside. Did we bring in the umbrella,

Mama? Um, no. We could take this one here, Mama. No, dear, that's called stealing. So, we get absolutely, positively soaked to the bone running to the car. We are already late getting on the road to the next party, but now we have to go home and change first.

Jack graciously decides to join us for the next party. We change, and I notice that my hair now looks like I just became the victim of a very bad perm (kind of like in fifth grade—do you remember when I did that?). There is no time to blow dry, and my mascara is all smeared. Beautiful. I fix what I can and we head out to Dallas for a swim party. In the pouring down rain. Jack laughs at my hair on and off for the whole ride down the toll way. He's so supportive.

We arrive pretty late-duh!-at the home of the birthday girl's grandparents, who have a fabulous pool. The girls look adorable in their swimsuits, Jack looks handsome in his casual shorts, and I look like little orphan Annie. The rain has downgraded from deluge to drizzle, so everyone at the party dives in to the pool.

My girls, who won't so much as put their chins in the water when I'm with them at the pool, magically transform into fish and need more supervision than the poolside observation I am offering. And the other parents in the pool keep beginning sentences with, "Claire, don't (insert various pool infractions here), honey." So as payback for ditching me at the previous party, I force Jack to change into his swim trunks to monitor drowning and such. I refuse to put mine on. The hostess resembles a stick, and I don't. Besides, I only wear swimsuits in foreign countries, if I can at all help it.

At one point, Claire tries to strip out of her swim top. No, honey, it's not okay to take it off. We don't really know all of these people. Emma spends much of her time teaching an 18- month-old how to swim in the hot tub. No, sweetie, don't push her head underwater, let her learn how to blow bubbles all by herself. Hopefully, her mother won't sue.

I engage in small talk with various family members and friends of the birthday girl while trying to observe my family in the pool for signs of distress and inappropriate behavior. Signs are everywhere. And every other sentence I am forced to interrupt myself or my companion to offer "instruction" to my children and, occasionally, to my husband, leading my companion to wonder, no doubt, whether I am ADD. And whether I gave myself that perm or actually forked over real money for it. I really need a margarita at this point. Sadly, this is an alcohol-free party. The birthday girl is, after all, only five.

The kids are called out of the pool to eat. Hissy fits ensue. Then Claire and Emma don't want to change out of their suits and back into their dresses. Oh, I know-let's run around the house naked. They very nearly succeed.

The meal goes flawlessly. Emma and Claire both want to sit next to the birthday girl, as does every other child there. Fights erupt. Feelings get hurt. Fish hats are torn. The hotdogs and hamburgers go largely uneaten. Emma insists that we peel every speck of browned skin off her hot dog before she will eat it. We finally succeed in doing that to her satisfaction on the third wiener. But by then she's lost interest in eating. Jack and I are forced to eat her rejects. Forced, I tell you. The kids all finish eating well before the adults and my two engage in that all-American past-time: whining. "When can we have cake?"

(Emma) "Can we open the presents now?" (Claire) "I'm sorry, is this your birthday party?" (exasperated Mommy).

After what seems like a month of torture, everyone is finally ready to open gifts. Emma appoints herself the chief gift bearer and won't allow anyone else to either give or take gifts to or from the birthday girl. She gets in the way of every single shot, so I fear that Emma's backside will be overly represented in the birthday album. Not to be outdone by baby sister, and as impatient as they come, Claire adopts the role of surrogate gift-opener. The birthday girl is perhaps less than thrilled with Claire's initiative. Claire and Emma's participation in the gift-opening proves very helpful to the general relaxed atmosphere of the party.

By this point, we are receiving pained looks from the birthday girl's family members that clearly translate into one of three questions: "Why can't you control your children?"; "Leaving soon?" and "How on earth did you rate an invitation?" Sadly, we are asking ourselves these same questions. After Emma knocks over someone's drink and Claire falls over in a chair, we are dying to leave. But we haven't even had cake yet.

The girls flank the birthday girl to sing to her and, amazingly enough, actually let her blow out her own candles without any interference whatsoever. That's a first. Cake in hand, we head back outside to eat it. Huge mistake. The girls now want back in the pool. No amount of insisting that it is time to leave deters them. We very nearly have to carry them back inside the house. But we manage to herd them out the door without much incident, party favors in hand. Said party favors (candy, paper, useless trinkets) end up all over the backseat and floorboard of my truck. Tangible evidence of our day in birthday party hell.

But I'm already planning Claire's fifth birthday party bash. Might as well spread the misery around. The last parent standing wins. It's one of those circle of life things.

Here's hoping you can stay off the birthday party circuit.
Yp

SUBJECT: RE: BIRTHDAY PARTY

Yvonne!

What chaos! I am doubled over and in pain from laughing so much. Mind you, I am not laughing at you, but with you, as I have in more than one instance been in the same boat-pool- party mayhem.

In the news recently, I have sworn off playgroups. I don't have time now, but remind me to relay that saga to you.

Take care and I'll talk to you soon. S.

SUBJECT: RE: RE: BIRTHDAY PARTY

Steph,

Ooh! Playgroup politics. Can't wait!
yp

SUBJECT: PLAYGROUP POLITICS

Hi there!

I am sharing this history with you in hopes of getting a little feedback...It's "The Playgroup".

Once upon a time, in a galaxy far, far away, I embarked on a mission to expose Maxwell to the finer arts in life. I signed him up for music class. We attended a small class of only four children, all of whom were about two years old. Initially, there were five children but one mother explained they would be dropping out after the first class, as her son was not the 'kum-bah-ya' type. I should have taken note and followed suit.

The class should have been called 'Frankenmusic' as we have a monster for a teacher. She is absolutely horrific. The instructor expects the kids to sit still during instruction. We are talking about two year olds here! She cannot carry a tune in a paper bag. Her nasally voice grates when she sings loudly and, oh so off key. And, she is quite vocal in expressing her disapproval when the parents of the class attempt to speak to one another. All of this glorious exposure to music in a room not much larger than a shoe box. I guess Maxwell's attempts to climb via the mini-blinds don't exactly exemplify model student behavior. Regardless of the admonishments from Franken-teacher, we (the parents) manage to become acquainted.

It is in this really awful music class that I meet two women who are obviously old friends. We would occasionally go to lunch to commiserate our Frankenmusic experiences and poke fun at the instructor. It was light and fun as the instructor was an easy target and we were all miserable in our experiences at music class.

In another galaxy, far, far away (well, not really) — I meet another woman with children similarly close in age. We became quite good friends, even outside the realm of our children. Actually, Pierce enjoys the company of her husband so it makes for a rare find. Through countless conversations, it became known that the two women in my horrible music class were also in a separate Gymboree class with this mom. Hence, the playgroup was born.

It was a relatively easy birth. We are all stay-at-home moms with children of like ages. We all like to socialize and stay hip. (That would be hip, as in cool, phat — not as in hippy and fat. Although hippy is definitely a better description right now.) Our kids got along mostly. There is only one child that likes to hit, but we chalk it up to the fact that he has an older brother and therefore hits in self-defense most of the time. I am the only brunette in the group. Ordinarily, this is a non- issue. However, for future reference I will take note. In this case, my non-conformance hair should have tipped me off to a storm a-brewin' — but it didn't. Like all in the infancy stage, we enjoy relatively uninterrupted fun time at each other's houses, destroying playrooms or otherwise dragging our ever- cooperative kids around the park in search of the infamous red snow cone.

During the toddler phase of the playgroup, we all learned to share. Much of that playtime is held over lunch with a bottle of wine or poolside, with a bottle of wine. I soon came to realize that quite possibly one in our playgroup is an alcoholic, one is married to an alcoholic, and one is in training to be an alcoholic (um…ok…two — me included!) While sharing information, I learned that Blond #1 is also a full-blown 'gusher'. But, boy is she fun! There are never dull moments in the conversation when she is present since she usually blurts out some really private tidbit of information. For example, while at a mixed playgroup with other people who were not a part of the inner circle, she asks Blond #2 how marriage counseling is going. Oops. In an effort to cover-up her faux pas, she goes on to say that she thought it was only Blond #2's mother-in-law that was not supposed to know, as she was the source of many problems. Oops again. On the third try, she says, "Was I not supposed to say anything?" A different occasion might bring out instances of Blond #1's attempts to please her sex-starved husband…I'll spare you the details. Regardless, there are always enlightening conversations in which to be privy. They truly bring joy and laughter to the day.

Blond #2 doesn't share much. She seems relatively stable albeit driven and focused on life outside the mommy kingdom. And there is Blond #3, a self-proclaimed clothes horse (with a substantial credit card bill to prove it). She cannot leave the house without complete makeup, hairstyle, nails, and perfectly pressed clothes. Talk about high maintenance! (Truthfully, I am motivated by her energy and ability to get dressed. That is a skill in my new mommy role I have yet to master.) Blond #3 is also the perpetual cheerleader. Just think about how befuddled I was when she proudly announces her role as a cheerleader in high school and then proceeds to do "the dance" she performed at football games. How old is she?? Or, maybe it's 'how old am I'?

After the toddler phase of the playgroup, where we all learned to share, we entered the teenage stage. We just skipped everything else. About two months ago, the playgroup decided to go on an overnight trip with kids and husbands. It should be interesting considering none of the husbands really like each other. Well, there is the husband of Blond #3 but they don't go.

The trip is relatively o.k. if you consider it felt forced. Although the moms got along fine, the hubbies sat in stone silence for the two, very long weekend days, all wishing to be elsewhere. The kids did their level-headed best to be loud and obnoxious at dinners and to run amuck throughout the hotel. It wasn't stellar but it wasn't a total disaster.

However, upon return to "the norm" back home, it soon became clear that Blond #3 felt rejected and left out. All the skills she learned in being a stereo-typical cheerleader of mustering the troops and identifying the enemy went into full force. In case you aren't reading between the lines: the enemy is me and the troops are everyone else in the playgroup.

Over the next few weeks, I notice I am no longer included in the playgroup invitations. In true high school fashion, I have been ousted via cunning, manipulation and downright lying. Apparently when 3/4 of a playgroup go on a weekend trip, someone must be the organizer and that someone must be shot! I am no longer privy to the inner circle of the playgroup. Is there not something seriously deranged here?

Anticipating that you may have experience in these matters considering your eldest is two years ahead of my eldest, I thought you might share some insight. If not, rest at ease as I have already written off adult attempts at friendship in order that my child has playmates. After all, I don't recall our mothers romping about in order that we could spend time together at the age of two. We were left to our own devices! Talk to you soon. S.

SUBJECT: RE: PLAYGROUP POLITICS

Steph,

Wow. So let me see if I've got this straight. You join an already formed friendship of Stepford Wives for the sake of your child (first mistake). Then you force the husbands to participate, who couldn't give a flying fig (second mistake). Then you go on a trip with Stepford Wives minus one (third mistake, even if not your fault). Then Stepford Wives close ranks and snub you. What to do? Hmm. This is a tough one. Oh, I know. GO FIND YOURSELF SOME NEW FREAKING FRIENDS! Preferably brunettes without loose lips. Who don't hail from Stepford. Good luck with that. That will be five cents, Charlie Brown.
And in case that sounded really insensitive, I do feel for you. Been there, done that. Which is why I can say that these are not your friends. Max, and you, will find new buddies to hang with.

Yp

SUBJECT: CLAIRE THE LAWYER

Steph,

Hey! How's it going? I'm suffering a bit of parental nerves at the moment. You know of my ambivalence toward the practice of law. There are so many more interesting things to do with one's life than be stuck in a law office or a courtroom. I would never want either of my girls to grow up to become lawyers. So, quite naturally, Claire will no doubt ignore my dire warnings and follow in my footsteps. Evidence in support:

— Today, she accused the company that makes "gogurts" of corporate malfeasance, indicating that she may pursue a career of dangerous, yet highly profitable, whistleblowing: "Yogurt is yucky. It's made up of spiders. They crush them up and put pink stuff with the spiders so we won't know." Investigation to follow.

— Recently, Claire explained to her friend Aaron (he's a mere three-years-old) the role of a husband in marriage, perhaps suggesting a career in family law: "You get married and have babies and you work all day and she stays home and in the evening you come home and she does client work and goes to client meetings and you keep the babies." Aaron's vigorous response: "I don't want to be a husband." She'll obviously need to work on her skills of persuasion.

— Then again, Claire may enjoy the challenges of litigating, as evidenced by an exchange she and I had over a year ago when she was almost four years old:
Mom: "Don't argue with me!"
Claire: "Okay. I'll go argue with Emma."
The ability to simultaneously recover quickly and be a smart mouth will take her far as a litigator.
— Claire's ultimate goal, however, may be to acquire her own bench. Last summer (before her fourth birthday), she came up to me and said, "I need a word with you. Now." Just add, "Counselor" to the end of that command, and we've got Judge Claire. Maybe she can take over from Judge Judy.

But I just had a thought. Maybe I can try reverse psychology on her. If I tell her she must become a lawyer, like her mommy, over and over throughout her childhood, then in the hallowed tradition of children turning a deaf ear to their parents where their "best interest" is at stake, she will no doubt rebel and seek out an altogether different career path. She's so hardheaded that it just might work. Let's hope her penchant for dancing while naked bears no relation to an alternate future career path.

Here's to parenting by subversion. Have a great week!
Yp

SUBJECT: RE: CLAIRE THE LAWYER

Hi Yvonne,

Seeing what our children will ultimately pursue will be an interesting thing to watch. Three days ago, Maxwell wanted to be a chef. Yesterday, Maxwell wanted to be a pilot. He wanted to fly planes and helicopters and space ships and rockets. Today, he wants to be his dad's partner. Pierce took him to a meeting and introduced Maxwell as his little partner. Apparently, Maxwell became very quiet until he and Pierce were alone in the car together. Then, Maxwell-in his most serious voice- said, "Daddy, I am not your little partner." Pierce acquiesced and in turn called him his junior partner to which Maxwell replied: "I am not your little partner. I am not your junior partner. I am not your partner yet. I have to grow up first and get old. You will just have to wait." There wasn't much more Pierce could say. We'll see what tomorrow's career path brings our way and I'll keep you abreast of his interests. At least you are on the straight and narrow, decision-already-made field of law with Claire! S.

SUBJECT: NAP TIME

Hi there!

I thought I might take just a minute (or as many as I can get away with) to say hi. This is, of course, much better than the alternative at this particular point in time. What is that? (I know you want to know!) Committing myself to an asylum and offering my children as gifts to the most-willing relative. The cause of my whacked-out behavior at this stage is simple. Maxwell is now three and, and has decided he no longer needs a nap. This is the third day in a row that he has forgone the much-needed nap. Well, I consider it to be a much-needed thing. He, however, thinks he is a big boy now and as such gets to make decisions on his own. Hence, I spend nearly an hour lying down with him in his room trying to get him to sleep. Of course, it is to no avail as Rose is also in the room shrieking out her version of "Home on the Range," or whatever song might be in her little brain. (I feel like I am living on a range. There are plastic deer, antelope, and a various assortment of other animals spread all over the floor along with every Hot Wheel and Matchbox car invented. These would be nicely put away if my three-year old wasn't so darned stubborn. I try to make it a positive trait by thinking it'll serve him well as an adult.)

I am the master of fielding questions from Maxwell during the pre-nap hour. "Mama, what is this?" "It's a corner dear." "What's it do?" "It holds the wall up." And so on. I could lick the Spanish Inquisition in one fell swoop. After I offered various bribes of treats, toys, games, painting (and that's a big one), I resorted to threats. Time outs, spankings, no play dates. You'd think I was talking to the corner that we discussed at length. The child acts as if not a word was heard in his little ears. No reaction to bribes, no reaction to threats. Maybe he is just heeding the words of the song his sister is insistent upon singing. (Where seldom is heard, a discouraging word. Doo dah…) I even resort to yelling! That gets a reaction, "Mama. You not supposed to yell inside. Yelling is for outside only." Oh those gentle words of instruction just re-delivered to me by my son, who by the way, has a Scooby Doo tattoo on his bicep and some unreadable stamp on his belly. I have a glimmer of the future—it doesn't look pretty. Unless, of course, you like the tattooed, earring infested, dregs-lock sort of guy.

Then comes round two: "Mama, I have to go potty." "Mama, I'm thirsty and hungry." "Mama, I need to take a bath. I'm dirty." Now, I'm exhausted and ready to fall into a self- induced coma just to avoid the battery of delay tactics. I think we should send three year olds to interrogate political prisoners. They'll beg for Chinese torture not to have to endure the relentless barrage of things a three year old can ask.

After an hour of this, I know to give up on the nap. I figure either I am going to sleep while my children run rampant about the house or I am going to go crazy trying to answer questions with no end.

So during this what would-be nap time, I have heard Elvis sing "Just let me be your teddy bear" from a stuffed bear that Pierce gave me while I was pregnant with the nap protestor. I can't even remember the words exactly as it was played so often that it has blurred into some weird melody with words of my own choosing. I'm sure at three o'clock in the morning I'll remember the words exactly as I am feeding Rose and then won't be able to go back to sleep due to the intolerable song.

I have heard Maxwell "play" the piano, beg for batteries to put in a toy, and basically destroy the house in less than fifteen minutes. Now, Rose is eating batteries—where did she get those, I wonder? Needless to say, I'm a little whacked. Well, I better run. Currently, the nap protestor is trying to teach his sister to crawl by pulling on her arms and legs all at once. She looks more like a foal trying to learn to walk at the moment with, you guessed it, a lovely version of Home on the Range belting out of those little lungs. Does any of this ring a bell with you? S.

SUBJECT: RE: NAP TIME

Steph,

Does it ring a bell? Does a child have to go potty the second the pediatrician walks in the door after a 45-minute torturous wait in the examining room? Of course! Emma gave up her nap earlier in the year, and I had as much fun with it as it sounds like you're having. But now the problem is when she does actually sneak in a nap. A mere half-hour snooze gives Emma enough juice to last until 11 pm. There is no getting her to sleep by 8:30–or even 10:30–if she naps. So afternoon naps are a two-edged sword. When she's melting down completely and really needs to sleep, I have to weigh whether I'm going to go crazy now, in the middle of the afternoon with no nap, or should I defer my lunacy until 9pm tonight when she won't go to bed because I just couldn't take it anymore and let her nap in the afternoon. And sometimes I get really lucky, and I go for the nap and con Jack into taking care of bedtime that night! Good luck to you.
yp

CHAPTER TWENTY-TWO: SHOP 'TILL I DROP

SUBJECT: MALL MISHAP

Oh my God. There is no other way to start this e-mail. I have just returned from the mall. It is a place I will not likely visit again with my two urchins. I was meeting two friends who also have children to pick out a baby shower gift for a mutual friend. I have to say, in retrospect, it started out relatively innocently.

We met at Pottery Barn kids. I was the first one there and my kids were actually well behaved. (Of course!) My other two friends arrived. One came with her three-year-old son and the other with her five year old and two year old. I could hear them coming. Just from the din, I should have taken note and fled but I was too interested in the cute little blender and coffee pot sets that were on sale. Anyhow, when the entourage entered, Max immediately joined the group of bandits-uh—kids. All the kids decided to partake in a game of "hot potato" with a stuffed beach ball that had been swiped from the summer display window. The first casualty was a cashier who was in the line of fire of this overstuffed, flying weapon of choice. Her glasses went flying off her face, which was contorted into a look that I cannot even begin to describe. The second casualty was the umbrella that stood over a cute toddler table and chair set. Well, that set off a chain of events as the table and umbrella crashed to the ground taking with them several picnic baskets filled with little plastic cups and plates. The cups rolled across the floor like ants on a mission only to find their way underfoot of an unsuspecting customer. Lady down! Casualty number three. As I rushed towards the woman to offer my assistance, I inadvertently rammed Rose's stroller right into the ceiling-high stack of cute coffee pots and blenders that had previously stolen my attention when I should have been high-tailing it out of there! Needless to say, a wall of pink and red kitchen appliances came tumbling down, into the stroller, onto other customers who were by this time trying to escape the chaos, and onto me. Whether or not it was intended, we were apparently taking no prisoners.

Once I uncovered Rose and myself, I found Max and removed him from the ball game. I think he was actually quite glad, having never been a part of mass destruction before. I think he was quite taken aback. Or at least, I hope he was. We made our way to the door, along with my other friends and their underlings, at which point in time any lady, man, or child left standing began to applaud our exit. Oh my God. S.

SUBJECT: RE: MALL MISHAP

Steph,

Holy cow. And I thought my shopping expeditions with children were nightmares. You win! I cannot stop laughing. But you know, you could have at least bought the appliance set. I mean, it was sort of the least you could do after destroying the store, don't you think?!
yp

SUBJECT: CPK INCIDENT

Hi there!

I have just been banned from yet another respectable establishment, the California Pizza Kitchen. Remember the two friends that successfully helped me get put on the "do not allow inside" list at Pottery Barn? Well, I met them for lunch. They had their children. Thankfully, mine were with their dad or I'm sure the scenario would have been worse. Granted, I do not know these two women well as we are in the infant stages of the friendship. However, I was certain things could not get any worse than the Pottery Barn incident.

When the hostess seated us, one of the women went over to the table adjacent and said "You might want to move down because my child throws things. I wouldn't want you to get hurt." I thought this was quite odd, after all, how painful could a noodle be?

The waiter took our drink and food order and things were progressing as any normal lunch date would. However, as the children finished their meals they became bored, as children do. (Mine usually whine.) Their kids had other ideas. The child whose mother issued the precautionary warning to the adjacent diner began throwing things. And they weren't just noodles! Forks and knives flew like we were at a circus show; straws surreptitiously filled with sticky, pink lemonade were flung about at unsuspecting patrons. I was mortified! Meanwhile, the children at the table found all this quite amusing. Naturally, they joined in the fun flinging anything within arms reach. We had an all-out, full-blown food fight on our hands, in our hair and on anyone within reach!

This was not enough for these kids however. Two of the boys decided a food fight would be much more interesting if it involved a search, raid, and destroy element. They jumped up from the table and began running around the restaurant, picking up pieces of pizza from strangers plates only to use them as target practice on one another.

I was ducking under the table, attempting to crawl out of the restaurant on all fours undetected. Meanwhile, the waiter and backup support descended on the table to clear any remaining food in hopes of saving the remainder of the diners. The manager called for a "lockdown" of the restaurant in order to separate the criminals from the victims.

Not wanting to be affiliated with the particular crowd I entered with, I rolled over on the floor and feigned an injury. Apparently, what works in the movies doesn't work in real life. I was tagged and listed as a 'banned diner'. Then, I was ushered out of the restaurant along with my dining companions. It was really embarrassing. You would've thought I'd learned my lesson from the Pottery Barn, but no… Needless to say, I won't be dining with that crowd again! S.

SUBJECT: RE: CPK INCIDENT

Steph,

Too funny! But I wouldn't sweat it. There are plenty of other restaurants in Austin still available to you to enjoy. Or in which to further humiliate yourself. Either way. Now, being banned from McDonald's or Chuck E. Cheese? That's a whole other problem. Can't have that.
yp

SUBJECT: WHY I SHOULD SHOP FOR LINGERIE ONLINE

Steph,

Hey, how's it going? My mental health is doing somewhat better today. I just got back yesterday from a relaxing mommy-only getaway, a one-night attempt to restore my sanity. My therapeutic destination? The swank, sophisticated, happening town of Muskogee, Oklahoma, where my cousin Liz lives.

We decide to see a movie right after I arrive. Since Liz turned 35 last week, I thought it'd be nice if I treated her. I really hope it's the thought that counts. Apparently, this Muskogee theater—a bastion of twenty-first century entertainment if ever there was one—doesn't take credit cards. As I stand at the ticket window, mouth agape, wondering if we're all in the same century together, I realize that I probably should not travel to Oklahoma anymore without cash. Not only does Liz have to pay for her own birthday movie, she has to pay to get me in as well. Ditto with the popcorn and drink (and chocolate, of course).

We happen to be the only two in the theater watching the movie, so we feel free to loudly comment and/or crack up every 2.3 seconds about what is happening onscreen. When we both need to pee in the middle of the film, the result of consuming vast quantities of Dr. Pepper, we yell up to the projection booth and request that they pause the movie for a potty break. We are ignored. As if it would kill them to pause the movie for three minutes. Please.

After the movie, we drive by the brand-spanking-new Super Walmart that had opened the day before. You would have thought the store was sponsoring a Shania Twain concert. I have never in my life seen so many cars packed into a Walmart parking lot — not even on my annual Christmas Eve, right-before-they-close-the-store pilgrimage (along with 500 panicked husbands) to purchase the last thirty things on my list.

Perhaps giddy from too much sugar and two hours of non- stop glib conversation during the movie, we decide to join the mob. As it turns out, this grand opening is Muskogee's see- and-be-seen, not-to-be-missed social event of the year. All around the store, we run into people Liz knows. What a great way to spend a mommy-getaway! Especially since we don't have a Super Walmart anywhere near my house here in Frisco-the closest one is a whole five miles away, a super straight shot down the highway that runs two blocks from my house.

Seeing as how back in Frisco I only get to shop at Walmart once or twice a week without the kids (usually around 11:00 p.m. when the stock boys pull out all the new merchandise and do a superb job of blocking every aisle), I decide to take advantage of this rare mommy getaway time to do something I might never,

ever get another opportunity to do: shop for new athletic bras. My current ones are not doing the job anymore. I know this because the last time I exercised (approximately four months ago, give or take), my multiple chins barely escaped bruising from all the bouncing . . . body parts. I'm sure I don't need to elaborate; you've nursed a kid or two. (I've come to the conclusion that bouncing body parts represent a surgical problem, but until the budget committee can afford to fund such a major renovation project, I'm forced to treat this situation as merely a containment issue).

Anyway, after finding a few that might work, Liz, the consummate saleswoman, persuades me to actually try the bras on in the store, rather than following my instinct and trying them on in my own bathroom at home, where I can be shocked and appalled in complete privacy. Stepping into said dressing room, I am immediately reminded why I should never let Liz talk me into anything and why I should NEVER use a Walmart dressing room. In a word: ceilings. Or, to be more exact, the complete lack thereof. How can you not have a cover over the top of a woman's dressing room when you hang a bunch of security cameras all over the freaking store's ceiling? Do they think we're stupid? Like we don't know what's under those domes? I can even see the nearest one off just a little ways from the dressing room if I stand on my tiptoes. I can't help but wonder: Can the high school guy manning the security cameras see me? Without my shirt on?

Despite feeling like a mermaid in a goldfish bowl with a lascivious cat hovering overhead, I decide to forge ahead. I am, after all, in Oklahoma, where I am decidedly anonymous (as if I'm a celebrity back home in Frisco…). Anyway. How hard can this be? Famous last words. If the security guy — and you know it's some acne-ridden teenage boy—is actually recording my image from the "hidden" camera, the floor show I put on for him is worthy of the grand prize on "America's Funniest Shopping Videos."

Endeavoring not to reveal my delicate bosom to the adolescent security voyeurs possibly hiding out in the ceiling, I first attempt to try on each bra while keeping my shirt hanging around my neck to cover my chest. This would pose no problem had I chosen back-closure garments. Naturally, the ones I had selected to torture myself with are the no-closure-over-the-head-only types. Now I don't know if you've ever tried to get one of those on or off while also wearing a shirt, but it's darned-near impossible. I try at least fifteen different ways before giving up and tossing the shirt in the corner, flashing the high school security guy in the process, no doubt, and sadly, taking his purity and innocence from him, (well, whatever was left of it after last night's fumbling attempts with some freshman in the band under the bleachers at the high school football game, anyway.) Hello, Mrs. Robinson.

Still endeavoring to be modest, I then attempt to wear my own bra while putting on the athletic ones, but strangely enough, a bra over a bra just doesn't work that well, especially when the one on top is waaaaay tighter, and besides, I can't figure out how to get mine out from under the new one to see if it actually fits. By now, Liz has come to the door three times to ask what on earth is taking me so long.

I give up. I strip it all off. At last freed from my bourgeoisie ideals of modesty, I begin to stuff my, ahem, body parts into said athletic bras in earnest. I swear my body parts haven't seen this much action since my honeymoon.

The cups on these bras all look enormous before I try them on, and I'm thinking there's no way I am going to fill these things out. But, as is so often the case, I am so wrong. In fact, I am pretty much bulging out in all directions (and from all sorts of unfashionable places) in practically every freaking one of them. And the few that do seem to fit somewhat give me a profile reminiscent of Madonna's "cone" period. Assuming I can live with that, and I'm not sure I can, they fail to pass the "jiggle" test. If the security kid hasn't noticed my nakedness up to now, my repeatedly jumping up and down in bra and jeans in the ladies' dressing room most certainly gets his attention.

Liz comes to the door again, asking if I'm ever coming out. I'm beginning to wonder that myself. I have one more bra left to try. What are the odds that this one will work? In my quest for a no-jiggle athletic bra, have I sacrificed my modesty — and perhaps led an innocent high school boy into prurience — for nothing? (Say it isn't so.)

I get naked one more time. Well, what do you know? It fits. And it doesn't give me bullet-shaped hooters that might poke out the eyes of anyone passing by me at a certain unfortunate height. Best of all, having bounced around for a full minute in it without knocking myself out cold, the bra appears to be jiggle-free. All hail Mrs. Robinson, victor in the quest for a fitting containment device.

To Liz's great relief, I finally emerge from the dressing "room," and we head off to pick up at least three more of these near-perfect bras. But, of course, the store only has the one in my size. Go figure. All that work and sacrifice for one lousy bra. But the worst part is, I no longer have an excuse to stay home from the gym. Now I have to start exercising. Bummer.

Not content to be seen (by everyone in Muskogee, you understand) walking around carrying just our bra selections, we head over to the underwear section. On the way, I disregard my own stern warning to myself and let Liz talk me into picking up a sexy red bra and panty set for Jack's enjoyment (as Gretchen Wilson's Redneck Woman runs through my head). It certainly wouldn't be for my pleasure, seeing as how I generally prefer to have at least five percent of my body covered at all times, and this set clearly wouldn't qualify. Since I'm not about to go back into that peep show masquerading as a dressing room to try on the top half of the red satin "ensemble" (and I'm being generous here), I just estimate and hope it's the wrong size so I can take it back as soon as possible. Jack might give me points for trying, anyway.

Our foray into the women's panty department turns out to be, if you can imagine this, even more entertaining for the security camera kid (and a few others as well) than my earlier topless peep show in the dressing room. After spending an inordinate amount of time discussing the relative merits of briefs vs. women's boxers. vs. bikinis vs. hipsters (my favorite), Liz and I attempt to make our selections. This proves more difficult than one might expect. You see, I can't remember what size I wear. Nor can I remember exactly how huge my hips are, which might hint at which size to purchase. What to do, what to do?

Liz comes up with a brilliant idea. She asks me where my tag on my current pair is. I state very clearly that I have no freaking idea. She insists that I check. "Just discreetly reach into your jeans and pull out the tag enough to read the size." Why do I let this woman talk me into this sort of thing? I try my best to reach, very discreetly, into the side of my jeans to grab the tag. No can do, at least, not without looking like some sort of exhibitionist pervert.

Liz decides to lend a hand. Literally. So there we are, in the ladies' underwear section of the new Super Walmart in Muskogee, Oklahoma, with gobs—and I do mean gobs—of people walking around, and just as a portly middle-aged man and his wife walk right by us, my dear cousin reaches into my jeans and pulls my underwear up to my waist to loudly announce the shockingly large number on the tag. The wife somehow misses this spectacle, but the middle-aged man sees it all and cannot contain his laughter, his belly shaking like a bowl full of jelly. Ho, ho, ho. Merry Christmas to you, sir.

We collect our underwear, laughing so hard that we can barely see, and then head over to the toy section. Where, of course, we run into the next set of Liz's friends and acquaintances, our arms overflowing with lingerie. Some of it embarrassingly sexy. Most of it just embarrassing, particularly as the sizes are imprinted in large numbers for all and sundry to see. My earlier decision not to get a cart now seems as ill advised as every other decision I've made since walking into this store. After this last encounter, we head off to grab a cart in an attempt to lower the humiliation factor as we navigate the rest of the store. Although, by this time, that ship has pretty much sailed.

So, that was my wonderful, relaxing, one-night-only mommy getaway in rejuvenating Muskogee, Oklahoma. And, for the record, I so do NOT want to hear that you've just gotten back from yet another Caribbean beach vacation, Tuscany wine tour, Mediterranean cruise, French biking tour, South American nature hike, or other equally exotic trip. Capiche?

Oh, good grief. Yes, you know I do. Just hit me with it. I can take it. I am, after all, a seasoned mom for whom torture is nothing new (just talk to the boobs).

yp

SUBJECT: RE: WHY I SHOULD SHOP FOR LINGERIE ONLINE

Hi there,

You are too funny. A mommy getaway sounds like a fantastic idea. Albeit going to Oklahoma is a stretch for a "getaway." I can only imagine the Wal-Mart's tapes of that day. Let's hope they don't retain them for posterity's sake!

Oh, and have a great time exercising. The time away from the kids could be used as medicinal and therapeutic. I "exercise" all the time. There's no need to report to your husband, however, the location of such strenuous activity. FYI-- Starbucks in the local Barnes & Nobles has the greatest workout regime ever! Just splash some water on your face before entering the house and he'll be none the wiser! Believe me on this—he won't even ask if you have gym fees! S.

CHAPTER TWENTY-THREE: BACK WHERE WE STARTED

SUBJECT: PLEASE IDENTIFY

Hi there!

Well, now that the New Year is upon us I have noticed something quite interesting. Perhaps it has been here all along and it has just taken a new wind to blow it into my view.

Everywhere I go, there is this funk. Occasionally, the smell is worse than at other times. Mostly though, it is just a presence that gets stuck in your nose. It reminds me of an annoying song stuck in your head in the morning, but on an olfactory level. Hence, I am forever scrunching my nose and looking around my surroundings like the odor has to be coming from somewhere else.

Everywhere I look there is a little cloud moving about my person. The cloud bounces along, obscuring my vision, so that I am constantly waving my hands about my face. Once in a while, it clears just enough to allow me to view the strangers that are pulling their young far, far away from the wacko-lady (me).

Always, I feel a little tugging on my legs. I feel the sensation at varying times. There are times I cannot move my own body due to the extra weight I feel.

So, here I am stuck in public, unable to move, scrunching my nose, looking about, waving my hands wildly about wondering what it is that follows me.

Is it a bird? Is it a plane? No-oh-wrong character. Is it Linus? Is it Pigpen? No-but they are much closer to the truth. In fact, it is Rose. The little Tasmanian devil that is my funk, my cloud, my weight.

But wait, there is still something more...it's a queasiness unwarranted. It is a sensation of a sixth sense, indescribable. It is a vague recollection of things past and things to come. It is a question, unanswered. That question being, 'did I tell you I was pregnant?'

Alas, here we go again...S.

SUBJECT: RE: PLEASE IDENTIFY

Oh. Crap. yp

ABOUT THE AUTHORS

Yvonne Parks lives in Dallas with her husband, two girls, two dogs, and her long-suffering mom. Since it took about 16 years for Yvonne and Stephanie to get their acts together enough to finish this book, her girls have long since graduated from challenging toddlers to impossible teens (and that's another book...or three--the authors are aiming to have them all done by the time they're eligible for Social Security). Yvonne has graduated from ambivalence to the law to a genuine love of the practice, finding a career with a great firm in Dallas. If she had any free time, she would write more, read, travel, brush up on her Russian and Spanish, and take up gardening. But that's just not going to happen any time soon (and plants everywhere are breathing sighs of relief). About the best she can manage between the office, the laundry, her kids' flute lessons and drivers' ed classes is listening to audio books (BEST INVENTION EVER!) She hopes you take pleasure in reading about all the bone-headed things she's done in this journey into motherhood. If nothing else, you undoubtedly feel better about yourself now!

Stephanie Duprie Routh, full of curiosity and wanderlust, is a gypsy soul that uses the world as a muse, travels with her husband and three kids in search of adventure, culture, and food! When not on the far side of the planet, she resides in Austin with the same motley crew and her trusty beagle Ranger Max. She enjoys gardening, beekeeping, yoga, and nourishing her inner foodie habits. Being a creative person, Stephanie uses her travels and her backyard, the strangers she's met and her own family as springboards for her photography and her writing. Once, in a lifetime far behind at a corporate job, someone told her she was loquacious. In the present moment, (how'd you like those buzz words?!) Stephanie is more thrifty with her words and tries not to be wasteful-- with anything--just as any self-respecting, tree-hugging, hippie should be.

www.ingramcontent.com/pod-product-compliance
Lightning Source LLC
Chambersburg PA
CBHW051646040426
42446CB00009B/998